001.942
HOU

Hough, Peter.
　　The complete book of UFOs : an investigation into
alien contacts and encounters / Peter Hough & Jenny
Randles. -- London : Piatkus, c1994.
　　304 p. : ill.

　　ISBN: 0749913991 :

1. Unidentified flying objects.　I. Randles, Jenny, 1951–
II. Title.

THE COMPLETE BOOK OF

UFOs

An Investigation into Alien Contacts and Encounters

Also by Peter Hough and Jenny Randles

The Afterlife: An Investigation into the Mysteries of Life After Death
Spontaneous Human Combustion
Looking for the Aliens
Mysteries of the Mersey Valley
Witchcraft: A Strange Conflict (Peter Hough)
UFOs and How to See Them (Jenny Randles)
The Unexplained: Great Mysteries of the 20th Century (Jenny Randles)
Aliens: The Real Story (Jenny Randles)
The Paranormal Year (Jenny Randles)
Crop Circles (Jenny Randles with Paul Fuller)
Time Travel (Jenny Randles)
Science and the UFOs (Jenny Randles with Paul Warrington)

THE COMPLETE BOOK OF
UFOs

An Investigation into Alien Contacts and Encounters

PETER HOUGH & JENNY RANDLES

PIATKUS

© 1994 by Peter Hough and Jenny Randles

First published in 1994 by
Judy Piatkus (Publishers) Ltd
5 Windmill Street, London W1P 1HF

**The moral right of the authors
has been asserted**

*A catalogue record for this book is
available from the British Library*
ISBN 0–7499–1399-1

Edited by Esther Jagger
Designed by Paul Saunders

Cover photograph: After the *Freedom of Information Act*, the Spanish Air Force
opened up their UFO files and revealed some amazing cases. The photograph,
taken over Maspalomas, Gran Canaria, in June 1976 depicts an object also seen by
the crew of a naval vessel.

Set in ITC Cheltenham and Plantin Light by
Create Publishing Services, Bath
Printed & bound in Great Britain at
The Bath Press, Bath, Avon

Contents

Picture Credits

Permission to use copyright photographs is gratefully acknowledged to the following:

Page 11 Mary Evans Picture Library; *page 15* Hulton Picture Company; *page 19* Mary Evans Picture Library; *page 36* Henry Thomson; *page 48* Mary Evans Picture Library; *page 55* Mary Evans Picture Library; *page 59* Mary Evans Picture Library; *page 72* Mary Evans Picture Library; *page 84* Fortean Picture Library; *page 90* Mary Evans Picture Library and *Fate* magazine; *page 101* Dennis Stacy/Fortean Picture Library; *page 111* Mary Evans Picture Library; *page 112* Mary Evans Picture Library/Daniel Fry; *page 117* Mary Evans Picture Library; *page 120* Crown Copyright, reproduced with the permission of the Controller of Her Majesty's Stationery Office, reference PREMII/855 XC 21498; *page 128* Mary Evans Picture Library; *page 129* M. Muyldermans; *page 131* Novisti/Science Photo Library; *page 145* Mary Evans Picture Library; *page 149* Reeves Studios; *page 152* Mary Evans Picture Library; *page 157* Jim Templeton; *page 162* Mary Evans Picture Library; *page 168* Peter Hough; *page 173* Mary Evans Picture Library; *page 177* Mary Evans Picture Library; *page 185* Paramount Pictures; *page 194* Mary Evans Picture Library/Ballantine Books; *page 197* Dennis Stacy/Mary Evans Picture Library; *page 205* Mary Evans Picture Library; *page 213* *News of the World*; *page 221* Mary Evans Picture Library; *page 227* *Fate* magazine; *page 234* Rex Features/*Today* newspaper; *page 237* Peter Hough; *page 239* Mary Evans Picture Library/Avon Books US; *page 251* Dennis Stacy/Fortean Picture Library; *page 259* *Today* newspaper; *page 263* Dennis Stacy/Fortean Picture Library; *page 278* NASA; *page 283* Keith Melia; *page 293* Fortean Picture Library.

Whilst every effort has been made to trace all copyright holders, the publishers apologise to any holders not acknowledged.

INTRODUCTION

The subject of unidentified flying objects (UFOs) is more popular today than it has ever been; its mounting interest to the general public has paralleled its increasing maturity and complexity. Sceptics were predicting in the 1950s that 'flying saucers' were just a fad that would quickly pass. Now, in the closing years of the twentieth century, that 'fad' has become an indelible mark, some would say stain, on world culture. UFOs are no longer a fringe interest, locked outside the mainstream of society and associated with 'cranks'. The phenomenon is now on the inside, woven into the fabric of day-to-day life. It has been a silent, subtle invasion.

UFO scenarios are used in television soap operas and major feature films. They appear in advertising and are the subject of late night discussion programmes. Men and women with scientific and military backgrounds talk openly and positively about the topic. The British Ministry of Defence has now publicly reversed its attitude: it regularly passes on cases to civilian organisations, and is ready to assist in providing relevant information to researchers. The subject is no longer derided but accepted as something 'alien', a phenomenon outside our understanding.

The release of official files in recent years reveals the seriousness with which UFOs were regarded at a time when government spokesmen rubbished them in public. Those files describe visual sightings and the tracking on radar of unknown aerial objects. They report the scrambling of military jets in futile attempts at chasing silver-coloured discs. These were not hallucinations or misidentifications. They resembled nothing on Earth. Sunlight often reflected off their hard shiny surfaces, and the best military pilots in the world found themselves out-manoeuvred.

UFOs may have always been around, but interpreted differently according to the culture of the time. This woodcut from a Swiss library describes an observation of strange globes that were seen in the sky by citizens of Basel on 7 August 1566.

We are not just talking from a historical perspective. Somewhere in the world, similar events are unfolding as you read these words.

In recent years UFO abduction experiences have come to dominate the subject. This has caused much controversy inside and outside of the UFO community. Abductions offer less objective evidence and some researchers believe it is a psychological phenomenon riding on the back of a genuine nuts and bolts anomaly. People are taken from their cars, or their beds, from crowded back streets, to a white room where they are experimented on by strange entities. Hidden 'memories' are accessed through the use of hypnosis. Is the abduction scenario a cover story for childhood abuse, as some sceptics believe, or does it demonstrate the complete control by an alien intelligence of the environment and every human being?

At last the prayers of serious ufologists are being answered. Specialists from all branches of science are becoming involved; they include psychologists as well as physicists. However, there is still no government funding for public research projects. Specialists give their expertise in their own time, at their own expense.

Our modern history begins in 1880. This was the time when UFOs were first perceived as futuristic flying machines, although in one form or another they have been with us all along. The book charts the development of the phenomenon and society's struggles to come to terms with something completely 'out of this world'.

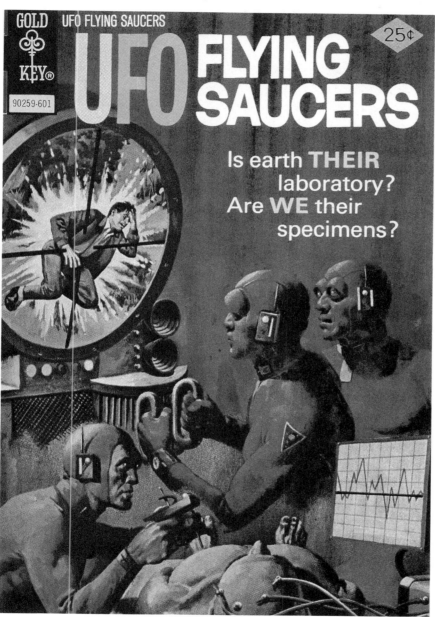

The cover of *UFO* magazine, dated January 1976.

Part One

1880:
ARRIVAL OF THE
AIRSHIPS

THE FIRST OF THE CIGAR-SHAPED OBJECTS

The modern UFO age began around 1880, at the height of the industrial revolution.

The modern UFO age began not in 1947, as many commentators suggest, but around 1880, at the height of the industrial revolution. Whether there is a link between the Western world's sudden advance in scientific and technological achievement and the simultaneous sightings of futuristic flying hardware is an intriguing speculation to which we shall return at the end of this book.

Of course, UFOs in essence have been around for much longer. Biblical history is littered with cryptic references to flying objects piloted by supernatural beings. But the period from 1880 up until the start of World War I saw one of the most clearly defined manifestations of the phenomenon. Our modern UFO history starts here. These early stories parallel modern-day UFO encounters, except that, instead of gleaming metallic 'spaceships' piloted by 'aliens', the sightings involved cumbersome dirigibles with human-looking crews.

Airship technology

Through the diligence of researchers on both sides of the Atlantic, numerous old newspaper accounts have come to light which describe sightings of mysterious airships. This was at a time when such machines were still on the drawing board, except for a few prototypes being tested in Europe.

Although the world's first powered, manned dirigible was flown on 24 September 1852, progress went haltingly after that. This steam-powered balloon (see opposite), designed by the Frenchman Henri Giffard, travelled approximately seventeen miles at 5 mph. Later attempts usually met with disaster, such as happened to the dirigible built by Dr Karl Wolfert in Germany; his machine, fitted with a small engine, crashed shortly after take-off. Dr Wolfert and his mechanic, Herr Knabe, died in 1897 during another attempt, when the gas envelope caught fire and exploded. In fact the first fully controlled air journey did not come about until 1903, when an airship flew thirty-seven miles over France.

It was after this date that airships slowly started to come into their own. On 15 February 1908, the US Army received its first tender for a dirigible from Captain Thomas Scott Baldwin. However, it was six years later before the *California Arrow* was built and tested. By this time the Germans had launched their first successful military mission using a Zeppelin, against the Dutch.

Aeroplane development was similarly beset with problems and disasters during this period. The first aeroplane to achieve man-carrying powered, sustained flight was the *Flyer* in December 1903. This was the culmination of four years' work by Wilbur and Orville

The first successful airship – constructed in 1852 by Henri Giffard.

Wright. Their aeroplane achieved flight for fifty-nine seconds and travelled just 852 feet.

As in modern UFO reports, the phantom airships of these times mimicked current flight technology but went several steps further. They attained remarkable speeds, demonstrating a manoeuvrability far outstripping anything built before World War II.

The sightings begin

Jerome Clark and Lucius Farish tell us that, according to the *Santa Fé Daily New Mexican*, a cigar-shaped craft driven by a huge propeller was seen by three men on the evening of 26 March 1880. These citizens of New Mexico described ten persons who laughed and shouted down at them from the strange object in an unrecognised language. Their general behaviour was of drunkenness. When one of them threw several items overboard, a beautiful flower and a slip of silk-like paper with oriental-type letters on it, together with a cup of 'very peculiar workmanship', were recovered.

The items were displayed at a nearby railroad depot. Within hours a stranger arrived and examined them. He pronounced them to be of Asiatic origin, and made the depot agent an offer of money he could not refuse. The man claimed to be a 'collector of curiosities', but it is common in modern accounts for strange men to visit UFO witnesses and procure any tangible evidence. These sinister figures are today referred to as Men in Black, because of their dark dress and strange demeanour.

All at sea

In that same year a close encounter occurred between a ship and an unidentified flying object, according to a Mr Lee Fore Brace writing in the December 1883 issue of the journal *Knowledge*.

On board the British India Company's steamer *Patna* while on a voyage up the Persian Gulf in May 1880, on a dark, calm night, about 11.30pm, there suddenly appeared on each side of the ship an enormous luminous wheel, whirling round, the spokes of which seemed to brush the ship along. The spokes would be 200 or 300 yards long. Each wheel contained about sixteen spokes, and made the revolution in about twelve seconds. One could almost fancy one heard the swish as the spokes whizzed past the ship, and, although the wheels must have been some 500 or 600 yards in diameter, the spokes could be distinctly seen all the way round. The phosphorescent gleam seemed to glide along flat on the surface of the sea, no light being visible in the air above the water. The appearance of the spokes could be almost exactly represented by standing in a boat and flashing a bull's-eye lantern horizontally along the surface of the water round and round. I may mention the phenomenon was also seen by Capt. Avern, commander of the *Patna*, and Mr Manning, the third officer.

The phenomenon spreads

Between November 1896 and May 1897, sightings were recorded in over nineteen states in America. Reports described large elongated objects with bright searchlights, and occasionally wings and propellers were noted. These apparently solid-looking machines flew against the wind; when sound was heard, it was a hissing or humming noise.

From October, newspapers began printing reports of unidentified craft in the backwoods of Nebraska. Late in that month a fruit rancher and his family near Bowman, California, observed an object with three brilliant lights, travelling at about 100 mph. Then on 17 November the phenomenon suddenly escalated into the airspace over Sacramento, with startling results. The *Sacramento Bee* recorded the flavour of those times:

Last evening between the hours of six and seven o'clock a most startling exhibition was seen in the sky. People standing on the sidewalks at certain points in the city saw coming through the sky over the house tops, what appeared to be merely an electric arc lamp propelled by some mysterious force. It came out of the east and sailed unevenly towards the southwest, dropping now nearer to the Earth, and now suddenly rising into the air again, as if the force that was whirling it through space was sensible of the dangers of collision with objects upon the Earth.

Some of the hundreds of witnesses who obtained a closer view said the object was enormous and cigar-shaped with large wings attached to an aluminium-type body. Shouts and laughter were also heard from the direction of the thing. A witness named R. L. Lowry and another man allegedly heard a voice call down: 'We hope to be in San Francisco by tomorrow noon!'

Airship reports also came from Canada. A glowing red ball was observed for fifteen minutes over Rossland, British Columbia, on 12 August, 1896. Many witnesses described how it approached the town, paused over a mountain peak, made several orbits then sped away.

The great plague of reports which followed took the press by surprise. These had all the trappings of a modern UFO 'flap' – a sudden rapid increase of sightings over a relatively short period. When occupants were seen, they appeared to be normal human beings. Usually they claimed to be secret inventors making test flights before unveiling their wondrous machines to the world. Needless to say, these 'inventors' were never heard of again.

A close encounter of the third kind

An incident comparable to a Close Encounter of the Third Kind, culled from the *Arkansas Gazette*, relates the experience of Captain James Hooten, a railroad conductor.

Not all of the airship pilots looked human. Two men told the Stockton Evening Mail *of their encounter near Lodi, California. They described three tall strange beings with large narrow feet and delicate hands. Each creature was hairless with small ears and mouth. Their eyes were large and lustrous. When they failed in their attempt to abduct two of the men, the beings fled into a cigar-shaped craft and left.*

I had gone down to Texarkana to bring back a 'special', and knowing I would have some eight to ten hours to spend in Texarkana, I went to Homan to do a little hunting. It was about 3 o'clock in the afternoon when I reached that place. Before I knew it, it was after 6 o'clock when I started to make my way back towards the railroad station. As I was tramping through the bush my attention was attracted by a familiar sound, a sound for all the world like the working of an air pump on a locomotive.

I went at once in the direction of the sound, and there in an open space I saw the object making the noise. To say I was astonished would but feebly express my feelings. I decided at once this was the famous airship seen by so many people.

There was a medium-size looking man aboard and I noticed he was wearing smoked glasses. He was tinkering around what seemed to be the back of the ship, and as I approached I was too dumbfounded to speak. He looked at me in surprise, and said: 'Good day, sir, good day.' I asked: 'Is this the airship?' And he replied: 'Yes, sir,' whereupon three or four other men came out of what was apparently the keel of the ship.

A close examination showed that the keel was divided into two parts, terminating in front like the sharp edge of a knife-like edge, while the side of the ship bulged gradually towards the middle, and then receded. There were three large wheels upon each side made of some bending metal and arranged so that they became concave as they moved forwards.

'I beg your pardon, sir,' I said, 'the noise sounds a great deal like a Westinghouse air brake.'

'Perhaps it does, my friend: we are using condensed air and aeroplanes, but you will know more later on.'

'All ready, sir,' someone called out, when the party all disappeared below. I observed that just in front of each wheel a two-inch tube began to spurt air on the wheels and they commenced revolving. The ship gradually arose with a hissing sound. The aeroplanes suddenly sprang forward, turning their sharp end skyward, then the rudders at the end of the ship began to veer to one side and the wheels revolved so fast that one could scarcely see the blades. In less time than it takes to tell, the ship had gone out of sight.

One can immediately see some remarkable similarities between this account and the more recent UFO scenario. Hooten came across the scene as if by accident, in an isolated area, and found the futuristic craft in some sort of mechanical trouble. This was a feature particularly of cases in the 1960s and 1970s: it was not uncommon for UFOs to suffer similar 'malfunctions', and provides a good excuse for someone to 'happen' to come across one.

A sketch of the 'airship' seen by Captain James Hooton at Homan, Arkansas.

As repairs are carried out by the crew, Hooten enquires about its motive power. The answer he is given fits the era and is tailored to Hooten's own interests, but is too general to be fully understood. Modern extraterrestrials prattle on about electromagnetic motors.

The British experience

Although the bulk of unearthed reports stem from North America, the phenomenon was not confined to that continent. Newspaper accounts have also been discovered in Britain, and searches made of newspaper files in other countries are showing that the airship phenomenon was global. In particular, many reports describe encounters in Scandinavia and New Zealand.

According to the Swedish newspaper *Dagens-Nyheter*, 'an unknown controllable airship' twice circled the Estonian city of Tallinn on Tuesday, 24 August 1909, before flying off towards Finland. Newspapers thought the object was 'probably Swedish', even though none like it existed. Exactly one month later a winged machine passed over the Castle Forest near Gothenburg in Sweden, just 100 metres above ground level.

The *South Wales Daily News* of 20 May 1909 referred to several Cardiff docks workmen who had sighted an airship in the early hours of the previous Wednesday morning. A little earlier, on the Tuesday evening, another witness got somewhat closer to the object.

Sweden and Norway, which was to be at the centre of a mystery aircraft wave in the 1930s, also played court to several airship reports around 1897. One of these featured a 'balloon' with an 'electric' or phosphorescent sheen.

Mr C. Lethbridge of Newtown, Cardiff, emphatically assured one of our representatives that on Tuesday evening while walking over Caerphilly Mountain, 'I saw a sight which frightened me, and which at first I thought was a big bird.' Lethbridge is an elderly man of quiet demeanour. He has a little Punch & Judy show, in which he travels about the country in the summer. He left Senghenydd with his show, on a handtruck, for Cardiff, and he reached the summit of Caerphilly Mountain when he saw the sight which frightened him.

'I saw,' said Lethbridge, 'a funny-looking object on the roadside, and two men who seemed to be at some kind of work close by. The object was long and like a big cigar. The men – two officers, were –'

'Officers? What made you think they were officers?'

'Well, they were tall men, military-looking men, and were dressed in thick fur coats and caps. Of course I didn't know they were officers, but they were two men – that's certain, and military-looking men, too.'

'How close did you get to them?'

'I was about twenty or thirty yards away when I first saw the men. The noise of my truck – it rattles a lot – must have disturbed them, for they commenced to speak very fast, some kind of lingo which I could not understand. They appeared to pick up something off the ground and jump into the object close by. Then it rose up like – like a switchback movement, and when it had got up a pretty good height it went straight in the direction of Cardiff.'

'What did you think it was?'

'I don't know. They frightened me. I thought first it was some big bird, but it must have been an airship.'

'What made you think that?'

'Well, after it had gone up a way two lights began to shine from it. They looked like electric lights. It made an awful noise – a – a whirring noise, and – '

The pressman had heard of that whirring noise. What did Mr Lethbridge mean by it?

'Well, ' he answered slowly, 'a noise like an engine working. Saw and heard it! I have no doubt about it, I was frightened I can tell you, and after watching it go away towards Cardiff I continued to walk home.'

Such is the story related by Mr Lethbridge of his strange experience between 10.30 and 11 o'clock on that Tuesday night. Interestingly, it received confirmation through the statements of residents in Salisbury Road, Cathays, Cardiff who said that: 'Between 10.40 and 10.50 they saw an object in the air which looked like an airship.'

The newspaper account goes on to narrate the testimonies of other witnesses to the airship. Lethbridge's vague description of the object as 'long and like a big cigar' has often been used in contemporary sightings. A search was made on Caerphilly Mountain at the location, where a red label printed in French was discovered along with a piece of mutilated notepaper and several other slips of paper – but these only served to confuse the issue.

The Caerphilly encounter was not an isolated incident but part of a huge flap lasting several months. On 21 May 1909, the *East Anglian Daily Times* came up with the headline: BRITAIN INVADED! AIRSHIPS IN EAST ANGLIA, WALES, AND MIDLANDS. PHANTOM FLEET. NORWICH AND SOUTHEND PAID A VISIT. What follows is a précis of the article uncovered by researcher Carl Grove.

The airship fleet which is invading England had a busy night on Wednesday. We speak of a fleet because, according to correspondents, there must be not only one, but half a dozen mysterious cigar-shaped machines with quivering lights and whirring mechanisms flitting about the country by night. Wednesday night's observers report manifestations at such widely divergent points as: Southend-on-Sea, Birmingham, Norwich, Tasburgh, Wroxham and Pontypool.

The mysterious airship has been seen in London. The fact has leaked out under extraordinary circumstances. The Aeronautical Society of Great Britain received a postcard on Thursday stating that a number of railwaymen at West Green had noticed the mysterious airship. They state they saw the airship on Friday last. The names of two of the men are George Walden and Joseph Cooper. Seen by a *London Evening News* representative, [Walden] said:

'Yes, it is quite true, we saw an airship. It was about 3.30am last Friday morning. We were at work coupling some trucks in the sidings. Suddenly my mate, Cooper, said, "What's that?" Pointing to a strange-looking object in the sky. "It looks like a policeman's truncheon, doesn't it?" I replied. "Yes, or a big cigar." It was travelling at a fast pace from the north-east. There were no lights attached to it. We were quite clear that it could not have been a cloud, as it was too regular in shape. It was also a very clear and cloudless night.'

A Southend correspondent telegraphs that on Wednesday evening at dusk, an airship was observed at a considerable height between Southend and Shoeburyness. It manoeuvred about for some time until darkness set in, and then disappeared.

Mrs Turner, of Norwich, was returning from the theatre on Wednesday night, and gives the following description of what happened about 11.30:

'As I came into my street, a flash of light came on me all of a sudden, and made the street look like day. There were two young people in the street – a youth standing near his bicycle, next to a young lady. I heard one of them say: "What's that?" I could hear a noise like the whirring of wheels. I looked up, and there I saw a big star of light in front and a big searchlight behind. It was flying very low, so low that it would have touched the pinnacle of Angel Road School had it passed directly over it.'

Mr Chatten, a grocer's assistant, was cycling home to the parish of Thurston about midnight on Wednesday night, when, he says:

'I was dazzled by a bright light shining from right above me. The trees and hedges were lit brilliantly. I have seen a naval searchlight at Harwich, and I should suppose that what I saw was something of that sort, but there was a bluish tinge about it, and it did not appear as strong as the naval lights. It seemed to be switched off after only a few

The major airship waves of the late nineteenth and early twentieth centuries lay undiscovered by ufologists for twenty years. Now they are the most widely researched historical cases in the field.

seconds. Getting off my bicycle I saw a long cigar-shaped object. It was soaring upwards, the tapering end going foremost, and was moving rapidly in the direction of Norwich. On the underside was what I should call a bar, supporting a sort of framework, a yellow light shining at each end.'

A Pontypool correspondent telegraphs that a mysterious airship was sighted at Pontypool on Wednesday evening by a number of people, including Mr Gath Fisher, architect, and his wife, who assert that it was cigar-shaped, and that it had a powerful light at each end. Men on night duty at Pontypool town forge declare that the airship floated over the forge and then darted off in another direction, frantically at right angles to that from which it arrived. It disappeared in the direction of Herefordshire. The airship carried a large sheet of canvas and a powerful light. Post Office officials and workmen corroborate the story.

For several nights people living in Small Heath, a suburb of Birmingham, have seen what is stated to be an airship passing over the district. It is described as cigar-shaped, but carried no light.

Barry Greenwood, editor of Just Cause *magazine, found a whole new group of airship sightings in Massachusetts as recently as 1992. The opportunity for newspaper archive research the world over still exists for dedicated people who do not mind eyestrain!*

Venus to enemy aircraft – the speculation continues

The airship sightings seemed to peter out after 1909, to surface for one final wave in 1913. Then, as now, Venus was cited as the explanation for some of the anomalous events. In the *Nottingham Daily Express* of 26 February 1913, the following appears:

In regard to the airship said to have been seen near Selby, Yorkshire. A glance at a map shows us Hambledon W to S, and Leeds W of Selby. These are precisely the azimuths of the plant Venus at the times given. Venus is now particularly bright, and suddenly appearing and disappearing behind wind-blown clouds, she gives the illusion desired. To hear the 'engines', shut your eyes, and a motorcar will rarely fail you. All the same it's rough on dear old Venus.

There must be no doubt that astronomical bodies accounted for some sightings, especially during a flap when people's awareness is heightened and they are more inclined to misidentify natural phenomena. Plainly, however, meteors burning up in the atmosphere, and bright stars and planets, could not account for the detailed description of nuts-and-bolts hardware witnessed at close quarters, sometimes by several people.

When the mundane failed as an explanation, society rationalised further and speculated that the sightings were of airships being test-flown by secret inventors. As we have seen, the phenomenon encouraged this belief by staging close encounters between witnesses and human-looking pilots. In the USA this idea proliferated, and individuals came forward claiming to be involved in the construction of the mysterious airships.

A character called Dr E. H. Benjamin confided to friends and relatives that he had constructed an airship near Oroville. The press began to hound him, and even his solicitors believed the story. A prominent San Francisco lawyer named Collins claimed to have seen the airship – some 150 feet long – ascend to about 90 feet under perfect control. The tale grew, although the only thing established with certainty was that Benjamin was a dentist from Maine.

There was also an enigmatic man named Wilson. According to witnesses in parts of Texas and Louisiana, a pilot aboard an airship had introduced himself as a Mr Wilson. During one of the encounters, Wilson mentioned an acquaintance called Captain Akers. When Akers was questioned, he admitted he had known a man of that name in 1876 and 1877, who was working as an aerial navigator. But Mr Wilson was heard of no more.

Modern UFO devotees will not be surprised to hear that airships were perceived as secret military aircraft. In Britain particularly, they were thought to be German reconnaissance ships. Arnold Lupton, MP for Sleaford in Lincolnshire and an explosives expert, sought to put people's minds at rest regarding a possible air attack. He pointed out that it would need 10,000 lb of dynamite to destroy the Bank of England. As this would necessitate a huge fleet of airships, it obviously was not practical, he stated in the *South Wales Daily News* of 20 May 1909.

Hoaxes

Some of the stories printed by American newspapers were hoaxes used by editors in the circulation war. Modern researchers have exposed several such tall stories.

On 18 April 1897 the Dallas *Morning News* printed a story of an airship which had allegedly crashed the day before at about 6am.

According to the story, the silver cigar-shaped object came down low over Aurora before crashing into the side of a hill. When observers rushed to the crash sight they discovered the disfigured body of the pilot; according to one man – an authority on astronomy – it was the body of a Martian! The alien was allegedly buried in Aurora cemetery.

In 1966 Dr Alfred E. Kraus of the Kilgore Research Institute at West Texas State University carefully investigated the story for the Condon Committee (see Chapter 18). He interviewed surviving citizens from that time, but they claimed to know nothing about the incident. Kraus discovered that, a few years before, an ageing telegraph operator had confessed to starting the hoax. A search of the crash sight with a metal detector uncovered nothing unusual, and there was no sign of the 'Martian's' remains.

Attempts to exhume the alleged alien body in the Aurora cemetry were met with fierce opposition by the local community. After a brief legal battle in 1973, the ufologists agreed not to pursue the matter.

Five days after the Aurora story was published in 1897 a prominent Kansas rancher, Alexander Hamilton, and two other men told reporters they had seen an airship hovering over a corral where he kept a herd of cows. They were startled to see a calf being pulled up into the cigar-shaped object, which then flew away. The following day a man called Lank Thomas found the remains of the animal, apparently dumped from the air. Other witnesses testified to Hamilton's honesty, and the tale became a classic case of animal mutilation by extraterrestrials.

However, the truth of the affair had been printed as far back as 1943, in an obscure Kansas newspaper. Apparently Alexander Hamilton and the publisher of the Fredonia *Daily Herald* had concocted the story between them – a tale that was to be retold in newspapers as far away as Europe. The article came to light in 1976 when it was brought to the attention of Bob Rickard, editor of *Fortean Times*, by Robert Schadewald. American ufologist Jerome Clark traced a survivor who knew the Hamilton family, and she confirmed the hoax but it was still being reported as true in some UFO books even during the 1990s!

The Clipper of the Clouds and other fictional inventions

Does art imitate life, or does life imitate art – or is one an interchangeable reflection of the other? In 1886 Jules Verne published a novel called *The Clipper of the Clouds*. Verne was already an internationally known writer with many previously successful works including *Journey to the Centre of the Earth*, *Twenty Thousand Leagues under the Sea* and

Around the World in Eighty Days. Clipper tells the story of a shadowy figure called Robur who builds a giant airship in which he has many adventures. Many people of the Victorian era must have been aware of Verne's futuristic romance. Indeed, he was not the first writer to propagate the idea – nor the last.

During the latter half of the nineteenth century a French painter and illustrator named Albert Robida produced a pictorial and written vision of the future. He described an imaginary world of the 1950s which included chemical and bacterial warfare, television, climate control – and airships.

In 1892 American writer Lu Senarens created a character called Frank Reade Jr, whose adventures were chronicled in the weekly magazine *The Boys of New York*. What was special about the adventures was Reade's mode of transport: he travelled about the world in a variety of airships. Many of them were electrically powered with rotors which operated similarly to modern helicopters. Remarkably, Lu Senarens was only fourteen when he made his first sale, and went on to produce an astonishing forty million words. When Reade had visited all the remote areas of the world, he built a new airship – one which transported him across the Milky Way!

One of those airships which never got off the drawing board was the *Avitor*, patented by an American called Dr Mariot. Drawings of the *Avitor* showed a cigar-shaped craft with fins and a smoke stack, indicating that it was steam-driven. It was against this background of human ingenuity and imaginative fiction that people believed they were encountering actual airships. After World War II the dream – or nightmare – was of visiting spacecraft; the UFO phenomenon obligingly structured itself accordingly.

A case, researched by ufologist Barry Greenwood, which illustrates in microcosm many of the components of the airship phase of UFO reports occurred in Massachusetts during the latter part of 1909.

It started with statements in the press that a man called Wallace E. Tillinghast had announced that on 8 September he had flown an airship from Worcester to Boston, then to New York where he circled the Statue of Liberty and back again, attaining a speed of 120 mph over a total distance of 300 miles. This coincided with sightings of an airship made at that time. Tillinghast was described as 'a prominent citizen and vice president of a Worcester Manufacturing concern' who offered 'the most remarkable claim ever made of the possibilities of human aviation'.

According to Tillinghast his machine was a monoplane weighing

In 1994 airships are once again filling the skies – only this time they really do exist. Hundreds have been exported from Florida around the world to be used for promotional purposes. They glow in the dark and have triggered dozens of new UFO waves that plague police, airports and UFO groups alike.

over 1,500 lbs, with a wing span of 72 feet. It was equipped with a 120 horse power gasoline engine, and in addition to himself carried a crew of two mechanics. Tillinghast claimed that while over Fire Island he developed 'motor' trouble. He flew up to 4,000 feet where repairs were carried out, the airship gliding unpowered for forty-three minutes!

Interestingly, William Leach, an employee of the Fire Island Life Saving Station, claimed that he had heard 'the rattle and hum of a high speed motor' passing overhead at 7.30pm on 12 December. If there had been no more sightings the story might have died there, but just a few days before Christmas the phenomenon returned in force.

The *Newburyport Morning Herald* reported that an 'airship' travelling at a rapid rate passed over Boston harbour just after 1am on 20 December. Immigration lawyer Arthur Hoe was alerted by a 'pandemonium' of ships' whistles in the harbour. According to the *Taunton Gazette* Hoe 'saw the dark frame of an aeroplane bearing lights come up against the wind and pass him going at a good pace. He heard the whir of some machine . . . and could plainly see the silhouette of some sort of large frame with the rays of the lights gleaming through its open work.'

It was suggested that Hoe had mistaken the masthead light of a steam liner, the *Whitney*, as she was sailing into harbour, but the lawyer was adamant that the phenomenon was high in the air, and sighted in a different direction from where the ship had berthed. But arguments over this particular sighting were quickly forgotten as a flap took hold of the Boston area during the next few days.

Below the headline AIRSHIP SEEN IN TWO CITIES the *Boston Globe* of 23 December said:

WORCESTER Dec 22 – Flying through the night at an average speed of 20 to 40 miles per hour, a mysterious airship tonight appeared over Worcester shortly before 6 o'clock, hovered over the city a few minutes, disappeared and then returned to cut four circles, meanwhile sweeping the heavens with a searchlight of tremendous power.

The glaring rays of its great searchlight were sharply defined by reflection against the light snowfall which was covering the city. The dark mass of the ship could be dimly seen behind the light which flashed in all directions.

The object attracted the customers of a restaurant and thousands more residents of Worcester who came out on to the streets to observe. After fifteen minutes the object departed, but returned just after 8pm, where

BOSTON EXCITED OVER PHANTOM AEROPLANE

Great Light Sweeping Skies Seen by Thousands

Following the report from Worc Wednesday night of the discovery that city of a strange moving apparently the searchlight of a d air craft, stories came from man of the observance of similar li evening from villages east of and even from Bo⸱⸱⸱on Comn

Scientists Think Venus Caused the Excitement

Some Claim Outlines of Craft Were Plain

While hundreds of people about Bos- ton saw what they declare was an air- hous⸱⸱ them

TILLINGHAST WON'T SAY WHERE HE WAS

⸱⸱ out of Worcester last night, up in the air. It may be that ⸱ over the city, but that is my business. hen I said recently that I had n from Boston to New York and rn I said nothing but what was I have an airship which will ⸱⸱ three or four persons and will ke the speed I claimed for it at is, about 120 miles an hour. When I get ready I shall speak ally, and not till then."—Wallace E. Tillinghast,

TILLINGHAST ADMITS FLIGHT

Meanwhile, Wallace E. Tillinghast, the ⸱⸱⸱ man who ⸱⸱⸱

Headlines from the *Boston Post*, 24 December, 1909.

once more it circled the city four times before disappearing in the south-east. It was also seen over Marlboro and Cambridge.

In Revere just after 7pm 'several responsible persons' also sighted the phenomenon. Samuel Gibby, Chairman of the Board of Sewer Commissioners, saw two fast-moving lights coming from the direction of Boston. He then saw that the lights reflected off the wings of an airship. He alerted a neighbour, and the two men then watched it hover overhead before turning round and disappearing. Fire Chief Arthur Kimball saw the object moving at the speed of an express train, and clearly saw its outline; this was witnessed by another fireman too. When the searchlight turned down on to the street, it made it as bright as day. Alexander Rampell, an aeroplane designer himself, told the *Boston Record*:

As the aeroplane approached the beach it apparently slowed up and began to drop. At first I thought it was going to land on an aeroplane station I have established on the roof of my garage. The aeroplane came down to within five hundred feet of the ground, its framework becoming plainly visible and the reports of its engines coming clear and distinct. The planes were, I should say, seventy foot across and the tail and propeller forty foot long. It became apparent that the aeronaut had come down merely to get his bearings, for rising rapidly as he passed over our heads, he passed out to sea towards Nahant.

In the small community of Lynn, Representative Matthew McCann and garage owner John Davis were emphatic on the physical reality of the airship. McCann told reporters: 'I saw it distinctly. I could hear the throb of the engine and could vaguely distinguish the outline. I could not tell how many persons were onboard. It had two lights on in front. It circled about in the air then disappeared in the direction of Salem, when it turned and went in the general direction of the Milton section of Dorchester.'

The sightings went on for several days, bringing some added colour to the Christmas festivities. Indeed, one newspaper suggested that the sightings were of Santa Claus! But what was it that drew thousands of American citizens out on to the frosty streets and convinced most of them they had witnessed a remarkable flying machine?

Anatomy of a phenomenon

A study of the Boston wave in the light of contemporary UFO flaps reinforces a truism believed by most responsible ufologists: that UFO encounters are never about just one thing. Once the belief – or real- isation – creeps into a society that human beings are confronted by a phenomenon beyond their own technological capabilities, all sorts of psychological and sociological factors come into play. These factors include misidentifications of natural phenomena, hoaxing, the possible sighting of secret terrestrial flying craft and a genuine objective 'alien' anomaly. In 1909, the events at Boston included all of these.

Venus

Without a doubt many of the more mundane sightings were of the planet Venus and possibly the stars Castor and Pollux in the constella- tion Gemini. These astronomical bodies were visible over Massachu- setts and the cold, frosty conditions would make them look spectacular. Certainly some of the descriptions sound like Venus. Professor William

H. Pickering of Harvard University told the press that the planet was visible from late afternoon until about eight in the evening.

Any object observed in the night sky for over two hours – as some of the witnesses claimed – has to be an astronomical body. But as Venus slipped out of sight over the horizon at about 8pm, it cannot account for sightings after that time. Although the psychological phenomenon of autokinesis can account for the apparent small movement of a stationary light, it is not an explanation for the obvious journey of an object across the sky. Nor can stars and planets project beams of light on to streets and buildings.

Hoaxers

The hoaxers were a combination of practical jokers and liars. For instance, there was evidence that someone – or several people – were sending up miniature hot air balloons. The lanterns which hung beneath these hot air-filled bags provided the spectacle of a light moving in the sky. The *Worcester Telegram* reported how one balloon had landed on a garage and started a fire; the remains of others were found around Worcester. Modern hoaxers also use this method. In a bizarre twist to the fire balloon theory, a man called C. D. Rawson claimed that the lights were lanterns attached to the legs of two large white owls! Rawson explained how he had ordered three dead owls for mounting, from North Carolina, but instead live birds arrived. He claimed that on deciding to release the owls he tied the small lanterns to their legs with string, so the birds could later free themselves.

Rawson told reporters he would publicly release the third owl in Only Square, Worcester, but first the weather and then other excuses were used to explain why the creature was not produced. Charles K. Reed, a taxidermist, stated that there were no white owls south of the Arctic, and in any case they would be incapable of carrying any weight.

'Secret' inventors

Were some of the sightings – particularly the close encounter cases – actual airships constructed by 'secret' inventors?

A man called G. F. Russell arrived in New York from Marblehead to announce he was the pilot of the mystery airship. Russell, who was only twenty-one, claimed that the machine operated on 'a new gyroscope-equilibrium invention'. However, when his employers were contacted – W. Starling Burgess, a yacht-building company – they denied the story. Although they had been working on several airships, none of them was ready for removal from the workshop – to say nothing of flying.

What was the truth behind the claims of Wallace E. Tillinghast, who told newspaper men he had made over one hundred trial flights in several machines?

With the upsurge of sightings in late December, Tillinghast found himself pursued by the press – which is perhaps what he had hoped for all along. Spies kept an eye on his movements, reporting that during the wave Tillinghast was sometimes at home and at other times missing. At one stage the press harassment became too much and he was reported to have slammed the door in the face of journalists. While not directly claiming to be responsible for the sightings, he did nothing to discourage belief either. When questioned about the phenomena observed over Worcester during the previous Wednesday evening, he told the *Taunton Gazette*: 'I was out of Worcester last night. Where I was is my own business. It may be that I flew over the city, but that is my own business too. I am not talking to the press or the public. When I get good and ready I will show the public that I have what I have claimed.'

Some newspapers saw the sightings as vindication of the engineer's earlier claims. A note was even secretly made of Tillinghast's car mileage counter to determine where the airship was based! While some newspapers carried stories supporting Tillinghast's story, others were openly sceptical – as were official bodies.

The Aero Club of New England issued a statement through its President, Charles J. Glidden, which was reported in the *Christian Science Monitor* and elsewhere. The statement related the results of the club's own investigation into the affair: Tillinghast's alleged speed of two miles a minute, and supposed gliding capability for over three-quarters of an hour, were impossible given the current technology. Other aeronauts in the Boston area had never heard of Tillinghast, and no one at that time was claiming to have seen his airship on the ground, taking off or landing.

Winston Churchill asked a parliamentary question about the airships in 1913. At the time it was speculated they might be German Zeppelins.

Under pressure Tillinghast announced that his airship would be exhibited at the Boston Aero Show, to be held in late February 1910. This was the result of a visit by the show's promoter, Percy Edgar. In the meantime there was speculation that the machine was garaged on a farm in Boylston owned by Paul B. Morgan, who had also provided financial backing for the project. Reporters tried to get near a long wooden building, but were arrested for trespassing. The Boston Aero Show came and went without an appearance by the two-mile-a-minute monoplane.

So was it all a practical joke by Tillinghast which got out of hand? Some months later, on 13 July 1910, the *Providence Journal* published a small piece that added some credence to the physical reality of an airship. It reported that Arthur M. Davidson, Secretary of the Worcester Board of Trade, had told them that he had visited Wallace Tillinghast at a secret location and been shown the airship. But when asked if he had seen it in flight, Davidson admitted that he had not.

The truth probably was that Wallace E. Tillinghast had built an airship. Equally probable was that the machine had never left the ground. The inventor hijacked the UFO reports out of vanity, and possibly in the hope that the publicity might attract additional backers for his project.

Fifty thousand people crowded the streets over Christmas 1909 looking for evidence of the phantom airship. Many of them, like witnesses today, mistook Venus. Did the rest really catch sight of an 'alien' phenomenon?

Ironically, the secret airship pilots are still with us, still taking credit for UFO reports! One of them approached Jenny Randles at a conference held in June 1993. He told her he was one of a network of inventors who carried out clandestine night-time flights over the British Isles. Apparently they wore silver jump suits to fool witnesses into reporting accidental sightings as UFOs. That way the Civil Aviation Authority would pay no heed to the reports, and they could evade prosecution.

Part Two

1919–39:
UP TO WORLD WAR II

GHOST FLIERS AND OTHER PHENOMENA

Reports of UFOs just before and during World War I are thin on the ground, although they do exist. Some of those that resembled airships have already been discussed; here is a selection of different-looking phenomena.

Fireballs over the Balkans

In 1913, over the Struma Valley in Bulgaria, a strange phenomenon was recorded just as the sun was sinking over the mountains. Prisoners in the valley saw a huge 'fireball' heading towards the frontier with Greece. What was remarkable was the slow descent of the object. According to a political prisoner named George Topîrceanu, it was as if it was descending on a parachute.

In the summer of that year, twenty-year-old François Zatloukal was travelling from Brnoyto Zidenice in Moravia (now part of the Czech Republic) when he was startled by something in the sky. It was between nine and ten in the evening when he saw six objects at high altitude resembling fiery red stars. They seemed to be under intelligent control, because they flew in an elliptical orbit in a clockwise direction. After six to eight minutes he continued on his journey.

A more bizarre series of encounters took place over the village of Bujoreanca in Romania, according to a schoolteacher. In the autumn of either 1914 or 1915 the man was having a meal in the garden with his family when everyone's attention turned to the sky. There they saw a spherical object with an 'exhaust pipe' protruding from it, not more than twenty-five metres above the ground, travelling east. As it passed over, the object caused some acacias and oak trees to bend in the turbulence. It left a trail of glowing sparks and made a whistling sound.

Over the next week the object reappeared several times and was witnessed by all the villagers. Strangely, it materialised over one house, then dematerialised over another. On one occasion it remained stationary over one of the houses, and a woman who lived there was afterwards found dead, apparently covered in burns.

A similar experience from these years was related by meteorologist Elizabeth Klarer of Natal, South Africa to investigator Cynthia Hind. In October 1917 Elizabeth and her sister were living on a farm in a valley nestling below the Drakensberg Mountains. It was near the Mooi River at sunset, at around 5.30pm, that they had their sighting. The girls were standing on a hill when an orange-red ball appeared in the sky; it seemed to be rushing in their direction, and Elizabeth thought it must be a meteorite. They then noticed a metallic sphere which circled around the ball three times, deflecting it from its course. In later years Elizabeth became a contactee and wrote a book about her experiences called *Beyond the Light Barrier*. It describes her regular contact with a non-human intelligence.

Back in the Balkans at a place called Colun in Romania, another interesting case occurred some time in 1926. A farmer called Ion Bunescu, was seeing to his horses at about 1am when over the pasture appeared an 'illuminated spear' which lit up the area. According to Bunescu it hovered for about twelve minutes, part of that time directly above him, before moving off towards Arpasul de Jos, some eight kilometres away. There it circled a small wood before suddenly becoming 'extinguished'. The farmer said it had made a whistling noise, was shaped like a boat, and was darker in the middle. He estimated it to be about three metres long and two wide. This is interesting in the light of modern animal mutilation cases where strange lights have been seen over fields just before the discovery of dead and injured animals (see Part Six).

That year also saw an early humanoid encounter. It occurred to a six-year-old boy in Lancashire, England, and was investigated by the authors in 1990.

The 'Three Wise Men'

Henry Thomson, a professional artist who has travelled around the world, has a photographic memory which allows him to commit to canvas with absolute accuracy scenes he witnessed decades ago. It also enables Henry to remember in vivid detail an incident from his childhood.

One evening in November 1926 Henry had been playing hide and seek with his pals. In their version of the game, half the group hid while the rest counted to fifty and then split up to begin searching. Grudgingly, Henry had had to leave the other boys because it was his bedtime.

As he lay under the covers he could hear the others outside, still playing, and he wanted to join them. He quickly dressed, then stealthily crept out through the back door to join his friends. This time he was one of the seekers, and volunteered to search the backs of Eustace Street and nearby Woodgate Street.

The back yards of the terraced houses all looked the same: dark and spooky, except where a chink of light spilled out through imperfectly closed curtains. As he walked down Eustace Street, something caught

'Standing, peering into the house, were three figures – and they did not look human.' This sketch by Henry Thomson depicts his mysterious encounter in November 1926.

his eye in the yard of number 21. He stopped and peeped around the opened gate. What confronted him was to remain indelibly etched on his memory for ever.

The light from the scullery window spilled out into the yard. Standing there, peering into the house, were three figures – and they did not look human. They were turned away from the boy, who stared in amazement. Two of them were around five foot eight, but the third, who stood in the middle, was several inches taller. They wore helmets and silver-grey suits ridged in thick padded horizontal bands, plus black boots. Tubes from a box mounted on each figure's back fed into the neck of the helmet.

Perhaps some small noise made by the boy alerted the figures, but they suddenly spun round. Three owl-like faces stared down at him. Their heads – or helmets – were doorknob-shaped, with two black slit eyes, no mouth, but a vertical slit where the nose should be. A loud gargling or mumbling sound issued from the tall one, and the three advanced towards Henry.

Henry ran home as fast as his legs could carry him. His parents thought his terror was due to being caught after slipping out of the house, and his story of 'three men in divers' suits' was met with disbelief. But Henry persisted, and over the coming months his family came to realise that something very peculiar indeed had happened to their little boy. Eventually his mother referred to the encounter as 'a visitation from the Three Wise Men' – a conclusion that Henry feels is a million miles from the truth!

High above the Himalayas

In his travel diary, published in 1929, Nicholas Roerich relates a very unusual experience. The book, entitled *Altai-Himalya*, records his expedition through India, Tibet, Sinkiang and Mongolia.

On August fifth – something remarkable! We were in our camp in the Kukunor district, not far from the Humboldt Chain. In the morning about half-past nine some of our caravaneers noticed a remarkably big black eagle flying above us. Seven of us began to watch this unusual bird. At the same moment another of our caravaneers remarked: 'There is something far above the bird.' And he shouted his astonishment. We all saw, in the direction north to south, something big and shiny reflecting sun, like a huge oval moving at great speed. Crossing our camp this thing changed in its direction from south to southwest, and we saw how it disappeared in the intense blue sky. We even had time to take our field glasses and saw quite distinctly the oval form with the shiny surface, one side of which was brilliant from the sun.

City sightings in the snow

In the winter of 1933 the *New York Times* published details of a sighting over the city which had occurred during a heavy snowstorm on Tuesday, 26 December. Witnesses described how they heard the sound of an aircraft circling above Park Avenue and 122nd Street at 9.30am; the phenomenon continued for five hours. Many witnesses contacted the National Broadcasting Company, and Newark Airport radio operators from the Department of Commerce offered help in the belief that a lunatic airman was trying to land. Field beacons were lit, and searchlights tried to probe through the falling blanket of snow. According to the newspaper, none of the flying fields had aircraft operating that day – indeed, the weather conditions made it impossible. At 2.25pm, when the sound stopped, nothing fell from the sky on to Manhattan.

Little more than two months later, on 2 February 1934, the London *Times* reported that the previous night an 'airoplane' had circled over the city continuously for two hours. The heavy note of the engines indicated it was a large machine, and its altitude was low enough for its lights to be seen. The Air Ministry stated it knew nothing of the flight, and civil aerodromes around London were equally baffled.

However four days later, when the matter was brought up in the House of Commons, Sir Philip Sassoon, Under Secretary of State of Air, offered an explanation. He claimed the aircraft belonged to the RAF and was on a training exercise in cooperation with ground troops. But on 11 June, two aircraft circled above the city, low enough for their outlines to be easily discernible. The Air Ministry admitted that the RAF frequently practised night flying, but it was forbidden to operate over London at less than 5,000 feet. They told *The Times* that the identity of the rogue aircraft was not known.

American researcher Charles Flood discovered a similar story dated 14 February 1936 in the *Oregonian*. It told how 'an unidentified airplane battled a raging blizzard and twenty below weather over Cody, Wyoming'.

The ship was heard roaring over the city at about 6pm. After it circled several times, the sound of its motors faded and it was not heard again for almost an hour. At approximately 7pm it was heard over the town again, the pilot accelerating his motor as he circled for several minutes.

Residents of the city fought their way through heavy snows to the airport, and circled the field with flares. Before the flares could be lit, however, the sound of the unknown plane's motor had again faded.

In a follow-up report, the newspaper stated that no explanation had been offered to identify the mystery aircraft.

The ghost fliers of Scandinavia

The last of Amundsen?

During the mid-1930s sightings of large grey aircraft were made by thousands of people across northern Scandinavia. They bore no markings and were the subject of intense searches by the military authorities of Finland, Norway and Sweden. These aircraft were able to outperform flying machines of that period and to operate in terrible weather conditions. The prelude to all this centred around an unidentified aircraft photographed on an island near the Arctic Circle.

In 1928 Roald Amundsen, the Norwegian explorer who in 1911 had been the first man to reach the South Pole, organised a fatal flight to the North Pole. His first attempt, in 1925, had nearly ended in disaster when one of the two aircraft his team were using crashed. This time, somewhere far north of the Arctic Circle his twin-engined Lathom aircraft must have come down, because it was never seen again.

Three years later a team of scientists flew over the Arctic Circle in the *Graf Zeppelin* on a photographic mission. Professor Paul Moltchanow discovered in one of his pictures an artificial object which no one had noticed at the time. Shaped like an aircraft, the object was resting on snow in the south-eastern part of the island of Novaya Zemlya. The professor told the *New York Times*: 'The plane was lying on a strip of snow. It is a monoplane with sharply rectangular wings and can be clearly seen. It is a two-seater and undamaged. It seems possible that it could be Roald Amundsen's plane, because he had a two-motor Lathom. We have no idea so far what it might be.'

However, Captain Walter Bruns, the founder of the Aero-Arctic Society, which had sponsored the expedition, disagreed with this hypothesis. He told the press that it was 'extremely unlikely' to be Amundsen's aircraft, as it had not carried enough fuel to have travelled

General Pontus Reutersward commanded the north Swedish military area. He wrote a secret seventeen page report to the Secretary of War concerning the ghost fliers. It said: 'The collected and analysed data ... has given me the impression that unauthorised air traffic has occurred.'

that far. Captain Bruns added that there was no record of any other aircraft missing in that area.

Further doubt was cast on the Amundsen explanation when German aviation experts announced that the object resembled a Dornier Wal seaplane. Was this the abandoned aircraft from Amundsen's first expedition? But it was thought impossible for the crashed aeroplane to have blown so far south – it had probably been crushed by pack ice where it lay. Then it was suggested that the mystery aeroplane was one of two Wals belonging to the Russian government. The Dornier factory in Friedrichshafen, Germany, who had sold the two planes to the Russians, stated that the aircraft were currently operating along the Siberian coast. The origin of the aircraft was to remain a mystery.

Invasion of the super planes

The parish priest of Lantrask in Sweden observed mysterious aircraft on several occasions during 1932 and 1933. In the summer of 1933 the craft flew over the area no fewer than twelve times. It always followed the same route, south-west to north-east. On four occasions it flew so low that he was able to observe it carried no markings or insignia. The machine was greyish with one set of wings. Once it skimmed just a few metres above the parsonage and he made out two figures in the cabin. As in the previous airship wave, the occupants were always described as normal-looking human beings.

Although there had been reports before 1933, the phenomenon intensified during Christmas week of that year. An article in the Swedish newspaper *Dagens-Nyheter* stated: 'A mysterious aeroplane appeared from the direction of the Bottensea at about 6pm, Christmas Eve, passed over Kalix, and continued westward. Beams of light came from the machine searching the area.'

The report was fairly brief, but it seems that the authorities must have received many similar unpublished sightings given that on the 28th the following announcement appeared in the press:

The ghost flier will be hunted by the Flying Corps Number 4 in Ostersund. Saturday, the Flying Corps received orders by telegraph to make contact with the police in the area. The flier was reported on Saturday, visible over Tarnaby, and this report was very interesting because the weather was clear.

The head of the Air Force received a telephone call asking for help in searching for the mysterious flier in Norrland. Information and detailed descriptions will be collected about the smuggler-flier.

An analysis was carried out by the General Staff in Stockholm of 487 Scandinavian cases between 1933 and 1934. They concluded that 46 were 'credible', 64 'probably credible', 273 'others' and 104 'unbelievable'.

At 6pm Saturday evening the ghost flier passed over Tarnaby. People saw it cross the Norwegian border, turn over Joesjo ... the place where he disappeared Friday evening. The last sighting was eastward towards Stensele.

On the day this report was released an aeroplane carrying three lights was observed at high altitude over Langmo Vefsn in Norway. Apparently it was similar to previous sightings from Hattefjallsdalen.

Two days later motorists near Gällivare in Sweden watched an aircraft which flew over the road at a height of around 150 feet. The authorities stated there were 'no ambulance planes or military craft in that area at the time'.

The New Year began with more reports and official comment:

The head of the Air Force, Major Von Porat, refused to speculate on the phantom flier except to confirm that he did exist. 'Specific details on this affair can't be published,' he said.

As late as Sunday morning a large grey aeroplane, bigger than any army plane, was seen in Sorsele. The machine flew in big circles over the railway station and vanished in the direction of Arvidsjaur.

Mr Olof Hedlund was taking a walk at 3.45am when he suddenly heard an engine roar from above. There was a full moon and visibility was very good. Mr Hedlund said the machine was about 400 metres up and in sight for about fifteen minutes. It was single-winged and enclosed, like a passenger plane, and was equipped with pontoons or some sort of skis.

No marks or insignia were visible. The engine stopped during the turns over the village. The noise seemed to emanate from the propeller. The machine was similar to a single-engined Junkers.

An old song set to a new tune

Over a hundred similar reports were uncovered in the 1970s by Swedish and American researchers. It is hard to imagine the impact of these reports on the Scandinavians, at a time when aviation lacked sophistication and was still a perilous pursuit. Like the phantom airships before them, the ghost planes seemed to be recognisable flying machines which possessed capabilities way beyond the technology of that time.

A feature of the mystery aircraft was to cast down blinding searchlights – a component of many modern UFO sightings. Arc lights came into being during the nineteenth century, but they required heavy generators and batteries which for a plane would have presented a weight problem beyond the technology of the 1930s. Aeroplanes were fitted with lights similar to car headlights, making night flying a rare and dangerous affair. The ghost fliers took to the air in appalling weather conditions, yet at that time instrumental and navigational equipment was so crude that most pilots preferred to remain grounded than to risk even a mild rainstorm. Over a third of reports referred to objects detected during snowstorms, blizzards and dense fog.

A lighthouse keeper named Rutkvist at Holmogadd in Sweden reported an aircraft which he had observed on two occasions. On Monday, 8 January 1934, he saw it hover over the island of Grasundet. After a time it spiralled towards the sea, stopped short, then ascended again – repeating the manoeuvre for an hour. On another date he observed an object flying in a blizzard against winds up to sixteen metres a second. He told journalists: 'I have never seen anything like it! It was a very strange action for an aeroplane.'

State of the art

Let us consider the evidence for where these craft might have come from. Most aircraft at that time had not advanced much since World War I: the majority were clumsy biplanes with open cockpits and a low range. But the ghost planes were larger than these. Radios were rarely employed, being heavy and difficult for a single pilot to use. Yet broadcasts by the phantom fliers were picked up all over Scandinavia.

The ghost fliers are a true mystery. It was not just a case of the misidentification of ordinary aircraft, or of secret military aircraft from a foreign country—although perhaps some of them were. In the 1930s Russia had no aircraft industry to speak of. Adolf Hitler broke the terms of the Versailles Treaty in 1933 when he began secretly building up the Luftwaffe; surely he would not have risked his meagre reservoir of ex-World War I pilots in pointless missions over Scandinavia. It was speculated that Japan might be the culprit, but that country was at war with China in the 1930s, and one would assume too busy to bother elsewhere. On top of that there was a worldwide recession.

Because of the very limited range of aircraft, any country carrying out a reconnaissance of Scandinavia would have had to set up fuel supply lines in hidden bases manned by aviation personnel. Aircraft carriers might be considered an alternative – but they were still only in the early stages of development. Even in America, the sighting of an aeroplane was still a rarity. Despite all this, the people of Norway, Sweden and Finland were observing large grey aircraft, sometimes in formations of threes, right up to 1937.

The military response

As far as the military were concerned, low-flying aircraft were over their territory for one reason only – to discover the location of forts, military and railway installations for a future war. The Swedish and Norwegian authorities were convinced they were dealing with a foreign power. They also knew the sightings were not explicable in terms of hoaxes and illusionary phenomena. In a report to General Virgin on 3 January 1934, Major Von Porat wrote: 'Many people of good reputation have seen the mysterious aeroplane with searchlight rays playing over the ground. Among the witnesses are two military men from the 4th Flying Corps.'

The ghost fliers seemed immune to accident – not so with their pursuers. When the 4th Flying Corps tried to shadow them across the mountains they lost two biplanes, which may have had something to do with the decision to call off the operation on 18 January. Army search parties nevertheless continued to search the snowy mountains on skis and snowshoes, and military investigators interviewed the many civilian witnesses. The same measures were being taken in Finland, while Swedish and Norwegian ships were busy exploring the surrounding seas and remote islands for the airbases necessary to equip the anonymous grey aircraft.

It is amazing how this hive of military activity has been mirrored in recent years by the hundreds of reliable sightings of phantom submarines which, with equal ease, have invaded Swedish territorial waters and escaped damage or capture. Before the collapse of the Soviet Union, these USOs – unidentified submersible objects – were thought to come from the Warsaw Pact countries. But Russia has always denied this. Despite the use of hundreds of depth charges, no USO has ever been forced to surface.

By February 1934 the authorities realised that the phenomenon was making fools out of them. They reasoned that if they were dealing with aeroplanes some of them would crash and a few of them would be captured, or at least their supply bases would be discovered. None of this had happened; so, they concluded, the ghost fliers were not aircraft. Many in the military preferred to think they did not even exist – a familiar story.

The authorities turned their backs, and the phantom fliers, as if sensing this, eventually lost interest and departed.

In 1937 the Finnish General Staff published a study of the 1933–1934 wave. Of 111 reports, 10 sightings and 5 sounds remained unexplained. The report said: 'The mysterious phenomena were usually observed for only a short time and never from two places at the same time.'

Part Three

1939–47:
WAR OF THE WORLDS

3

FOO FIGHTERS FROM MARS?

Whilst scattered sightings occurred throughout the war and across the globe, it was late 1943 before air crews began to realise that something odd was going on.

D uring World War II thousands of aircraft were flying above Europe and the Pacific on bombing raids, reconnaissance missions and other operations. Never before had so many people been above the clouds, scanning clear skies with eagle-eyed intensity on the constant look-out for enemy action. It is hardly surprising that the UFOs, which had probably always been 'up there', suddenly got spotted in great abundance. But as some worried people soon came to ask: were they fighting enemies from only *this* world?

Confusing the enemy?

Whilst scattered sightings occurred throughout the war and across the globe, it was late 1943 before air crews began to realise that something odd was going on. At first, those who reported these incidents were laughed at or told they must be suffering from battle fatigue. But such easy rationalisations soon had to be rejected.

Hilary Evans reports a sighting on 14 October 1943 when a bomber raid on an industrial plant at Schweinfurt in Germany was mounted by the American 384th. On their final bombing run many crew members observed 'a cluster of discs' dead ahead. These were 'silver coloured, about one inch thick and three inches in diameter'. They were 'gliding down slowly' in a tight group. One B-17 pilot, unable to avoid contact, feared imminent disaster as his plane sliced through the small lights. But to his intense relief the bomber continued on its way, unhindered and undamaged.

It is quite conceivable that some reports of this kind referred to 'chaff' – clumps of aluminium foil released by aircraft in an attempt to confuse enemy radar screens by producing false reflections. Yet this possibility does not seem to have prevented official investigations by worried intelligence units, particularly with the American forces based in Europe.

According to rumour, there was also a British investigation into the foo fighter reports called the Massey Project. However Air Chief Marshal Sir Victor Goddard – who was an outspoken believer in alien craft during the 1950s – flatly denied this and said that Treasury approval for such a minor exercise at a time when Britain was fighting for its survival would have been ludicrous.

More certain is that the sightings continued to bemuse pilots and were occurring not only in European skies. On 10 August 1944 there was a sighting from a bomber unit near Sumatra in Indonesia, who observed an object pacing their aircraft's wing. It was a red-orange sphere that kept up with all the evasive manoeuvres executed by the pilot. After several minutes it shot away at a 90 degree angle and accelerated into the night. Captain Reida of 792 Squadron filed an in-depth report with US Army/Air Force intelligence, 'thinking it was some new type of radio-controlled missile or weapon'.

More explanations have been suggested for foo fighters than any other UFO type – including meteors, ball lightning and small comets.

Not St Elmo's Fire

By autumn 1944 reports were so commonplace over France, Germany and surrounding areas that crews had nicknamed the lights 'foo fighters', apparently after a comic strip popular at the time. 'Foo' was, presumably, a corruption of the French word *feu*, which means fire.

Jenny Randles interviewed comedian Michael Bentine, who in late 1944 was an intelligence officer stationed in eastern England dealing with Free Polish troops. He had to debrief bomber crews after a raid on the German secret weapons site at Peenemünde on the Baltic coast where deadly aerial technology was developed.

Bentine reported how they described seeing these lights. He did not take them seriously until several crews had come back and told identical stories. They spoke of being 'pursued by a light which was pulsating and had flown round the aircraft'. He suggested that they were observing St Elmo's Fire, a static electrical discharge that sometimes creates balls of light around pointed metal objects like ship's masts. But the crews were insistent that they had seen St Elmo's Fire elsewhere and that these phenomena were nothing like it.

Bentine continued: 'As far as they were concerned it was some form of weapon. So I said: "What did it *do* to you?" And they said "Nothing." So I said it was not a very effective weapon!'

Foo fighters photographed over the Pacific theatre during World War II. These mysterious balls of light were some of the earliest officially investigated UFOs.

A couple of days later an American intelligence officer visited Bentine's unit to hear what his crews were observing. By now there had been more than half a dozen cases in just a few weeks. The American said that his men were seeing the same thing and added: 'They appear in daylight as well. We don't know what they are.' Michael Bentine told us that, in his view, 'It was probably the manifestation of what is now called a UFO.'

Tales of the 415th

The most widely quoted sighting occurred on 23 November 1944 and involved the 415th, an American night fighter unit flying out of France. They seem to have been the location of most of the best-known 1944–5 reports and were the source of the 'foo fighter' nickname.

On this date, Lieutenant Edward Schlueter was going from Dijon on an intercept mission to Strasbourg and Mannheim, flying mostly above the Vosges Mountains. With him were Lieutenant Don Myers and an intelligence officer, Lieutenant Ringwald. It was Ringwald who first spotted about ten balls of orange-red fire moving at great velocity in formation. The sky was very clear and Ringwald was an excellent and experienced observer: he had just spotted a freight train miles V-rockets then terrifying southern England, and the frantic Nazi race to develop intercontinental missiles to strike the American mainland away from their flight path, despite the fact that its boiler was shielded by blackout and only a plume of steam had given its location away.

The crew debated the lights. Were they misperceptions of stars? Could they be meteors? Perhaps their own aircraft was reflecting off clouds? They dismissed each idea in turn.

Then, as they closed in for the kill, the red fireballs simply melted into nothingness. Minutes later they reappeared, then vanished again. It was as if they were playing tag. The crew gave up and got on with their raid.

Many similar sightings followed. Radar stations and on-board radar in the aircraft showed that nothing was actually there. Yet the lights climbed up, chased the bombers, matched them for speed and man-oeuvrability and then disappeared instantly. It is not surprising that the possibility of a 'secret weapon' became popular, despite the innocent nature of the events.

Three weeks later, on 2 January 1945, stories appeared in the press in many countries, using the term 'foo fighter' and still implying a weapon, but adding that nobody could identify what it was. Given the V-rockets then terrifying southern England, and the frantic Nazi race to develop intercontinental missiles to strike the American mainland

A montage of press cuttings about the 1945 foo fighters.

'Foo fighters' are what UFO experts now call 'lights in the sky' or LITS. They are the most common UFO type in the world, accounting for over sixty percent of all sightings.

(near to perfection when the war ended), the idea of an unknown German threat was far from absurd.

There were ground-based witnesses, too. We have a report from a former prisoner of war at the Heydebreck camp in Upper Silesia, Poland. At 3pm on 22 January 1945 a number of men were being paraded by the Germans before being marched away to evade the liberating Russian Army. A bomber appeared overhead, flying at about 18,000 feet, and the men gazed in horror at what seemed to be fire pouring from its rear end. Then they thought it might be a flare caught up in the slipstream of the aircraft. Finally, they realised it was neither of these things: the object was a silvery ball hugging the bomber, which was desperately trying to evade it. The foo fighter was still right on the tail of the aircraft as both passed into the distance.

A few weeks later the war ended, and nothing more was said. No secret weapons of this kind were found in German hands. Captured air crew, scientists and intelligence officers affirmed that Nazi fighters had also been seeing foo fighters (they called them 'feuer' balls). The Germans and Japanese had both assumed these things to be American secret weapons!

An undiscovered secret weapon?

When the first 'flying saucers' arrived a couple of years later, the secret files on foo fighters were re-examined by the US Army and Air Force to see if they might be the same phenomenon. Foo fighters were concluded to be rare electrical activity, such as ball lightning.

However, novelist W. A. Harbinson took a very different view in his fictional epic *Genesis*, based, he reports, on research initiated by foo fighter stories. He contends that there really was a German secret weapon – a small, jet-powered, remote-controlled disc, effectively a prototype of larger (manned) versions that would have flown had the war not ended when it did.

According to post-war German accounts that Harbinson traced, the device was designed by Rudolph Schriever in spring 1941, first tested in June 1942 and flown in earnest in August 1943. Schriever reportedly built a full-scale circular craft some 137 feet in diameter that was scheduled to fly in April 1945. The test was abandoned with the advance of the Allies on Berlin, the death of Hitler and the end of the war in Europe. But Harbinson found evidence that the working full-scale prototype was built in the Harz Mountains during 1944 and secretly flown on 14 February 1945.

Schriever originally believed that his papers and the prototype had all been destroyed to stop them falling into Allied hands; but subsequently, right up to his death in the late 1950s, he wondered if that were true. He had concluded that the by then persistent sightings of disc-like UFOs were the result of continuing secret development of his own invention, perhaps by Nazi scientists who had fled Germany and set up a base in some remote region.

Eventually, in January 1992, the truth about foo fighters and the USAF was revealed when Barry Greenwood, an excellent and objective UFO investigator specialising in digging into government files, gained limited access to still classified records on American war activity. Initially this comprised the unit summary and war diary of the 415th night fighter squadron – certainly the most involved of the US flight crews.

These papers credited Don Myers of the 23 November 1944 sighting with the first use of the term 'foo fighter' (although, oddly, this event was cited as having occurred in late October, and not the date the crew themselves had given in a December 1945 service magazine interview). Assorted lights (often red, sometimes green and also white) were encountered on frequent missions. Lieutenant Schlueter saw them more than once.

In September 1992 Greenwood started reading a three-feet-thick file of all the mission records for the 415th between autumn 1944 and spring 1945. He found that sightings continued right up to the end of the war. Intriguingly, among these documents – which were many years older than Harbinson's bizarre novel – were the records of American foo fighter sightings during February 1945. There were two of them – both within a few hours of the purported flight of that amazing Nazi flying disc from the reputed complex in the Harz Mountains!

By 1945 pulp science-fiction comic books were very popular with adolescents and often featured alien contact and even, occasionally, saucer-shaped objects in the sky.

4

GHOST ROCKETS IN THE SKY

Throughout the summer of 1946 the sightings escalated.

It was left to science fiction readers and tabloid speculators to think that there might be something supernatural behind the quickly forgotten foo fighter stories. The war ended and there were far more pressing matters for most people to contend with.

However, the UFO mystery was not about to go away. Whilst nobody had yet recognised how scattered pockets of activity, from the phantom airships to the foo fighters, reflected an unidentified aerial phenomenon that had been appearing in the sky for decades, another wave of strange events was about to hit the world.

These latest UFOs were not perceived as a scientific riddle to be resolved. They were not pursued with open and enthusiastic vigour. These new lights in the sky were decreed a military secret and treated yet again as a possible source of threat from a power very much of this earth – not one that was thought to come from somewhere decidedly off it.

Crowded skies over Scandinavia

The reports began as early as 26 February 1946, when a Helsinki radio story described 'inordinate meteor activity' in the far north of Finland. But it was late May before they spread further south and into Sweden, where greater population density ensured almost daily reports. Throughout the summer of 1946 the sightings escalated. By the autumn 996 reports had been officially logged by the Swedish defence authorities alone. A conservative estimate for sightings in Scandinavia that summer would probably reach several thousand.

Most witnesses referred to a light at night, briefly emitting flame from the rear. The speed varied from very rapid to quite sedate. There were daytime reports also, often describing missile—or dark lozenge-shaped craft. Often there was a short tail of fire. The objects moved horizontally but then often fell vertically downwards. However, mixed in with these reports were occasional sightings of spindle shapes or eggs and ovals – accounts more reminiscent of modern-day UFOs.

A good account in early August came from a meteorologist who had the good fortune to be using a telescope for observational purposes when he saw one of the lights above Stockholm. He watched it carefully as it passed overhead for about ten seconds, describing it as being 'at least 90 feet long. The body was torpedo-shaped and shining like metal. It had a tapered tail that spewed glowing blue and green smoke and a series of fireballs.'

The media reported the events quite extensively from late May – until ordered by the defence authorities in late July to stop for what they called 'strategic' reasons. Their fear was clear – these 'ghost rockets', as the media had named them, were believed to be secret weapons being test flown in (or – in some more hysterical quarters – deliberately aimed at) Sweden. There was only one realistic possibility for the sender of these missiles – the Soviet Union.

By 1946 scientists were making their first tentative searches for extra-terrestrial life by scanning the heavens with radio telescopes.

Indeed, in summer 1944 the first V-2 rocket successfully tested by Germany had landed in Sweden, crashing and exploding in a farmer's field. Debris had been collected, analysed and then sent to Britain for Allied assessment. This prototype ballistic missile was the first taste of the successor to the Nazi V-1 (or 'doodlebug') which was already devastating London. The V-2 (and the longer-range V-3, under development as the war ended) could carry bomb payloads hundreds of miles from their remote launch sites, such as Peenemünde.

High-level intelligence briefings

Worried defence chiefs in Scandinavia now believed that the USSR (which had captured control of Peenemünde in 1945) might have developed the technology and started trying out enhanced V-2s by 'bombing' supposedly friendly countries – although, thankfully, minus the warheads. There are persistent stories that during August 1946 top-level intelligence experts visited Sweden to discuss the problem, under the guise of trade missions or proffered aid for radar equipment. British war hero Douglas Bader and the general who had led the US bomber squadrons that had reported most of the foo fighters, James Doolittle, were two who visited Stockholm and had meetings at this time.

Legends about what they discussed have since abounded. But in 1984 Barry Greenwood attempted to find out directly. He wrote to Doolittle, who replied unambiguously on 29 August that he 'did know' about the ghost rockets, but seemed to scotch the claims that he had access to any higher-level data by saying that he had 'no firm knowledge of actual … "ghost rockets" in Sweden' and that what he did know came 'largely by the press'. Of course, he may simply have been being discreet, given the fact that the matter has never received an official airing in the US public archives.

A British Air Ministry intelligence report, dated 8 September 1946, referred to 'bright, shining, luminous or fiery balls, or else cylindrical or cigar-shaped objects, sometimes with a bright light in the tail, occasionally in the nose …'. It is interesting to note the phrase 'cigar-shaped' being used here in an official report a year before there were such things as flying saucers or UFOs. Some sceptics still cling to the view that colourful language like this is a product of imaginative witnesses in the modern age, basing their accounts on science fiction. But in fact it was originally used in a government report, and probably for the same reason that witnesses still use it fifty years later: it well describes what they see. Exactly the same applies to the term 'saucer-shaped', which has nothing to do with images of extraterrestrial spaceships, as has been assumed. It was first used, in fact, in a witness account during the 1896–7 airship wave!

Meteors – or lumps of coke?

The most impressive sighting from among all these ghost rocket events occurred on 9 July 1946, when over 250 reports were made in Sweden and the only known photograph was taken. A man named Erik Reutersward managed to obtain a single dim picture. The thing was described as being silvery but changing to blue-green in coloration as it plunged near-vertically towards the ground. The photograph opposite depicts a teardrop object with a short tail.

Most analysts have concluded that this sighting and the photograph relate to a bolide – an unusually bright daytime meteor – and it does have many of the characteristics of one. Indeed, there is little doubt that quite a number of the ghost rockets were probably a case of mistaken identity: other reports suggest meteors at night, yet others may be flocks of birds reflecting moonlight, and so forth. In fact, in the end even the defence authorities suggested that some 80 per cent of the reports came from people alerted to watch the skies in unprecedented

During 1946 Scandinavia was the subject of a wave of 'ghost rocket' sightings which received considerable attention from the military authorities but was never resolved. The only known photograph was taken on 9 July by Erik Reutersward and despite its limited quality was evaluated by investigators as probably depicting a daylight meteor.

numbers by the media hype, but who were seeing as a result what we would now call IFOs (identified flying objects).

But there were some real anomalies. For example, there were accounts where the object supposedly crashed into the ground. Many people saw an object plunge into Lake Kolmjarv in northern Sweden on 19 July. The authorities scoured the lake for days, but found nothing. Yet in a few other cases debris was picked up from the ground at the site of a supposed ghost rocket impact; it resembled lumps of blackened slag of some sort. For instance, at Bjorkon in Sweden on 10 July a rocket smashed into the beach, leaving a three-feet-wide crater with powder that burned the hands when it was touched.

Professor R. V. Jones, an expert in V-1 and V-2 rockets, and an Air Ministry scientist in Britain analysed some of the slag and other residues from such landings. Jones later reported that he was utterly unimpressed and that in his view these were irrelevant materials such as lumps of coke. People had found objects on the ground after seeing lights in the sky, but the materials had probably been there long before the ghost rockets flew and were completely unconnected.

It has recently been discovered that some ghost rocket sightings occurred in Soviet territory but were kept secret for many years.

On 10 October, with the sightings now far less frequent, the Swedish defence authorities issued their main public 'conclusion'. This dismissed all stories of crashes and residue, said that most sightings were unreliable misperceptions of mundane things, but that in a few cases 'clear, unambiguous observations have been made which cannot be explained as natural phenomena, Swedish aircraft or imagination . . .'. They added that precautions were being taken. In effect, all military authorities were under orders to report sightings of 'ghost rockets' (which some did make), and a low-level alert of the armed forces was in operation for a time afterwards.

An extensive investigation of ghost rockets, involving the scouring of official records in Stockholm, was made possible after declassification of these files in 1983. Swedish ufologists Anders Liljegren and Clas Svahn, who undertook this task, noted that the team of scientists and intelligence officers which the Swedish authorities brought together ended their work in December 1946. In their final report the team affirmed the high IFO ratio and said that 'despite the extensive effort which has been carried out with all available means, there is no actual proof that a test of rocket projectiles has taken place over Sweden . . . Even if the main part of the report can be referred to as celestial phenomena, the committee cannot dismiss certain facts as being merely public imagination.' In other words, some were *real* UFOs.

Conclusions from the evidence

So, what were the ghost rockets? In hindsight two things are obvious. The official conclusion that 80 per cent (plus) were really mundane things such as meteors is clearly valid; yet the unsolved cases were almost certainly not Soviet rocket tests. As later events were to demonstrate, most of the Nazi secrets and experts gravitated to the Americans, giving them a clear lead in the field of rocketry during the 1950s. Had the USSR been capable of launching ghost rockets in May 1946 it seems rather unlikely that they would have fallen as far behind in this aspect of the arms race as they quickly did.

Nor did the ghost rockets vanish after autumn 1946. Sightings of the same phenomena appeared all over the world in years to come, and reports are still being made as the millennium approaches (see pages 274–6 for some worrying modern-day examples).

We simply call these lights something other than ghost rockets . . . Today we call them UFOs.

Part Four

1947 onwards:
INVASION OF THE
FLYING SAUCERS

5

LIKE SAUCERS SKIPPING ACROSS WATER

The day of 24 June 1947 began like any other for businessman Kenneth Arnold.

Over Washington State on the west coast of America, 24 June 1947 was a clear, sunlit day. The purity of the atmosphere enhanced the natural beauty of the Cascade Mountains which were visible from the cockpit of Kenneth Arnold's light aircraft. Arnold, with over four thousand hours' flying experience, was a thirty-two-year-old businessman who sold and installed the Great Western Fire Control System – an apparatus he had designed and patented himself. He was also a flying deputy for the Ada County Aerial Posse, an acting deputy Federal United States marshal, and a member of the Idaho Search and Rescue Mercy Flyers.

Searching for wreckage

That day started just like any other, as Arnold was later to explain.

> I had just finished installing some firefighting apparatus at Chehalis, Washington. The job finished, I began a chat with Herb Critzen, chief pilot for Central Air Service. We talked about the possible location of a lost Marine transport which had gone down in the mountains. I decided to look for it. It meant a $5,000 reward, and I hoped that via my proposed route to Yakima, Washington, I might be lucky enough to find it. I decided to spend enough time in the air in the vicinity of Mount Rainier to make a good attempt at locating the wreckage.

His own aircraft, a single-engined Callier, was specially designed for mountain work – capable of landing in rough fields and pastures. At 2pm Arnold took off to start his search for the Marine Curtess C-46

On 24 June 1947 pilot Kenneth Arnold observed a formation of UFOs flying over the Rainier Mountain range in Washington, USA.

Commando transport plane which had disappeared somewhere in the mountains and had so far eluded discovery. He figured his journey to Yakima would be delayed by about an hour while he searched the 14,400-foot-high plateau of Mount Rainier. Kenneth Arnold never did find that aircraft. But he found something else instead – or it found him.

It was during this search, and while making a turn of 180 degrees over Mineral, Washington, at approximately 9,200 feet altitude, that a tremendously bright flash lit up the surfaces of his aircraft. He was startled, and thought he was very close to collision with another aircraft whose approach he had not noted.

He spent the next thirty seconds or so searching urgently for that 'other aircraft' in an attempt to avoid an accident. He did indeed see another aircraft, which he identified as a DC-4 – probably on its regular flight from San Francisco to Seattle. But this was to the port side and rear of him, and surely much too far away to have caused the light phenomenon. So he conjectured that a P-51 – a USAF jet fighter – might have buzzed across his nose to give him a fright, and that the sun had reflected off its wings.

As he continued his search for this speculative other aircraft a second flash occurred, and this time he was able to pinpoint the direction it had come from. He followed the line of sight, and his brow furrowed in puzzlement. From the north, near Mount Baker, flying close to the mountain peaks at incredible speed, was a formation of very bright objects.

Arnold felt they were about a hundred miles away and therefore too distant to make out any features. However, they were approaching him at an angle and steadily nearing the snow line of Mount Rainier. 'All the time I was thinking that I was observing a whole formation of jets. In group count, such as I have used in counting cattle and game from the air, they numbered nine. They were flying diagonally in an echelon formation with a larger gap in their echelon between the first four and the last five.'

Tail-less aircraft

But Arnold noticed something disturbing. None of the aircraft had tails! Once more his rational mind sought out an explanation. He knew the Air Force were very good at camouflage. Had they perfected it to a degree that appendages such as tailplanes on an aircraft could be rendered as good as invisible?

They were now about twenty miles away. If they carried on their present course they would pass between Mount Rainier and Mount Adams. Using the mountains as markers, Arnold timed the passage between them using his wristwatch, hoping to work out their speed later.

I was fascinated by this formation of aircraft. They didn't fly like any aircraft I had seen before. In the first place, their echelon formation was backward from that practiced by our Air Force. The elevation of the first craft was greater than that of the last. They flew in a definite formation, but erratically. As I described them at the time, their flight was like speed boats on rough water or similar to the tail of a chinese kite that I once saw blowing in the wind. Or maybe it would be best to describe their flight characteristics as very similar to a formation of geese, in a rather diagonal chain-like line, as if they were linked together.

Another characteristic of these craft that made a tremendous impression on me was how they fluttered and sailed, tipping their wings alternatively and emitting those very bright blue-white flashes from their surfaces. At the time I did not get the impression these flashes were emitted by them, but rather that it was the sun's reflection from the extremely polished surface of their wings.

The direction of the flight never varied, although the individual objects did swerve in and out of the mountain peaks – flying in front of some, disappearing momentarily behind others. Between the two mountains lies a very high plateau; Arnold observed that, as the first unit of craft cleared the far southernmost edge of the plateau, the second part of the echelon was just entering the opposite, northern edge. That meant the formation was five miles long!

Captain Tom Brown, public relations representative for the Army Air Force said they did not know what the saucers were, but they did not believe that 'anyone in this country, or outside this country, had developed a guided missile that will go 1200 miles an hour as some reports have indicated'.

As the nine objects flew out of sight, he unsuccessfully tried to explain them away in his own mind as some sort of technological wonder belonging to the Air Force. They made him feel 'eerie', and he tried to focus his mind on the search for the downed C-46 which had crashed some months earlier with thirty-two Marines aboard. Somehow the $5,000 didn't seem important to him any more. 'I wanted to get to Yakima and tell some of the boys what I had seen,' he explained.

A flight of guided missiles?

At around four o'clock Arnold landed at Yakima, went straight to see Al Baxter, general manager of Central Aircraft, and asked to see him alone. When he had related his story and drawn some pictures, Baxter was bemused. He knew Arnold was neither crazy nor the type to pull a stunt: he was in fact a level-headed character and an experienced pilot. Besides, he had nothing to gain from making up such a story, and everything to lose. Yet Baxter could not disguise his feelings of incredulity. It was written all across his face, and Arnold saw it. *Was* there a rational explanation for the experience?

Baxter called in several of his helicopter instructors and flight pilots for their opinions. After listening carefully to the story, they discussed it amongst themselves. Arnold related what happened next. 'The high point of my enthusiasm got its top knocked off when one of the helicopter pilots said: "Ah, it's just a flight of those guided missiles from Moses Lake." '

Arnold returned to his aircraft and took off for Pendleton, Oregon. Was that the explanation? He was not even aware of a base at Moses Lake. Besides, he had not mentioned the incredible speed of the objects, nor the fact that one of the craft looked different from the rest. This had been darker, crescent-shaped, with a small dome on top. If they had indeed been missiles they were of a completely new and previously unknown design. The other eight objects had resembled pie pans – so shiny that they reflected the sun as well as a mirror.

As a matter of routine, the officials at Yakima had to notify those at Pendleton of Arnold's imminent arrival. With this information went news of the businessman's strange sighting. So when he landed a group of people were waiting for him, anxious to hear the story. Using the figures Arnold had recorded at the time of the incident, it was calculated that the objects had been travelling at around 1,300 miles per hour! The pilot was now certain of one thing. If they were terrestrial they were remotely controlled. The human body could not survive the terrific gravity forces generated at such speeds.

Armed with his maps and calculations, Arnold decided he should report the incident. 'I kind of felt I ought to tell the FBI because I knew that during the war we were flying aircraft over the Pole to Russia, and I thought these things could possibly be from Russia.'

The birth of the flying saucer

Ironically, when he arrived at the local FBI office he found it shut. So instead he went to see Nolan Skiff, editor of the 'End of the Week' column in the *East Oregonian*. Initially Skiff was sceptical, but the pilot's credentials and sincerity convinced him. Another journalist, Bill Becquette, was also present and, realising that the story would have national interest, sent off an Associated Press despatch. It was while Arnold was trying to explain the strange movement of the aircraft that he unwittingly gave the media a phrase they grew to love, but one which later ufologists loved to hate. 'They flew like a saucer would if you skipped it across water.' With those few words, the term 'flying saucer' was born.

The despatch which was to ensure Kenneth Arnold's place in history said:

PENDLETON, ORE, June 25 (AP) – Nine bright saucer-like objects flying at 'incredible speed' at 10,000 feet altitude were reported here today by Kenneth Arnold, Boise, Idaho, pilot who said he could not hazard a guess as to what they were.

Arnold, a United States Forest Service employee engaged in searching for a missing plane, said he sighted the mysterious objects yesterday at three pm. They were flying between Mount Rainier and Mount Adams, in Washington State, he said, and appeared to weave in and out of formation. Arnold said that he clocked and estimated their speed at 1200 miles an hour.

Enquiries at Yakima last night brought only blank stares, he said, but he added he talked today with an unidentified man from Utah, south of here, who said he had seen similar objects over the mountains near Ukiah yesterday.

'It seems impossible,' Arnold said, 'but there it is.'

A Gallup Poll of 19 August 1947 revealed that nine out of ten Americans were now familiar with 'flying saucers'.

It said a lot for Kenneth Arnold's credibility that the story was reported seriously and in a matter-of-fact way. But even Bill Becquette could not have realised the international ramifications of the incident, which captured the imagination of the media across the world. Arnold, like so many unprepared victims of anomalous phenomena, had unwittingly opened up his life to the media circus.

I could have gone to sleep that night if the reporters, newsmen, and press agencies of every conceivable description had left me alone. I didn't share the general excitement. I can't begin to estimate the number of people, letters, telegrams and phone calls I tried to answer. After three days of this hubbub I came to the conclusion that I was the only sane one in the bunch. In order to stop what I thought was a lot of foolishness and since I couldn't get any work done, I went out to the airport, cranked up my airplane, and flew home to Boise.

Arnold was naive if he thought the interest would leave him behind at Pendleton, and until he spoke to Dave Johnson, aviation editor of the *Idaho Statesman*, he was still convinced that the objects were of advanced terrestrial origin.

When I caught the look in his eye and the tone of his words, 'flying saucers' suddenly took a different and serious significance. The doubt he displayed of the authenticity of my story told me, and I am sure he was in a position to know, that it was not a new military

As a result of Kenneth Arnold's story about crescent-like objects skipping through the air like a saucer across water, the term 'flying saucer' was invented by a journalist. Most people assumed that this meant that UFOs were saucer shaped and this motif soon dominated. A few years later even the cover of Arnold's own book, pictured here, portrayed the UFOs as more saucer-like than he had described them.

guided missile, and that if what I had seen was true it did not belong to the good old USA. It was then I really began to wonder.

Dave Johnson told him that the Wright Field Base wanted a report so they could check it out. They were not the only ones. Journalists and TV crews besieged the home of Doris and Kenneth Arnold.

Other sightings

Around that time there were other sightings too. United Airlines pilot Captain E. J. Smith and co-pilot Ralph Stevens observed something unexplained during one flight. On 26 June, the *Chicago Tribune* reported a sighting made by a Pendleton couple. On the same day as Arnold's sighting, a prospector from Portland called Johnson claimed to have witnessed five or six discs around the region of the Cascade Mountains. There were 850 sightings reported between June and July.

All of this left Arnold confused. It seemed that everyone was jumping on the bandwagon. It was true that, prior to his headline sighting, the phenomenon of 'flying saucers' was not generally acknowledged. Why were all these reports coming in *now*?

Did Arnold's sighting act as a catalyst? No doubt some people caught up in the excitement were going out looking for saucers and then misidentifying aircraft landing lights, bright stars and weather balloons. Others, however, were perhaps observing something truly mysterious. All Kenneth Arnold had done was give people the confidence to speak out instead of skulking away afraid of ridicule.

Not that Arnold escaped ridicule himself. Once people started interpreting his experience as proof of an extraterrestrial invasion, the debunkers were not slow in coming forward. As he told ufologist Greg Long in 1981: 'These nameless, faceless people ridiculed me. I was considered an Orson Welles, a fraud. I loved my country. I was very naive about the whole thing. I was the unfortunate goat who first reported them.'

Investigation and theories

Some months later, he sent a detailed report to the Air Force, which carried out an investigation. At that time, astronomer Dr J. Allen Hynek was their UFO consultant. Many years later, after realising the government were hoodwinking the American people, Hynek founded CUFOS – the Centre for UFO Studies.

Dr Hynek found several discrepancies in the story. Arnold's estimate of a hundred-foot 'wing span' did not bear out for the alleged distances involved. At twenty miles away – never mind a hundred – something only 100 feet wide would be invisible to the human eye. This meant the distances must have been much less, which also reduced the calculated speed of the formation to subsonic figures. Therefore the objects could have been terrestrial aircraft. There was only one problem with that: everyone denied there were any aircraft in the area at that time. However, if it was the estimate of *size* which was wrong and the distance was about right, but the objects were much larger than Arnold had thought, then the speed of around 1,300 miles per hour was about correct.

The case was never solved, although there have been plenty of theories, including that of mirages. More recently it has been suggested that what Arnold observed were 'earth lights' – luminous balls of electromagnetic energy allegedly released into the atmosphere along fault lines in the Earth's crust during periods of underground stress.

As far as Kenneth Arnold was concerned, the formation of nine objects he saw moving across the crystal-clear Washington skies 'like a saucer would if you skipped it across water', was only the beginning of several more similar experiences. Although this is not generally known, Arnold experienced many more sightings. His eighth, in 1952, was of two objects – one of which was transparent. 'They looked like something alive,' he said. 'I've had the feeling with these things that they are aware of me, but they made no effort to come close.'

Then in 1966 he took some 16mm cine film of a glowing 'cylinder' over Idaho Falls, Ohio. Although the object looked similar to an atmospheric balloon, it was travelling at speed into a northerly wind.

Whatever he saw during the long day of 24 June 1947, Arnold retained his passion for the subject right up until his death in 1984. This would suggest that his experience was something much more tangible than just imagination. An FBI agent who saw Kenneth Arnold at the time thought so, too:

It is the personal opinion of the interviewer that [Arnold] actually saw what he states he saw in the attached report. It is also the opinion of the interviewer that [Arnold] would have much more to lose than gain and would have to be very strongly convinced that he actually saw something before he would report such an incident and open himself up for ridicule that would accompany such a report.

—6—

IT CAME FROM OUTER SPACE

The Roswell incident of July 1947 is believed by experts to be the single most significant incident in UFO history.

The FBI are unimpressed

On 22 March 1950 Guy Hottel, a field officer with the FBI in Washington, sent a bizarre memo to his boss J. Edgar Hoover. Headed 'Flying Discs or Flying Saucers', it ran:

An investigator for the Air Force stated that three so-called flying saucers had been recovered in New Mexico. They were described as being circular in shape with raised centres, approximately 50 feet in diameter. Each one was occupied by three bodies of human shape but only 3 feet tall dressed in metallic cloth of a very fine texture ... the saucers were found in New Mexico due to the fact that the Government has a very high-powered radar set-up in that area and it is believed the radar interferes with the controlling mechanism of the saucers.

Such an extraordinary story seems not to have been taken too seriously by the FBI hierarchy. They note that 'no further evaluation' was undertaken. Many researchers think the leak came via an unreliable source and related to a dubious story of an alleged UFO crash at Aztec, New Mexico. That event is widely considered a hoax. But the official memo is quite real.

March 1950 is very early for allegations about a UFO crash in this state, with the entities being small, humanoid and wearing silvery suits. The science fiction of the day did not feature this type of alien – which soon became the norm for American UFO reports of alien contact and abduction. When this memo was secretly circulating, the first UFO book – *Flying Saucers are Real*, a sensational charge of cover-up by ex-Marine officer Donald Keyhoe – had only been in print a few weeks.

Strange hieroglyphic markings

Another possible source for the memo is the Roswell, New Mexico incident of July 1947. This affair received minimum attention outside the American West and was rapidly forgotten even by ufologists. It would be thirty years before they researched it in earnest. From the declassified files we can now see what 'officially' happened and couple this with the evidence from the few public revelations in 1947.

On the night of 2 July 1947, barely a week after the Kenneth Arnold sighting, William Brazel heard an explosion in the sky above his large property near Corona, New Mexico. Corona is a fascinating location – a scrub desert area surrounded by rocky ridges, with the Los Alamos nuclear facility a hundred miles north, Socorro just west, and the atom bomb and missile test facilities of White Sands and Alamogordo/Holloman Air Force Base only a short distance south. It is also twenty-five miles from Vaughn – home to the startling green fireballs that were set to erupt upon the landscape some sixteen months later (see page 86). Anything odd going on within this sensitive area would shake the defences of the United States.

The explosion that Brazel heard came in the middle of a fierce thunderstorm but sounded unlike thunder, so next day he rode around the property to check on his sheep. He and a neighbour were amazed to discover an area about three-quarters of a mile across scattered with very odd-looking wreckage. A gouge in the earth looked as if some craft had skidded upon impact. The debris included a very light metal that could easily be lifted, yet was very tough. Bits of material were akin to balsa wood, and would not burn, plus some brown, parchment-like substances. Some of the debris bore hieroglyphic or geometric symbols, seemingly stained with a purplish or pink coloration.

House arrest and secrecy

Mystified, the men took pieces of this material back and showed it to family and friends. Someone thought he might get a reward for handing in the remains of a military device to the authorities, and Brazel was persuaded to take it into the town of Roswell on his next visit, on 6 July. When he told the sheriff, two deputies were immediately sent off to the 80-mile-distant site as vaguely described by Brazel. The rancher was then directed to the town's air base, which in 1947 was the only location in the world with an active bombing unit flying atomic weapons.

The Roswell deputies found no debris in the area, but did see a burnt circle as if a craft of some sort had touched down. An intelligence officer from Roswell, Major Jesse Marcel, together with a junior officer, Sheridan Cavitt, drove to Corona with Brazel. At the same time the bits that Brazel had brought in were flown to a regional command centre at Carswell Air Base in Forth Worth, Texas for expert analysis.

Back at Corona, Brazel, Marcel and Cavitt soon gave up the idea of collecting the rest of the debris – there was just too much of it. But they loaded some of it into the back of a pick-up and late on 7 July drove back to the base. Next morning base security met Brazel at the site to cordon off the area, and even turned away the local police. They collected up all the remaining debris and, to Brazel's surprise, took him back to Roswell where they kept him under voluntary house arrest for about a week. Friends who saw him during this time say he looked 'strange' and walked past without acknowledging their presence.

A rapid (or hasty) evaluation of the bulk of the debris was made at Roswell Air Base during the early hours of 8 July. Colonel William Blanchard arranged for Marcel to load up a B-29 and fly the stuff to Wright Patterson Air Force Base in Dayton, Ohio (soon to become the hub of all Air Force investigation into UFOs), calling off at Carswell to collect the test samples.

Blanchard appears to have been unable to identify the wreckage. As no government rules about UFOs were yet in force, the commander chose to tell the world what had been discovered. He was quickly censured for doing so by Pentagon sources keen to put the lid back on, but not before base officer Lieutenant Walter Haut had issued a wire message reading:

Apart from the UFO crash in the Roswell desert, about twenty other claims exist for similar accidents. Most of them are in the desert somewhere!

The many rumours regarding the flying discs became a reality yesterday when the intelligence office of the 509th bomb group of the eighth air force, Roswell Army Air Field, was fortunate enough to gain possession of a disc through the cooperation of one of the local ranchers and the Sheriff's office at Chaves county. The flying object landed on a ranch near Roswell sometime last week. Not having phone facilities, the rancher stored the disc until such time as he was able to contact the Sheriff's office, who in turn notified Major Jesse A. Marcel of the 509th bomb group intelligence office ... It was inspected at the Roswell Army Air Field and subsequently loaned by Major Marcel to higher headquarters.

Hughie Green's unfinished story

The story was picked up by local radio and press. It was these reports – and the subsequent retraction – that gave ufology all it knew before 1978. The one exception was the account of Hughie Green, later a leading TV entertainer in Britain, whose story first appeared in the UFO press in 1955.

Green said he was driving across the USA from west to east and heard the original radio broadcasts, which then suddenly stopped. Upon arrival at Philadelphia he tried to discover more but failed. He has intimated to both authors of this book that there may be more to his story, but has unfortunately not elaborated upon that point.

'National security item. Do not transmit...'

The next breakthrough occurred in 1978 when the USAF, FBI and CIA files on UFOs, including the original official release from the base and its subsequent retraction via the Pentagon, had just been released under new freedom of information (FOI) laws. Major Marcel, by then retired, and Lydia Sleppy, a teletype operator at a radio station in Albuquerque, had both been traced by UFO researchers and had a lot more to say about the matter.

Sleppy related how she had been receiving incoming data on the retrieval of the flying disc via Roswell when a further message came through reading: 'Attention Albuquerque: Cease transmission. Repeat cease transmission. National security item. Do not transmit...' At this point data stopped coming in from the base and she had to curtail all plans to release it through the news networks to the rest of the world.

This second official message came some hours after the first, with media sources already swamping Roswell. Marcel was now at Carswell with all the debris and General Roger Ramey had taken command upon his arrival, ordering Marcel off the B-29, instructing him to say nothing, replacing him as courier for the onward leg but (Marcel insists) still flying the wreckage on to Wright Patterson. Marcel was then flown back to Roswell immediately, and the story was issued that the flight to Dayton had been cancelled.

Ramey now sent out a second press release, stating that the whole thing had been a mistake. The debris was from a weather balloon with a radio device attached. A hurried press conference that afternoon showed the supposed weather balloon debris to the rapidly disenchanted media (see page 72).

In 1978 Marcel told ufologists that this balloon story was invented to

See opposite
A copy of an FBI teletype about the Roswell crash that first told the world about the UFO incident in July 1947, before it was hushed up and there was a backtrack to claim it was a balloon.

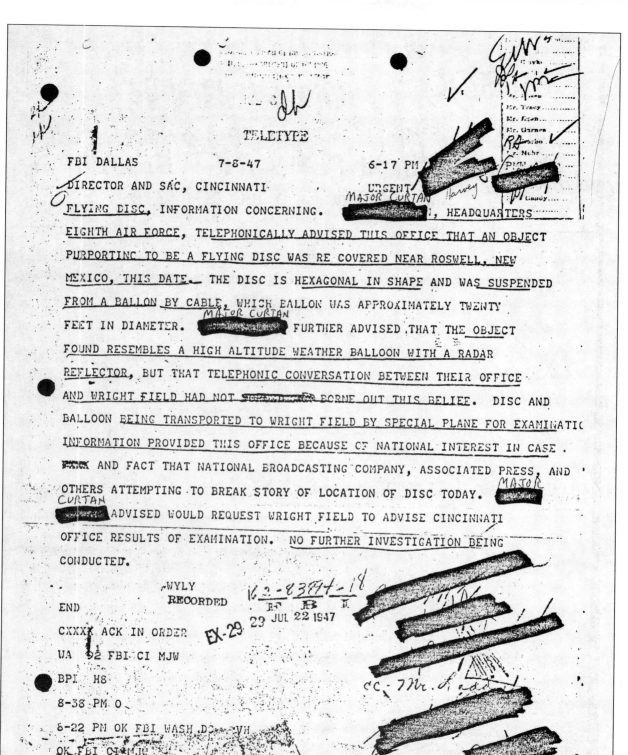

TELETYPE

FBI DALLAS   7-8-47   6-17 PM

DIRECTOR AND SAC, CINCINNATI   URGENT

FLYING DISC, INFORMATION CONCERNING.   , HEADQUARTERS

EIGHTH AIR FORCE, TELEPHONICALLY ADVISED THIS OFFICE THAT AN OBJECT

PURPORTING TO BE A FLYING DISC WAS RE COVERED NEAR ROSWELL, NEW

MEXICO, THIS DATE. THE DISC IS HEXAGONAL IN SHAPE AND WAS SUSPENDED

FROM A BALLON BY CABLE, WHICH BALLON WAS APPROXIMATELY TWENTY

FEET IN DIAMETER.   FURTHER ADVISED THAT THE OBJECT

FOUND RESEMBLES A HIGH ALTITUDE WEATHER BALLOON WITH A RADAR

REFLECTOR, BUT THAT TELEPHONIC CONVERSATION BETWEEN THEIR OFFICE

AND WRIGHT FIELD HAD NOT   BORNE OUT THIS BELIEF. DISC AND

BALLOON BEING TRANSPORTED TO WRIGHT FIELD BY SPECIAL PLANE FOR EXAMINATIO

INFORMATION PROVIDED THIS OFFICE BECAUSE OF NATIONAL INTEREST IN CASE.

     AND FACT THAT NATIONAL BROADCASTING COMPANY, ASSOCIATED PRESS, AND

OTHERS ATTEMPTING TO BREAK STORY OF LOCATION OF DISC TODAY.

          ADVISED WOULD REQUEST WRIGHT FIELD TO ADVISE CINCINNATI

OFFICE RESULTS OF EXAMINATION. NO FURTHER INVESTIGATION BEING

CONDUCTED.

                    WYLY
END   RECORDED

CXXXX ACK IN ORDER   29 JUL 22 1947

WA 92 FBI CI MJW

BPI H8

8-38 PM O

8-22 PM OK FBI WASH D   VH

OK FBI CI MJW

Debris from a weather balloon displayed to the media at Roswell.

deflect attention from the truth. Nobody knew what the debris was, but it was definitely not from a balloon. The US government wanted the opportunity to investigate the wreckage in secret, so it had to silence the media. On 9 July a dazed-looking Brazel was wheeled in front of the local press in Roswell to claim he had found the material on 14 June – not 3 July – and had discovered weather balloons on his land before. He later told friends, as confirmed by them in interview, that the military had asked him to say this.

Marcel was always adamant that the material he collected and handled for over twenty-four hours was incredible. All who saw it and who have been tracked down (at least a dozen people since 1978) confirm that it was very strange and unearthly. They talk of trying to dent some metal bits with a sledgehammer but failing, despite its extreme lightness and flexibility. Crates containing huge amounts that were carried on to the aircraft reputedly weighed almost nothing. And, as Marcel always argued, a weather balloon would not scatter over the huge area of desert which he saw in this case. He felt sure that some solid craft had exploded in mid-air and rained pieces down upon the landscape.

The secrets of Hangar 18

A second story surfaced in about 1950, and may be related to the March 1950 memo to the FBI. This came via Grady Barnett, a civil engineer with the Soil Conservation Service, who told friends that at the time in question he had been at Magdelena on the plains of San Agustin near Socorro, New Mexico, over 100 miles west of the Brazel ranch. He reputedly saw a crashed disc with small human-like bodies. They had no hair and large domed heads, and were lying dead outside the craft. A group of archaeology students led by a professor were in the area and saw this evidence too, but all the witnesses were ordered to remain silent by a team of military men who arrived to secure the site and take the bodies away.

This story has been influential within ufology. Rumours are persistent that it was the main craft which hit trouble over Corona and then impacted in San Agustin. The bodies were taken to Wright Patterson, where a secret 'Hangar 18' complex is supposed to have housed technology and bodily remains even before Project Sign was launched there some weeks later. It then moved, and is still at, Area 51 in the Tonopah Air Base complex, nestling within a remote area of Nevada 200 miles north of Las Vegas.

Indeed, many ufologists in the USA claim, as a result of this, that the alien nature of the UFOs was proven by the Roswell crash nearly fifty years ago. All the twenty-two years of Air Force study were a sham – a team of uninformed, low-level people putting on a public pretence of investigation. In 'truth' the greatest secret *never* told has been kept from the world ever since.

Unfortunately, the evidence to support the alien body claim within the Roswell story is hard to find. Many ufologists, even if they believe that an unknown craft did crash in the desert at Corona (as most do after extensive perusal of the evidence) are unpersuaded by the San Agustin allegations.

The Roswell Incident, a book published in 1980 by William Moore and Charles Berlitz, reported what little we knew about the matter at that time. It did enough to establish that a case had to be answered. Unfortunately Grady Barnett had died in 1969, and so was never interviewed by the Roswell investigators; the alien story remained a

The film Hanger 18 *(1980) was loosely based on what might have happened if a craft was captured at Roswell and kept under military guard ever since.*

secondhand, unsupported yarn. But the crash of some kind of object was established beyond reasonable doubt.

A debate arose about new witnesses who appeared after an NBC *Unsolved Mysteries* feature on the case in September 1989. In February 1992 a series of meetings were held in Chicago between both those favouring and those sceptical of the alien side to the story, and the debate was published in a monograph. Also in 1992 CUFOS published a whole series of reports, many by their investigators on the case, ex-Air Force officer Kevin Randle and researcher Don Schmitt, who discussed their continuing work, including field searches for debris scraps in the Corona scrub. Sadly forty years on nothing was found.

There are some claims that Brazel actually helped the Air Force discover a second location near Corona via aerial reconnaissance flights during the week that he was in custody. Not only the main 'disc' was found but also alien bodies – but, again, these are just unsupported rumours.

Schmitt and Randle cite some intriguing circumstantial evidence to verify this. A Roswell mortician fielded several enquiries from the base that week about preservation of bodily tissue, leading him to believe an air crash had occurred. He was then asked about the smallest coffins available! A base nurse later told the mortician that she assisted in transporting these child-sized bodies. The pilot of the aircraft that flew Marcel and the debris to Fort Worth also says he later took the bodies to Wright Patterson. This man ('Pappy' Henderson) kept the story even from his wife until 1982, after the Moore and Berlitz book had appeared. Feeling it was evidently no longer a secret, he chose to talk about it – though with circumspection.

Consistently these claims are that the entities were about four feet tall, had large domed heads, no hair, tiny mouths and big slanted eyes. The opinion of all those who claim to have seen them is that the affair proved the existence of alien craft arriving on Earth. The technology from the crashed object was so far beyond us that much is still undeciphered.

Japanese balloon bombs

Of course, there are critics of the case. Most sceptics argue that the weather balloon 'cover story' is true and the mistake came from excited air base officers presuming something stranger amidst flying saucer hysteria in the press. Others' ideas include a V-rocket astray from a nearby range.

By far the best-argued critical theory comes from within ufology itself – research by the influential writer John Keel. He says that the object that crashed in the Corona scrub was a Japanese balloon bomb!

In fact there is strong supporting evidence for his claim. During the latter stages of World War II the Japanese did launch large balloons packed with explosives across the Pacific. They drifted for days at great heights and, although most never completed the journey, some descended on the USA. The US government kept the fact secret because they did not want the Japanese to know their flights were a success. In an incident in the summer of 1945 six people were killed by an exploding balloon when it fell near their picnic area in Oregon.

Some years after the war balloon bombs were still being found – mostly in the western states, where they had lodged in rocky crevices. From late 1945 censorship was removed and people were warned what to look out for, but the story of the balloon bombs was fairly obscure even by mid-1947.

Keel's idea that the Roswell debris was from a Japanese balloon certainly has its advantages. The balsa wood, thin metal foil, parchment and rod-like metal bits covered with pink and purple stained picture writing (not unlike Japanese, one senses) all sound far more like a balloon than a spaceship that has crossed the universal void. Indeed, the very fact that the US government's blatant cover story about a weather balloon worked at all was only because the debris found by Brazel was rather balloon-like.

But Randle and Schmitt argue against Keel's thesis in their 1992 book, *UFO Crash at Roswell*, noting the most damning evidence such as the seeming indestructibility of the metal, the reputed gouge on the ground which no balloon could make, and the finding of the larger 'craft' and bodies. One would also expect the military authorities at Roswell to have recognised a balloon bomb. Nor does there seem to be any obvious reason why a cover story would be needed when the full truth could easily have been told in 1947 – or today, half a century after the war has ended.

It was Keel who proposed a rather fanciful idea of the balloon circling the globe for two years before descending on Corona – something that Randle and Schmitt find implausible. But Keel has since suggested a renegade Japanese military figure launching a solo attack on the USA because he could not accept his nation's defeat. If that idea were true (or even if suspected of being true at the time) it might indeed have incited a cover-up back in 1947. But why not release the records about this matter now, if that is all that took place?

Another idea that occurs to us is that the balloon bomb may have stuck in a ridge near Corona from 1945 but was released by the storm winds on 2 July 1947 and then hit by lightning as it drifted away. This would have caused the huge explosion in mid-air that Brazel heard, and the balloon may have rained its debris down on his ranch. But again – if this was what occurred – why not simply tell us so? The fact that there was, and remains, a cover-up and the insistence on the ludicrous weather balloon story implies that the truth was rather more startling.

The jury is out

In January 1994 Steven Spielberg was reported to be working on pre-production of Project X – *his film about the Roswell crash, to be prepared in time for the 50th anniversary in July 1997.*

With the multiplicity of books already published, the Roswell case is far more important to the ufologists of the 1990s than it was at the time of its occurrence. Most American experts believe it to be the single most significant incident in UFO history – the one that will eventually prove an alien presence on earth. Calls for congressional hearings periodically surface and, following the making of a movie and a TV documentary about the case, both scheduled for 1994 release, the fascination of this extraordinary event can only continue to grow.

Whether the truth will ever be known is quite another matter.

— 7 —

A Sign of the Times

The waves of flying saucer reports in 1947 led to a top-secret investigation by the US Air Force.

Kenneth Arnold's sighting and the waves of flying saucer reports that followed had a serious effect on the US military authorities, regardless of the truth behind the Roswell affair that dominated its first few weeks. They had entered World War II after being caught with their pants down at Pearl Harbor. The danger of doing so again was not to be underestimated. So flying saucers were treated to a top-secret investigation in the hands of the US Air Force.

Few people outside the Pentagon knew how during the previous three years foo fighters and then ghost rockets had come to maximum strategic attention, both being perceived as potential secret weapons. Now exotic craft were being observed above the US mainland and had all the signs of being another rung up the ladder of technology, with capabilities well beyond anything the Americans possessed. If they were in the hands of an enemy power they were a major threat.

It would have been irresponsible not to take such a threat seriously. As a result, the investigation that was mounted and the secrecy that surrounded it were inevitable. Unfortunately, there were two unforeseen consequences.

Preconceived ideas

Once the mechanics of secrecy were in place they became almost impossible to dismantle, giving rise to whispers of cover-up and conspiracy – in effect that the US government knew the 'truth' (the alien origin of the discs) but were afraid to admit it. It seems unlikely that this was the case, unless there was a spaceship at Roswell. Bureaucratic secrecy feeds upon itself and breeds conspiracy theory. It was to be a long time before governments woke up to this and became more open about their UFO data.

The other problem is more subtle. By placing UFO study in the hands of military authorities from the start the answer to the mystery had been predetermined. These flying saucers were craft – that is, machines – powered by some living intelligence. As a result of such a premature conclusion it was equally presumed that the craft probably had pilots. In other words, UFOs were perceived by everyone – from governments to tabloid newspapers – as being products of a controlled and very strange technology.

This was an understandable, but serious, misjudgment. Whilst some UFOs may prove to be craft of unknown origin, by far the great majority of them are not. That lesson could have been learnt from the foo fighters and ghost rockets, where eventually it was found that the source of most reports was natural, not even supernatural, and certainly not extraterrestrial.

Yet the mind-set of 'UFOs as flying craft' gripped hold of popular imagination, and its stranglehold is scarcely broken today. Most people still regard UFOs and alien craft as synonymous terms. The question everyone asks is the same one that those first military investigators had posed in 1947: not the more correct and definitely more helpful 'What are these strange phenomena that people are seeing?' but 'Where do these frightening *machines* come from – and who the heck is flying them?'

Uneasy cooperation

Within a week of Kenneth Arnold's sighting there was furious military activity. We can piece together what went on from hundreds of documents released decades later under the US Freedom of Information (FOI) Act and from interviews with some of those who were involved at the time.

By early July Brigadier General George Schulgen, an Army/Air Force intelligence officer, was already requesting various military bases and intelligence agencies to cooperate in collating reports on the waves of UFO sightings. The press was full of them, but he wanted first-hand data.

On 10 July 1947, E. G. Fitch from the FBI circulated a memo under the heading 'Flying Disks'. He told how Schulgen had urged that every effort must be undertaken in order to run down and ascertain whether the flying disks are a fact and, if so, to learn all about them. According to General Schulgen the Air Corps intelligence are utilizing all of their scientists in order to ascertain whether or not such a phenomenon could in fact occur. He stated that this research is being conducted with the thought that [they] might be . . . a foreign body mechanically devised and controlled.

Key people within the FBI appended their comments as to whether such cooperation with the military was appropriate. Assistant Director David Ladd was reluctant, referring to recent cases in which small discs had been found and investigated by military bodies but which as a rule were 'found to have been pranks'. The top man, however – none other than J. Edgar Hoover – added his own thoughts in a handwritten note, saying that he would recommend cooperation but that 'before agreeing to it we must insist upon full access to disks recovered. For instance in the La. case the army grabbed it and would not let us have it for cursory examination.'

This remark created all sorts of rumours when the file was declassified in 1977. Was Hoover referring to real UFO debris which had been captured by the US Army/Air Force in summer 1947, such as at Roswell? Sadly, the truth is more mundane:'La.' is the abbreviation for Louisiana, and from other declassified files we know that on 7 July, three or four days before Hoover penned these words, a case had occurred at Shreveport in that state. A small aluminium disc, not much more than a foot wide, was found amidst smoke on the ground. The military arrived and discovered that it was covered in wires and bore a crude motto on the side reading 'Made in the USA'. It was obviously a hoax – someone's idea of a joke following two weeks of intense flying saucer coverage by the press.

On 30 July the FBI issued instructions to all its agents to cooperate fully with the military – an arrangement which was to last barely a month. On 3 September an unfortunately phrased memo was circulated to Air Force bases, suggesting that the Air Force should do all the serious work and FBI agents be left to sift through the 'many instances which turned out to be ash can covers, toilet seats, and whatnot . . .' Not surprisingly, the FBI were not impressed and their cooperation ceased forthwith! Sadly, the level of tact and skill with which the US Air Force were to handle the UFO problem during the next twenty or so years was to show very little improvement. Nevertheless, the FBI involvement did bring in some impressive cases.

'Something is really flying around'

On 8 August a London agent reported an incident that had occurred on 16 January 1947 – five months before the Kenneth Arnold sighting. At 22.30 hours an RAF Mosquito was on night flying practice 100 miles out over the North Sea near the Dutch coast when a radar tracking was made of an unknown target. The aircraft was ordered to intercept at 22,000 feet and 'a long chase ensued'. This concluded at 23.00 hours over Norfolk. Two airborne radar contacts were established with the unidentified object, which took 'efficient controlled evasive action'. The British Air Ministry conclusion had been that the encounter was unexplained. UFOs were clearly nothing new.

It was strong evidence like this that formed the basis of a very early appraisal of sixteen American cases made by Lieutenant Colonel Donald Springer of Hamilton Field Air Base in California. All were dated between 19 May and 20 July 1947 and were very impressive. His analysis, dated 30 July, showed that ten of the sightings had occurred in daylight and almost all had been made by well-qualified observers. This was a sample of the 'best' of possibly dozens of cases received by military sources by that time.

These sort of reports show how the popular misconception that UFOs were 'flying saucer'-shaped was now taking root, thanks to the media. Of these sixteen cases, only one came close to being what we might now call disc-shaped. The rest were a mixed bag including 'a bright light', 'flat on base with top slightly rough in contour', 'like barrel head' and 'a wagon wheel'.

The conclusions of this first-ever attempt to conduct a serious investigation into UFO reports were amply supported by the data. The following remark was included in an appendix: 'This "flying saucer" situation is not all imaginary or seeing too much in some natural phenomenon. Something is really flying around.'

Springer further noted that he was puzzled by the 'lack of topside enquiries' – a decided disinterest from the highest level in government. Many similar statements have been made since then by military personnel or witnesses to major events. Springer became the first in a long line to speculate about a conspiracy, arguing five weeks into the UFO mystery that flying saucers might well be something 'about which the President, etc. know'.

Project Sign

Although sightings were falling off by late summer (as Schulgen himself rightly concluded, largely because the media were reacting less fervently towards them), analyses of data such as that made by Springer became very influential. They had persuaded Lieutenant General Nathan Twining, head of the AMC (Air Material Command), to request action. So on 23 September he wrote to Schulgen to conclude firmly that 'The phenomenon reported is something real and not visionary or fictitious.' He urged that a codenamed secret project should be mounted to study the data on a permanent basis, so as to allow the 'information gathered [to] be made available to other branches of the military and to scientific agencies with government connections'.

Twining's suggestion was endorsed by Schulgen; on 30 December the chief of staff at the Air Force, Major General Craigie, approved the project and ordered the creation of Project Sign. It was to be based at Wright Patterson Air Force Base at Dayton, Ohio (where the Roswell wreckage had been flown), and coordinated by AMC. Although its name was classified, the existence of the project was not secret because it needed reports. To the public it became known affectionately as Project Saucer.

Project Sign was officially launched on 22 January 1948 and got off to a traumatic start. A few days earlier, Captain Thomas Mantell had died as he climbed high into the air in his F-51 aircraft in pursuit of a silvery mass. This object was also reported by ground observers near Godman Field, Kentucky. His last words described seeing a large silvery metallic object trying to close in on him, and then there was silence. His plane was found smashed to fragments on the ground some hours later.

Sign employed various experts to assist – they ranged from intelligence officers to scientific consultants who were asked to comment on relevant cases. One of the first employed on an ad hoc basis was a young astronomer then at Ohio University, and later to become Professor at Northwestern University in Chicago. This was Dr J. Allen Hynek – roped in, as he admitted, for two principal reasons: he did not believe in flying saucers and would try very hard to find an answer to all sightings, and, by chance, he was the closest astronomer to Wright Patterson Air Force Base at the right moment. None the less, this invitation changed his life.

Speculation as to what 'Project Sign' stood for is rife. Was it a 'sign of the times' or a 'sign in the sky'? In fact it was simply next in the list of code words in the USAF manual.

The Skyhook tragedy

Hynek did his best with many sightings, but never compromised his scruples. If he could not find a credible solution, he said so. He could not find one for the Mantell crash and told the hierarchy at Sign of this failure. They had the media baying at their doors for a statement and desperately needed a solution, so they came up with the idea that the silvery object was the planet Venus.

Had a brave (if perhaps foolhardy) Mantell died trying to do the impossible and fly towards the stars in his plane? If so, eventually lack of oxygen in the cockpit would have led him to have suffered a blackout; the plane would then have gone into a steep dive and ultimately disintegrated.

There was only one thing wrong with this speculation. It is almost impossible to see Venus against a clear blue sky in the middle of the day – and even if you could do so it would definitely not look dramatic enough to qualify for the description of a large metallic object. The public refused to be fobbed off with a ludicrous solution cooked up to enable Sign to play for time, and this latest public relations disaster merely fuelled the belief that the government knew all about UFOs but would not tell the truth.

In reality, we now know that Mantell was almost certainly chasing a 'Skyhook' – a huge silvery device that was floating far too high in the atmosphere for his F-51 ever to have reached it. The Navy were testing these monster aerial devices secretly and had not told the Army/Air Force about their exercise.

Warring factions

Project Sign was soon convinced that some sightings were real, but its members split down the middle as to what that meant. The idea that they were Soviet missiles was quickly rejected – because it seemed ridiculous to imagine that the USSR would test secret devices deep within the US mainland.

This really only left one option – that the technology was not from any terrestrial source but from an extraterrestrial one. The UFOs, in other words, were alien spacecraft. Any Project Sign staff who could not stomach such a startling idea concluded the opposite: that the sightings were real enough, but must all be mistaken identity for various ordinary things like stars and planes.

For months the two factions were at loggerheads. Then an incident

An early case that impressed the official investigation involved an aircraft which engaged in a aerial 'dog fight' with a glowing disk over North Dakota. Sceptics argued that it was a balloon, but it convinced many of the investigators.

happened which was to tip the scales heavily in favour of those backing the aliens.

'A Flash Gordon rocket ship'

At 2.45am on 24 July 1948 Clarence Chiles and John Whitted were piloting an Eastern Airlines DC-3 at 5,000 feet on a beautiful moonlit night not far from Montgomery, Alabama, when they spotted a strange aircraft rushing towards them at great speed. In fact it was a ghost rocket, encountered for the first time at such close range. It was torpedo-shaped with two rows of windows on the side, glowing bright blue and with flames shooting out of the back. Whitted excitedly described it as a 'Flash Gordon rocket ship'.

The thing shot past them in just a few seconds without creating any air turbulence – something sceptics would use to show that it must have been much further away than the pilots believed. Yet it was so bright that it almost blinded them. Most of the passengers were asleep.

The most likely explanation for this event was a sighting of a very bright bolide, or fireball meteor. However, Chiles and Whitted categorically rejected the idea, saying they had often seen meteors in mid-air. In any case they were adamant that the object they saw was 'a man-made thing'. It was a flying craft built and flown – by somebody!

These witnesses were highly experienced air crew whose testimony therefore carried considerable weight. Indeed, Sign was quickly aware that there was still more to the story, because about an hour earlier a near-identical object had been secretly reported by a ground engineer at an air base in nearby Georgia. The object had a phosphorescent glow and was moving horizontally – exactly as the air crew had described their 'rocket ship'. A meteor or bolide descends at an angle into the atmosphere, so that answer looked shaky.

Sensibly, Hynek hedged his bets. He pointed out that if you took the report at face value there was no astronomical interpretation. However, he added that the ground engineer might have made a timing error and seen the object at the same moment as the Eastern Airlines crew. If so, this might support the view of an 'extraordinary meteor' giving off incandescent gases.

Few at Sign agreed with this theory. Edward Ruppelt (pictured on page 84), a later leader of the US Air Force project who had access to these secret files, said in 1956 that this case 'shook them worse than the Mantell incident'. It gave the believers in the ETH (extraterrestrial hypothesis) all the incentive they needed.

Captain Edward J. Ruppelt.

Codename Grudge

Within two weeks these people had produced a summary 'Estimation of the Situation'. Dated 8 August 1948, it used the Chiles-Whitted sighting as a cornerstone in its case, arguing that the best answer to the escalating evidence was that the flying discs were alien in origin. The file went to chief of staff General Hoyt Vandenberg, who rejected it, cogently arguing that it was based upon eye-witness testimony alone and had no physical evidence in support. Staff from Sign tried to change his mind, but he refused to budge.

The other faction at Project Sign now seized the upper hand and began to press their case that all sightings were explicable. The 8 August report was destroyed, although a few pirate copies appear to have been retained and Ruppelt read one of them about four years later. This 'holy grail' of ufology has never been found when requested under the FOI Act.

Staff who had backed the ETH hypothesis were reassigned. Six months later, in February 1949, Sign produced a rapid 'final' report. This stressed how many cases could be readily explained, suggested an increase in staff so as to place UFO officers on every air base, and implied that, given this sort of effort, most cases could probably be resolved and the entire mystery soon eliminated. But it did admit that it had failed to find a workable solution for about one in five of the 237 sightings it had investigated.

The Air Force chose to downgrade the project rather than increase its status. Effectively it became part of another, larger study and was given a new codename – Grudge. This word, some said, may have been intended as an expression of how the Air Force now felt about its UFO headache.

Grudge was a low-key affair with a clear brief. Captain Edward Ruppelt, who took over its reins in October 1951, minced no words in describing its role: he said that the team's task between 1949 and his takeover was to get rid of as many UFO sightings as possible. Grudge tried very hard to persuade responsible journalists to write negative stories in exchange for access to 'secret files', but the people they approached had examined the mystery and could not be convinced there was nothing going on.

By August 1949 Grudge published its final results – assessing 250 sightings and failing to identify 23 per cent (actually a worse performance than Sign, despite the new tactics!). Grudge warned that sightings might be used by Communist infiltrators to mask an insurrection – a curious argument which was to resurface later.

On 27 December 1949 the Pentagon announced that Grudge was to be axed (although in truth it was simply reduced to just one low-rank officer, effectively a filing clerk). It was to stay in limbo for two more years until Edward Ruppelt rode in like the cavalry to the rescue.

TWINKLE, TWINKLE, LITTLE UFO

During the political games of the late 1940s and early 1950s, one of the best-kept secrets of the day had a profound effect on Washington's judgment of the UFO mystery. If there had merely been tales of lights in the sky, appearing randomly, doing nothing in particular and showing no threat, then no long-term investigation would have been maintained. But there was an extraordinary pattern developing that terrified the authorities: one secret memo used the term 'grave concern'.

Green fireballs – a new kind of spy

A specific type of UFO which came to be called the 'green fireball' was literally haunting key installations. These included top-secret missile sites, nuclear research facilities and atomic weapons testing grounds. It was as if an enemy surveillance of America's best-guarded facilities might be under way. The problem was that nobody knew who the enemy was – or indeed if that enemy was human!

On 31 January 1949 a secret FBI memo to J. Edgar Hoover summarised data accrued to that point from a conference headed 'Protection of Vital Installations'. This had involved the OSI (an Air Force intelligence unit) and the ONI (the Office of Naval Intelligence). The military had reported how lately there had been 'day-time sightings which are tentatively considered to possibly resemble the exhaust of some type of jet-propelled object. Night-time sightings have taken the form of lights usually described as brilliant green, similar to a green traffic signal or green neon light.'

One witness – a pilot from Sante Fé, New Mexico – offered a graphic account to an Air Force investigator some time later: 'Take a soft ball and paint it with some kind of fluorescent paint that will glow a bright green in the dark. Then have someone take the ball about 100 feet out in front of you and about 10 feet above you. Have him throw the ball at your face as hard as he can. That's what a green fireball looks like.' The January 1949 memo added that the objects were moving at between three and twelve miles per second – in other words, astonishingly fast!

As the document wrily noted, '... these phenomena have not been known to have been sighted, however, at any intermediate point between Russia and Los Alamos, but only at the end of the flight toward the apparent "target" ...'. Los Alamos in New Mexico was a highly sensitive nuclear facility. It is no wonder the US government were worried by all of this.

Although superficially these swift-moving green lights are similar to meteors , the report added that 'some nine scientific reasons are stated to exist which indicated that the phenomena observed are not [meteors]'. It then concluded that scientific opinion amongst the intelligence staff was that the green fireballs were either 'hitherto unobserved natural phenomena or that they are man-made. [But] no scientific experiments are known to exist in this country which could give rise to such phenomena.'

Thus, as Project Grudge was telling the public that UFOs were all easy to explain away, some of the top intelligence experts and scientific advisers to the US President were studying a stream of repetitive sightings of unknown objects overflying secret atomic bases. Their conclusions were that these objects were not only unexplained but also highly disturbing.

The experts are baffled

Piecing together the story of the green fireballs, we see that they began in late November 1948, although it seems that the first major events took place on 5 December. Within days so many experienced personnel, including Air Force pilots in mid-air and scientists on the ground, had seen these things that nobody at Los Alamos ever doubted that a mystery was afoot.

The man called in by the military intelligence was Dr Lincoln La Paz, a world authority on meteorites and a professor at the University of Albuquerque. La Paz had top-secret clearance and, some evidence suggests, had been one of the advisers consulted by the US government in July 1947 regarding the infamous Roswell UFO 'crash' (see Chapter 6).

La Paz and his team tracked down witnesses, interviewed them, plotted bearings on maps and followed a technique they had used successfully many times before to find meteorite debris on the Earth's surface. Again and again they visited the spot where green fireball debris should be. Again and again they found nothing. Yet reports were showing an alarming and very consistent flight pattern. The green fireballs overflew the atomic and nuclear facilities at Los Alamos, Sandia and so on – and then simply vanished!

Within one week, on 12 December 1948, Dr La Paz saw a green fireball for himself. It moved horizontally across the sky and had many other characteristics that did not match those of a meteor. He estimated its light output as 5218 angstroms, and inferred that the colour resulted from a high copper content. Much later that view was affirmed when considerable copper dust was recovered from beneath green fireball flight paths. Copper is hardly ever found in meteorite falls.

From all this evidence Dr Lincoln La Paz had absolutely no doubt that the green fireballs were unknown objects. In a secret report he wrote down his preliminary findings: the fireballs were moving too slowly, were too low in the sky, gave out no sonic boom despite their supersonic speed and proximity to witnesses, and did not leave a trail of sparks from the rear as meteors do. These things were utterly baffling.

On 8 February 1949 Dr Joseph Kaplan, a leading geophysicist and specialist in phenomena within the atmosphere, visited Albuquerque. He too had security clearance and was allowed to examine the now extensive data, after which he told the Air Force scientific advisory board that he found the matter 'unsettling'.

A home-grown mystery?

It was now felt necessary to convene a Conference on Aerial Phenomena, as it was termed, to debate this matter. The top scientists who attended included Edward Teller, one of the masterminds behind the building of the atomic bomb. At last UFOs were getting the right kind of respect, though they have never fully recaptured it since. Project Grudge were invited, but amazingly did not bother to send a representative – a fact that upset the scientists, who decided to keep Grudge only summararily informed in the future.

The problem was that Grudge's newly reconstituted operation was still reeling from the rejection of their 'estimate of situation', and the team were under orders to explain as many cases as possible as mundane things. This meant focusing on easily resolvable sightings – of which ufology, then as now, had plenty. It may have had no choice but to distance itself from something being endorsed by world-famous scientists.

As Edward Ruppelt said, when head of Air Force investigations into UFOs, this February 1949 gathering at Los Alamos was 'one conference where there was no need to discuss whether or not this type of UFO, the green fireball, existed. Almost everyone at the meeting had seen one.'

La Paz tried to persuade the assembled scientists that the objects were no known natural phenomenon, but Teller and others felt that they had to be some new process such as plasmas or electrical effects in the atmosphere. Teller added that the characteristics of the report suggested an optical rather than a physical phenomenon, akin to an ionised glow.

Teller, in particular, had access to data that would have told him had these objects been secret test launches – perhaps guided missile experiments with a 'need to know' classification. He assured the meeting they were not US technology. In the end La Paz carefully phrased his own conclusions – saying, in effect, that the fireballs were not meteors, nor did he, personally, believe they were natural phenomena. He felt that they were projectiles of an unknown technology, he hoped American. If 'friendly' they need not then be investigated – a view he 'doubted will be taken seriously' – but, if the powers above his head *knew* that these things were not American projectiles, as he clearly thought they did, then 'intensive, systematic investigation should not be delayed'.

Project Twinkle

One hint that the Americans were perhaps behind the green fireball sightings after all comes in several references from FBI memos; intelligence staff reported that they were twice warned of the probability of new sighting waves being imminent, including just prior to the first outbreak in late November 1948. A wave of reports had followed each tip-off. The warnings came from sources 'high up' in the chain of government, causing one to question how they knew what was about to happen unless they themselves were in control of the green fireballs?

However, this attractive solution is countered by the fact that Dr Kaplan was charged with the responsibility of a further detailed study in the wake of the Los Alamos meeting. A codename, Project Twinkle, was assigned and he spent much of 1949 setting up ideas for a further discussion meeting held in October – visiting, for example, the Cambridge scientific research laboratories of the AMC in Massachusetts to devise practical experiments.

'Project Twinkle' was the first scientific experiment to seek UFOs but it was not to be the last. The quest for proof is never ending.

The green fireballs pictured on the front cover of *Fate* in July 1957 were seen by thousands over the stadium at Santa Fé, New Mexico.

Following the October 1949 meeting Twinkle contracted Land-Air Incorporated to develop an automatic system to enable the fireballs to be filmed by two cameras at once, which would provide much useful data about the objects. Spectrographs and equipment to measure electromagnetic emissions were also obtained. Twinkle operated the cameras near Holloman Air Force Base in New Mexico during 1950 and 1951 for a total of eighteen months. If they were US weapons this expensive government-funded project makes no sense.

Sadly, a whole host of things went wrong with Twinkle. The Korean War intervened, taking away the military personnel who had been trained to use the more sophisticated equipment. There was much human error, lack of inter-departmental communication and sheer inefficiency, which meant that even when green fireballs did appear they were not adequately documented by the experiment.

Worst of all, the fireballs played games and Project Twinkle was led by the nose around the New Mexico landscape, rather than staying put and waiting for the UFOs to fly past their equipment. They set up their twenty-four-hour monitor where most green fireballs had been seen. But the numbers had dwindled by early 1950 when the project finally got up and running. After fruitless weeks they heard of sightings now occurring some distance away and so they upped sticks and followed the trail, only to arrive at their new stake-out soon after the wave was over! Then the fireballs returned to Vaughn, and so the game continued.

By late 1951 Twinkle closed down without reaching any firm conclusions. In 1953, when Edward Ruppelt had taken over the helm at a newly invigorated Air Force UFO project, he saw Dr Joseph Kaplan at a meeting. The professor's first question was 'Whatever happened to Project Twinkle?' Ruppelt did not know, as the work had largely been routed past his predecessors at Grudge, but this encouraged him to find out what he could.

Kaplan, whilst saying that he disagreed with the findings of Lincoln La Paz, suggested that Ruppelt (a man passionately interested in the truth behind the UFO sightings) should visit the meteor expert in Albuquerque. Later in the year Ruppelt visited Los Alamos and spent several hours discussing the matter with scientists and technical staff at the atomic research centre there. They came up with various ideas about the fireballs, but each worker accepted the reality and strange nature of the objects, which were still occasionally seen. All of them had witnessed at least one, and some had seen several. The consensus at Los Alamos was that these were possible projectiles fired from an alien craft in Earth orbit as some kind of long-range surveillance probe!

In his memoirs, published in 1956, Ruppelt reported that 'Two years ago I would have been amazed to hear a group of reputable scientists make such a startling statement. Now, however, I took it as a matter of course. I'd heard the same type of statement many times before from equally qualified groups.'

Ruppelt finally did meet Lincoln La Paz. He was very forthright, but considered carefully before he answered the key question as to what he thought the green fireballs had to be. According to Ruppelt: 'He didn't think that they were a natural phenomenon. He thought that some day one would hit the Earth [i.e. crash] and the mystery would be solved. He hoped that they were a natural phenomenon.'

The fireball enigma continues

In September 1954 Dr La Paz had said that sightings of green fireballs had disappeared. But the archives of UFO research groups contain records of many such phenomena from around the world, and from far more recent times than the days of Project Twinkle. Often they are associated with major military or industrial complexes, exactly as they were half a century ago.

In May 1978 an RAF pilot was driving near the massive oil refinery plant at Carrington in Greater Manchester when he saw three green fireballs whizz past. He was later 'regressed' by hypnosis to see if he might have been abducted by them! This enthusiastic, if improbable, experiment ended in failure. The man recounted in detail the passage of the fireballs, but there was no hidden story of an alien kidnap – just another sighting to add to the ever-growing list of a mystery intractable as ever even after fifty years.

Again green fireballs focused in October 1983 around the controversial nuclear plant at Sizewell in Suffolk, an area ringed by secret establishments with strong British and American connections. These facilities include electronics research centres, over-the-horizon radar and the twin NATO air bases of Bentwaters and Woodbridge.

It may well be very significant that two US air bases make persistent claims that they have hosted contact between aliens and the US government in modern times. These are Holloman Air Force Base in New Mexico (1964) and Bentwaters in Suffolk (1980) – see pages 212-18 – both are focal points of the most intensive green fireball activity known. Indeed, during the infamous close encounter at Bentwaters in December 1980 the sighting of many 'comets in the sky' – a new wave of strangely behaving fireball activity – proved a vital part of the story.

The green fireball mystery is far from a thing of the past.

In 1993 a new attempt was mounted by a group called CSETI who tried to establish contact with aliens at key UFO and crop circle sites by beaming light up at the sky. It had scientific support.

—9—

THE ALIEN INVASION OF WASHINGTON

1952 saw the biggest ever wave of UFO activity in the USA, triggering massive global interest in the subject.

After two years in the wilderness Project Grudge received a massive shot in the arm when in October 1951 Captain Edward J. Ruppelt became the latest Air Force officer to pick up the task. Like his predecessors, he was not a believer in UFOs but a thorough investigator who would seek out rational explanations. He was brought in, as he was told, 'for just a few months' in order to 'sort things out'.

It took little time for Ruppelt to realise that something unexplained was going on, and before long he was recommending improvements and better resources. The Air Force hierarchy liked him. Some thought he could get rid of the problem of UFOs entirely. Others – in the minority, but a strong view none the less – remained sure that behind these pesky UFOs lay an alien vision and that Ruppelt could be just the man to prove it.

Project Blue Book takes off

So, for a variety of reasons, the top brass assisted in fulfilling some of Ruppelt's requests and the project became more active and more responsible than before. He secured its independent status again as the Aerial Phenomena Group, with a new codename – it became Project Blue Book in March 1952. As Ruppelt said; 'The word "grudge" was no longer applicable ... the code name "Blue Book" was derived from the title given to college tests. Both the tests and the project had an abundance of equally confusing questions.'

The great 1952 wave

Hardly had Ruppelt's feet got under his desk at Wright Patterson Air Force Base than the USA was hit by the biggest wave of UFO activity ever. Although reports escalated from April onward, it was the last two weeks in July 1952 that were to see the height of the 'great flap'. This event was to have very profound effects: it would permanently alter the US government approach to UFOs, a term that Ruppelt first started to use as replacement for the presumptive 'flying saucer', and typical of his sensible approach. However, perhaps more important, the 1952 wave would create massive global interest in the subject – triggering official (and secret) investigations in countries like Britain which had been content to sit and watch what happened in the USA. The wave was also to make a deep impression on the minds of young children then growing up alongside regular accounts of these strange things in the sky – particularly given their widely perceived origin as alien craft.

The ufologists, the space enthusiasts who catapulted humanity towards the moon and the lovers of science fiction were all enraptured by the events of July 1952. A flood of UFO-related movies swiftly followed, notably *Earth Versus the Flying Saucers* of 1955. Without the 1952 wave space travel might have been slower in arriving, and very possibly the UFO mystery would have gradually ebbed away. As it was, this dramatic course of events virtually assured immortality for the dream of alien contact. The UFO mystery just happens to be a convenient mode of expression for a huge public desire that as a species we should have companions out there in the vastness of space.

A vital prelude to the wave was an article called 'Have We Visitors from Outer Space?' which appeared in *Life* magazine in March 1952. Coming from such an influential and unsensational publication, it was stunning. Ruppelt tells of the media clamour and how he had to issue what he called a 'weasel worded' public statement that *Life*'s opinions were their own, when in truth he knew that 'the Air Force had unofficially inspired [the article]'.

Indeed, Blue Book had supplied the best case material. The article cited key figures as saying: 'Maybe they're interplanetary.' This Ruppelt insists, reflected the personal opinion of several very high-ranking officers in the Pentagon at that time – 'so high that their personal opinion was almost policy'. The gradual escalation of all the evidence, despite every attempt to wish it away, was a factor in this shock verdict, as was the realisation that attention was settling on the seat of government – Washington DC.

Visitors to Washington

In May 1952 a high-ranking member of the CIA held a garden party not far from headquarters in Langley, Virginia. Suddenly a UFO flew right overhead, put on an aerial ballet and disappeared in front of many gaping influential guests. The impact was, of course, enormous.

After rushing quickly to nearby Washington to investigate the matter, Ruppelt notes that there was not very much he could do except stamp the file 'Unknown'. Then a CIA scientist told him that analysis was suggesting that a major event was imminent. It would occur in the capital. Blue Book had been monitoring the build-up also and had come to the same conclusion.

On 14 July, at 8.12pm, a Pan-Am DC-4 flying through the Washington area had a close encounter. Its veteran pilots, William Nash and William Fortenberry, had a close view of six coin-shaped objects that glowed red on top. At first these were below the aircraft; then they moved in a strange path across the sky, switching direction and finally climbing upwards to shoot away past the passenger aircraft as it flew south en route to Miami. The pilots last saw the lights 'flip' off one by one, possibly as they came out of range of the sunlight that was creating these reflections.

Hardly had the concerns about this worrying case died away when radar screens all around the capital started to pick up UFOs. This

In the summer of 1952 Washington DC was struck by a major wave of sightings that shook up both the US and British governments. Later this photograph appeared reputing to show the lights above Washington encircling the Capitol building. Investigation revealed them to be 'lens flares', ie street lamps outside the Capitol bouncing off the camera lens system.

began at 11.40pm on Saturday, 19 July, and lasted until after dawn. The sets were checked for faults within minutes of the blips appearing, as the control of air traffic over this location was a vital matter. The radar was working perfectly.

There were three systems in the area – the long-range set-up, which tracked aircraft passing through; the short-range radar at Washington Airport tower, which dealt with local landings and take-offs; and a military installation just across the Potomac River into Virginia. All three recorded the objects that night, often simultaneously. They comprised various targets moving slowly like aircraft, which then suddenly accelerated and zipped off-screen – one tracked at the then fantastic speed of 7,000 mph (about six times what Concorde can achieve today).

The 1952 Washington waves had more impact on the world than any other sightings in history. They also produced record numbers of witnesses – over 2000.

Many experienced radar officers viewed these targets and they were all baffled. When the UFOs started to fly through restricted airspace over the White House and Capitol, panic resulted. The nearest military base was undergoing runway repairs and was out of action. Three calls were made to urge the Air Force to send some interceptors into the area. Finally, one jet was scrambled – but it was nearly 3am before it reached Washington. By then aircraft arriving, departing and passing through the city's air space were seeing strange lights cavorting about the sky in total disregard of the tight security.

As the senior radar controller, Harry Barnes, said in his report: 'We knew immediately that a very strange situation existed.' Howard Cocklin, the radar controller in the tower at Washington Airport, looked out above the city as the blips rushed around the sky. He could see a big orange light right where one of the targets was indicated. A similar object 'like an orange ball of fire trailing a tail' was reported by phone by an airman to Andrews Air Force Base; an officer at the base went outside and saw it too, 'unlike anything I had ever seen before'. As he tried to bring others to watch it stopped dead, then shot off at an incredible speed and vanished.

A Capital Airlines DC-4 was vectored towards the lights from radar trackings. This was at about 1am. They saw several, but each time they closed in on the objects they shot away, both visually and on radar. Later Barnes described the UFOs' behaviour as 'like a bunch of small kids out playing'.

Government inactivity – or was it?

The radar and Air Force personnel were extremely puzzled by the slow response of the government authorities, who took a very long time to do very little. Indeed, when the interceptor from Delaware finally arrived, three hours into the affair, the UFOs had vanished – just minutes before, in fact. The jet flew around Washington for a while, using up fuel and seeing nothing, then returned to base. Almost as soon as it left the area the UFOs returned to the radar screens!

The events subsided as the sun rose, leaving a lot of baffled people. Yet nobody told Blue Book. In fact, Ruppelt flew by chance into Washington Airport just over twenty-four hours after the incident. When he bought a paper from the news-stand he found himself reading about these close encounters for the first time. He called his contact at the Pentagon from an airport phone booth to ask what was going on, but everyone there seemed as much in the dark as he was!

Although later that morning Ruppelt did interview personnel who were involved, this incredibly lax performance by the powers that be is as mystifying as the sightings themselves. But it has happened in other crucial cases since. This leaves the strong suspicion that in such instances there is a higher-level, top-secret, investigation unit, so far above operations like Blue Book that the small fry have no 'need to know' about its activities.

In cases such as this one – above the nation's capital city – someone must have been doing something. One wonders if for once they simply forgot to tell the dummy in the shop window what went on at the back of the store.

Official obstructiveness

Ruppelt tells how at the Pentagon that Monday every journalist and his cat was calling to get more information. Opinion was divided on whether to put out any solution they could think up or just to say they were investigating. The end result was 'No comment', which not surprisingly provoked accusations of a cover-up. Eventually it was accepted that Blue Book had to investigate, so Ruppelt agreed to extend his one-day visit to Washington and 'work all night' if necessary. He called back to Dayton, where nationwide sightings were pouring in – many better than the ones of the past thirty-six hours above Washington. But Ruppelt decided that national interest was best served by focusing on the case that the world's press were clamouring after.

So he planned his visits – to the three radar sites, to airline offices to speak to air crew, to the interceptor bases and to the weather bureau to check out possible solutions. Then he hit a brick wall. Nobody would give him an Air Force car to get to these sources as quickly as possible. He tried to hire one, but his expenses chits were refused. Instead he was told to take the bus – impossible, as speed was vital that morning. Finally he was reminded that he had written orders only to visit the city for the day, and would be classified as AWOL unless he went back to Dayton right away!

The by now deeply frustrated Ruppelt – supposedly the one person charged by the US government with handling the most significant UFO sightings yet on record – was aware that he was being manipulated. He called his boss at the Pentagon, told him what he thought and added: 'I decided that if saucers were buzzing Pennsylvania Avenue in formation I couldn't care less . . . I caught the next airliner to Dayton.'

In Earth versus the Flying Saucers *the sightings over Washington were given liberal interpretation as a UFO crashes into the monument!*

An unlikely theory

A week later, on the evening of Saturday, 26 July, the radar screens went crazy again and Washington was hit by a second flood of lights. Yet again Ruppelt, busy dealing with reports of nationwide UFO activity back at Dayton, got the news secondhand from a journalist who called him to ask what the Air Force were doing about the 'invasion'. One can sense his anger when he reports that instead of the expected 'No comment' he told the reporter: 'I have no idea what the Air Force is doing. In all probability it's doing nothing.'

Being the good investigator that he was, of course, Ruppelt put the case ahead of his personal feelings. He alerted Washington and within minutes three officers connected with Blue Book were on their way to the airport – a press officer, Al Chop; Ruppelt's right-hand man, Major Dewey Fournet; and a navy intelligence electronics expert called Holcomb. They all got to the airport in time to see the majority of the radar trackings (again recorded by all the area radars that night) and the arrival of two F-94 interceptor jets who were in constant radio contact with these men.

The media had arrived at the airport as the lights in the sky were being reported publicly. Ruppelt describes how they were ordered out of the operations room 'on the pretext that classified radio frequencies would be used' that night. Actually this expulsion occurred because 'not a few people in the radar room were positive that this night would be the big night in UFO history – the night when a pilot would close in and get a good look at a UFO – and they did not want the press to be in on it.'

An incredible game of cat and mouse resulted. At first there was a duplication of the previous week's farrago. As soon as the jets reached the area the UFOs vanished, both visually and on radar. They turned up instead at Langley, Virginia, where a passing Air Force jet and several people on the ground saw them. When the interceptors left Washington, the UFOs returned there – so more F-94s were scrambled! This time they got a radar lock on one of them, but as they closed in the UFO sped off too fast to catch. Finally one jet managed to get a good visual close-up of the object, so the pilot put the jet on afterburner and flew straight at the thing. As he approached it, the UFO shot away at an incredible speed. The pilot, Lieutenant William Patterson, later reported: 'I chased a single bright light which I estimated about 10 miles away. I lost visual contact with it at about 2 miles.'

Fournet briefed Ruppelt the next day as he headed for Washington to handle the expected media flak. It was clear that all of the experienced personnel working in the radar room that night were satisfied that the targets they were tracking were real. They were not radar equipment defects or the result of a temperature inversion that was causing a mirage – one theory that had been mooted as a possible solution. Fournet added that these men thought the objects were 'metallic'.

Two days later the biggest-ever peacetime press conference was held by the USAF, but with none of the officers who had been eye witnesses. Instead, a radar expert was flown in that day. He had met no witnesses but tentatively put forward the inversion theory. It was gratefully embraced by the Air Force.

The Blue Book conclusion, thanks to Ruppelt, was that these reports were unexplained. The radar experts at Washington who had seen the targets insisted that inversion echoes regularly appear all summer long and look quite different from those appearing on their scopes for those two nights.

Indeed, and possibly far more relevant, the US Weather Bureau failed to back up the vaguely proffered temperature inversion/radar mirage theory – noting that the radar experts who described the targets were reporting things unlike the behaviour commonly known in the weather trade as an 'angel'. It seems that – whatever the Air Force wanted the public to believe – these 'angels' were not caused by the forces of nature.

Fifteen years later, the men in the radar rooms at Washington DC told the same story to experts from the University of Colorado funded by the US government to try to debunk UFOs into oblivion. The radar officers were again adamant that the July 1952 sightings in Washington DC were quite inexplicable. They insisted that, whatever occurred on those mysterious nights, they are amongst the most important UFO sightings in history.

10

ENTER THE CIA

The aftermath of the Washington DC wave was incisive. Some people were bought off by the weather inversion theory, but not within the corridors of power. The CIA, for example, were sufficiently perturbed to get involved in the matter.

Their concern stemmed less from what UFOs might be and more from what they might do to the harassed intelligence network. After the Washington debacle an Air Force general had pointed out that normal communications channels were clogged by the flood of incoming UFO data. This was the era of the McCarthy witch-hunts against Communist sympathisers, and the height of the Cold War: the CIA perceived a real danger to its operations. A UFO wave would provide excellent cover for any enemy invasion, which made UFOs a big threat – whatever they were.

An analysis based on newly recovered records of the time was recently made by ufologist Barry Greenwood (pictured opposite). This suggests that to some extent the hysteria over the Washington flap may have been manipulated. It was difficult to persuade citizens to participate in ground observer watches for Communist activity, yet in the wake of the UFO sightings recruitment shot up and everyone started watching the skies. Perhaps, Greenwood suggests, the wave was allowed to develop so as to fulfil that function. Were the slow response times in sending interceptors and seeming disinterest in bringing Blue Book into the picture part of a CIA scheme?

In early 1952 Ruppelt made a number of suggestions to improve Blue Book. One of the most important was to employ a prestigious scientific research facility – the Battelle Memorial Institute – to make an intensive statistical appraisal. This impressive long-term project ran until 1954.

Ufologist Barry Greenwood, speaking at a conference.

High-level deception

When the US Air Force subsequently informed Ruppelt that a panel of top scientists would be convened to review the best UFO data, he thought this was another success for his attempt (backed by Allen Hynek) to upgrade the science within Blue Book. What he did not know was that the CIA were behind this latest initiative, and that the experts would be working for them towards a hidden agenda.

Battelle were by this time well into their far more detailed project and when they heard about the planned CIA meeting they urged that it be put on hold until their data was ready. Like Ruppelt they falsely assumed that the panel would meet to discuss UFOs, not secrecy behind them. The Battelle scientists' plea was ignored and the CIA team met for five days in Washington in January 1953. Even Hynek, Air Force science adviser since 1948 and the only scientist at that date to have real experience of UFO investigation, was merely invited to some sessions and excluded from others because he had no CIA clearance.

The Robertson panel, as this team were called, was headed by Dr H. P. Robertson, a relativity physicist who had been involved in the Manhattan Project to build the atomic bomb. The four others were

Luis Alvarez (a future Nobel prize winner), Lloyd Berkner, Sam Goudsmit and Thornton Page – all experts in physical sciences, emphasising the government view that UFOs were a material phenomenon and not hallucinations. Hynek, Ruppelt, Fournet and others directly involved in the data gathering at Blue Book presented evidence to the conference – which lasted for only twelve hours. The entire last day was spent writing and rewriting the statement to be issued in conclusion.

Thirty cases were investigated, with only a few minutes devoted to each one. Probable solutions were offered for some. Others were left as insoluble.

Ruppelt, sadly unaware of how he was being duped by his superiors, was optimistic about this group. He said: 'Although the group of scientists would not be empowered to make the final decision, their recommendations were to go to the President if they decided that UFOs were real. And any recommendations made by the group of names we planned to assemble would carry a lot of weight.' The betting in an unofficial sweepstake at the Blue Book office just before the panel met was 5 to 3 in favour of them finding UFOs real (which in most eyes meant finding them extraterrestrial). In the end, of course, the panel were never interested in such questions.

In the wake of the Roberston panel meetings in Washington, Project Blue Book began to explain away as many sightings as possible. It is now accepted by most serious ufologists that they were often right to do so and that ninety percent of all UFOs are really IFOs (identified flying objects). This UFO, photographed in Spain, is actually an unusual cloud formation.

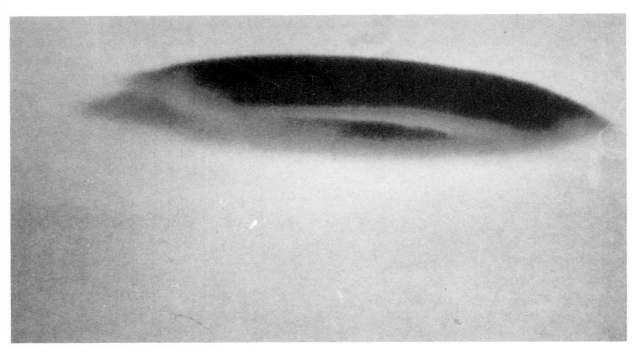

Manipulating the public

Their carefully discussed conclusions (again kept top secret, of course, even – it seems – from Ruppelt) were extraordinary. They agreed that communication channels could become 'overloaded', and that the US government should start a campaign to debunk the subject so as to 'result in the reduction in public interest in "flying saucers"'.

Suggested methods included allowing Walt Disney to make propaganda films, as well as TV programmes and press articles. The object of their two-year plan was to 'reduce or eliminate' public concern about UFOs as far as possible. However, the panel did warn that the newly founded civilian UFO groups 'should be watched because of their potentially great influence on mass thinking if widespread sightings should occur'. Adding to this was the curious idea that enemy agents could infiltrate UFO groups and use them for devious ends!

Such CIA tactics were rapidly put into play. Less than a year later, on 17 December 1953, a secret memo notes how 'the definite drop in the number of sightings' was 'attributed to the actions following the [panel's] recommendations'. Amazingly, Blue Book statistics suddenly showed that from unknowns totalling 20 per cent or more in previous years, only 1 or 2 per cent of cases per year were now being considered unidentified. The public were told that this showed how the UFOs had gone away. The real truth emerges from a careful study of the files, released in 1976. Identifications were being invented with abandon so as to wish away countless cases on a whim. Evidence to support each conclusion was regarded as an unnecessary luxury.

Nor is this a thing of the past. A CIA memo from 1976 tells how the agency is still having to 'keep in touch with reporting channels' in ufology (in other words, to spy on UFO groups). And in a November 1983 conference at the University of Lincoln, Nebraska, where Allen Hynek and Jenny Randles were amongst the lecturers, delegates were confined to the campus for the duration of the event following warning phone calls. A claim was made by an influential critic that the thrust of the conference could inadvertently aid Communist sympathisers by daring to discuss whether there was a cover-up of UFO data!

The Battelle results

Ruppelt knew none of these things. He was simply told that Blue Book was being upgraded in the wake of the Robertson panel, but his 1955 book makes it clear that he was never told of the secret directives. However, he quickly sensed the new regime. He left the Air Force in late 1953, writing positively on the subject and two years later publishing his devastating memoirs in which, ever the loyal officer, he pondered: 'Maybe I was just the front man for a big cover-up.'

It should be stressed that Ruppelt never became a member of the UFO community. He remained outspoken against the claims of writers such as Donald Keyhoe – then openly making charges of major conspiracies – and was greatly disillusioned by the contactee movement in the mid-1950s. This took hold just after the Robertson panel had met, and its value to the debunking cause was recognised in secret CIA memos. Some historical analysts think that the sudden arrival of countless Americans claiming contact with 'space brothers', and the quirky behaviour of some of them, may not be coincidence. Were some of the more extreme cases planted by the CIA as a way to speed up the Robertson panel requirements? They definitely tarnished UFO credibility.

If so, the move certainly paid off with Ruppelt. Four years after publishing his excellent book he produced a 'revised' edition in which he completely changed its emphasis. Now he said that UFOs were a space age myth and were all explicable. So dramatic was the turnabout that some think he must have been leaned on by the government, which may have threatened his new career in the aviation industry. Sadly, he died soon afterwards from a heart attack, aged thirty-seven, and was never able to answer the charges. But his widow insisted that it was the extent of the lunatic fringe within the contactee movement in California which demolished his faith in UFO reality.

This summary of the Robertson panel has excellent support. A fuller version was previously read by a panel member, Dr Thornton Page, who affirmed that it accurately portrayed what he recalled.

In contrast to these manipulations the Battelle study – by sceptics, it should be said – was a masterpiece of scientific research. It was subjected to intense secrecy. Hynek was told that even to mention it in public would result in him losing his prized contract with the Air Force.

The study was secret partly because its results were so positive – although, noting the lack of physical evidence, the Institute argued that they failed to prove an alien reality. Special Report 14 – as it was called when later released – took all 4,000 cases on Blue Book files to the end of 1952, selected the 2,199 that had the best data, and subject these to intense scrutiny. Every one was tabulated according to minute factors such as age, sex, observational experience of the witness, size of the object and so on: a very tough task when computer technology was not what it is today.

A Battelle scientist then assigned each case to one of four categories – excellent, good, doubtful and poor, according to quality of the evidence. Next it was put into an evaluation category. Every case was then given to an evaluation panel of Battelle scientists who met regularly to study batches of cases and reach their own conclusions. They did not know the outcome of the first evaluation. A team of experts – in fields like astronomy, radar and meteorology – were called in by the panel when significant cases appeared.

If the evaluation of the panel matched that of the lone Battelle analyst, then that conclusion was adopted. If not, discussions focused on that single case alone until a consensus was reached. On every case where the conclusion 'unknown' was adopted by either party, a full meeting of personnel was called to thrash it out until everyone was satisfied.

The results of the study provided some startling data. Most people expected the unknown cases to offer the least information (they were considered unknown only because there was insufficient data to identify them). When such missing data was provided, the case would be far more likely to be explained away. Sceptics still cling to this view.

In fact just under 10 per cent (about 200 cases) were rated as excellent data by Battelle. Of these, one third qualified for an unknown classification after rigorous investigation. Yet of the cases rated poor less than half were ultimately considered 'unknown'. All told, Battelle found that in just four years no fewer than 261 cases where the calibre of data available was viewed as either excellent or good qualified as an unknown phenomenon. This was overwhelming scientific evidence that something unexplained lay behind the UFO data. Yet the Robertson panel were only given a brief glimpse of a handful of these baffling cases.

Before freedom of information made the data available, the Air Force used the Battelle analysis to bizarre effect to try to counter Ruppelt's book. They reported that a study had proved UFOs to be invalid, because its data included only 'a few surviving unknowns'. In fact Battelle considered 22 per cent of its 2,199 cases to be unknown – which hardly justifies the tag 'a few' survivors! A government memo soon afterwards noted that the disclosure of this finding from Battelle was 'serving well the purpose for which it was intended'.

More dramatic still was a parameter for parameter analysis that Battelle had carried out. They looked at factors such as duration, shape and speed of the reports in both the identified and the unidentified categories. When an unknown case has no explanation, logic suggests

Despite claiming no interest in UFOs, Freedom of Information Act *requests for data show that the CIA have regularly collected reports of UFOs.*

The 1993 American TV series X-Files *is a drama based, reputedly, on 'true' files from the secret services. The agents regularly confronted UFOs and aliens in claimed reflections of genuine intelligence unit investigations – labelled the 'X-Files' – where X stands for the Unknown.*

that it may well simply be an example of an identifiable event which has not yet had the fortune to be resolved. But if so, then it would match up on this kind of parameter study.

For instance, all oranges are round and are coloured orange. If you have an object that you think might be an orange but you cannot prove that it is one, it will still match up to all other oranges in a parameter study of its shape and colour. Of course, things are a lot more complex in terms of multi-faceted UFO data, but the principle is the same.

Battelle studied its many cases to find the chances that the unknowns were identifiable objects (such as aircraft) but which had not had the fortune to be resolved. The outcome was that the chances were rather low – in fact the odds were an incredible one in a billion!

Such results imply that the unsolved cases were going to remain unsolved whatever investigation was carried out. They were genuinely unknown phenomena. But this could not prove, or even support, the view that the reports were describing an alien technology. That required a very different level of as yet unseen physical evidence. Even so, the Battelle results were a vital step forward.

Part Five

1950s:
ALIEN CONTACT

11

THE CONTACTEES

Controversy still rages over the contactees of the 1950s – men and women who were the precursors of the New Age channellers. Where modern channellers describe mental communications, much in the way that clairaudient mediums converse with 'spirits', the contactees actually met aliens and took trips in their flying saucers.

The contactee phenomenon is a rich treat for anthropologists, sticky with conscious and unconscious deceit, naive romanticism, and both sincere and sincerely deluded individuals. Were the contactees in touch with anything other than their own internal fantasies? Were the core experiences – stripped of all the third rate science fiction trappings – evidence of genuine 'alien' contact?

In the 1950s space exploration had hardly begun, and little was known even about our nearest neighbours. The contactees encountered extraterrestrials from planets in our own solar system – humanoid beings who apparently lived on Venus, Mars, Saturn and Neptune. It was conceivable at that time, because mankind was yet to learn how inhospitable these planets really are. Does this make the contactees tall story-tellers, or, as some ufologists believe, were the contactees being lied to?

The man who met a Venusian

The most famous contactee of all was George Adamski, a Polish American whose adventures with the 'space people' were chronicled in several books beginning with *Flying Saucers Have Landed*. This self-made man, who had an interest in astronomy and oriental philosophies, was out with some friends on 20 November 1952. They were picnicking in the Mohave Desert in California when they noticed a cigar-shaped object which was chased away by military jets – but not before it had ejected a silver disc which landed some distance away.

Adamski drove out near to where the saucer lay and was approached by a 'man' dressed in a one-piece suit. They communicated using telepathy, and Adamski learned that the being was from Venus. He said his race were concerned about the radiation from atomic bombs reaching into space and harming other worlds. The alien also informed Adamski that Earth was being visited by races from other planets in the solar system and beyond.

The witnesses to this encounter, observed through binoculars, signed affidavits. Meetings with other humanoids ensued, who took him on flights into space and around the dark side of the moon. But his description of wooded valleys was not borne out by subsequent space missions from Earth.

Adamski's photographs of cigar-shaped 'mother ships' and close-ups of the smaller disc-shaped 'scout craft' (see page 110) caused a lot of controversy. Critics compared the latter variously to part of a vacuum cleaner, a chicken feeder and a bottle cooling machine made in Wigan, Lancashire. This turned out to have been designed *after* the photographs were released, and purposely engineered by a fan of Adamski's to look like the scout craft. However, none of these items exactly matched the image captured on film.

In his defence, even sceptics were impressed with Adamski's apparent sincerity. Science journalist Robert Chapman wrote in *UFO – Flying Saucers Over Britain*: 'Adamski was so damnably normal and this was the overall impression I carried away. He believed he had made contact with a man from Venus, and he did not see why anyone should disbelieve him. I told myself that if he was deluded he was the most lucid and intelligent man I had met'.

Others around the world who have never heard of Adamski had sighted identical objects to the scout craft. One of them was a school-boy named Stephen Darbishire, who with his cousin took two pictures in Coniston one day in February 1954 (see page 111). Leonard Cramp, an aeronautical engineer used a system called orthographic projection to prove that the object depicted in Darbishire's and Adamski's photographs were proportionally identical. In a recent interview with Darbishire, now a professional artist, he confirmed to Peter Hough and Dr Harry Hudson all the details of his original story.

On his first trip into space Adamski observed 'manifestations taking place all around us, as though billions upon billions of fireflies were

According to Flying Saucers Have Landed, *Adamski had his first sighting in 1946 – a year before Kenneth Arnold's.*

George Adamski was the first man to become famous as a claimed contactee with alien entities. To back up his story he produced many controversial photographs reputed to show the UFOs flown by the Venusians and Saturnians that he met. Many investigators doubt the credibility of images such as this 'mother ship' disgorging several 'scout ships' taken near Mount Palomar in California.

flickering everywhere ...'. This is not something that would readily emerge from the imagination to be included in a space yarn. When astronaut John Glenn orbited Earth on 20 February 1962, he commented that '... a lot of the little things I thought were stars were actually a bright yellowish green about the size and intensity as looking at a firefly on a real dark night ... there were literally thousands of them'. Russian cosmonauts reported the same phenomenon, which turned out to be caused by billions of reflective dust particles. How could George Adamski have guessed that?

This son of a Polish immigrant generated a worldwide following. By the mid-sixties, however, his popularity was on the wane as his claims became more and more outlandish. Just months before he died, on 26 February 1965, he was staying with a couple at their house in Silver Spring, Maryland. That afternoon Adamski and Madeleine Rodeffer saw something hovering through some trees. A car drew up and three men told Adamski: 'Get your cameras – they're here', before driving

off. Adamski grabbed the Rodeffers' ciné camera and produced some 8mm colour footage of a scout craft which seemed to be suffering a distortion effect down one side. Was this meant to revive public interest in Adamski, or was it evidence that the contacts, on some level at least, were 'real'?

Stephen Darbishire's famous photograph, taken in Coniston in 1954. Some UFO researchers feel that the in focus upright object in the front right of the picture is the pin or stick holding up a UFO model or drawing. Stephen Darbishire, however, denies this.

Daniel Fry

George Adamski may have been the first contactee to maximise his commercial potential, but Daniel E. Fry pre-dated his initial contact by two or three years. Fry was employed at the White Sands Proving Grounds in New Mexico. Like some contactees, he exaggerated his credentials: he described himself as an 'internationally known scientist, researcher and electronics engineer, recognised by many as the best informed scientist on space and space travel'. But Philip Klass discovered that Fry was in fact a skilled instrument maker who had designed and built small devices used in missile control systems.

Fry had his first contact at White Sands on 4 July 1949 or 1950 – ten years later, he was not certain of the date. That night, he said, he missed the bus which was to take him into town to see the traditional fireworks, so he walked out into the desert instead to enjoy the cool night air. As he looked up he noticed that the stars were being blotted out by something descending. Shortly afterwards a metallic object, oblate spheroid in shape, settled on the desert floor about seventy feet away from him. As he approached to investigate, a voice speaking in American slang warned him to keep away from the hot hull. At this Fry fell over a root, and the voice attempted to calm him. It belonged to an extraterrestrial called A-lan who was communicating with him telepathically. In fact the craft was remotely controlled from a mother ship orbiting the Earth, and was there to collect air samples.

A-lan invited the Earthman inside, whereupon the craft took off and travelled to New York City and back in half an hour. This would have meant attaining a speed of 8,000 miles per hour, yet Fry felt nothing except a slight motion. He was released back into the desert with the promise that there would be further contacts. Fry was given the task of preaching the aliens' philosophy of 'understanding' to human society. The beings turned out to be the descendants of a previous Earth civilisation which had emigrated into space in the distant past.

One of Daniel Fry's 'spinning UFO' photographs.

Fry produced several books and clear daylight photographs of space-craft (see opposite) and founded a quasi-religious order called Under-standing, in order to spread the word. His first book was published just after Adamski's, and given his scientific background should have up-staged his rival's. However, Fry agreed to take a lie detector test on live television – and failed it. The result of a polygraph test is open to interpretation by the operator, but it damned Fry in the eyes of the media. Yet it is hard to conclude that the scientist was a hoaxer: he had a good, well-paid job and must have known that his claims of meetings with the space brothers would ruin his career.

George King – 'primary terrestrial mental channel'

Born in Wellington, Shropshire on 23 January 1919, taxi driver George King had a strange experience in his London flat when he was thirty-five. But having practised yoga since 1944, he was mentally prepared when a voice commanded: 'You are to become the voice of the inter-planetary parliament.' His first contact was with an alien from Venus called 'Aetherius', and out of this grew the Aetherius Society. It still thrives in many countries including Britain, the USA, Canada, Australia, New Zealand, Nigeria and Ghana. Many years ago 'Sir' George King vacated the damp London climate for the foothills of California.

After that initial contact King became a direct voice medium for the extraterrestrials. One of his contacts was Jesus Christ, who apparently now resides on Venus. He claims to have met Christ on a hill where he emerged from a spacecraft; the Messiah gave him some new teachings called 'The Twelve Blessings' to pass on to mankind.

The Aetherians use various paraphernalia including a 'prayer bat-tery'. Richard Lawrence, the society's European secretary, described the apparatus in an interview with Peter Hough: 'With this we can do something which the Vatican cannot. Two hundred members highly trained in Buddhist mantra and Christian prayer regularly meet, charg-ing up the battery with great prayer energy. In a matter of minutes, this beneficial energy can be directed to any location in the world.'

Indeed, the Aetherians claim that many natural disasters around the world would be even worse if it was not for the release of prayer energy from these batteries. The internal construction of the apparatus is secret, and no outsider has been allowed to examine it.

In his book *You Are Responsible*, written in the fifties, King describes a visit in an out-of-body state to Mars, where he is wounded by a dwarf with a ray gun. Later, he is commandeered to help the Martians destroy an intelligent meteorite which is attacking their space fleet. King finally defeated the sentient lump of rock 'with a weapon of love'.

Many Aetherians, including those with a scientific background, believed and continue to believe this rather far-fetched sounding scenario. How did the Aetherius Society cope with the information from space probes in the sixties and seventies, when it was discovered that conditions on Venus and Mars could not support advanced, oxygen-breathing life forms? Their answer was that the Master Aetherius and his colleagues became spiritual entities, not beings of flesh and blood. But in that case, why do they need space vehicles? Lawrence claims that the beings can manipulate energy and matter by tuning it to different vibrations, making it appear sometimes 'solid' and at other times more insubstantial and 'ghostly'.

Richard Miller and the spaceship *Phoenix*

One of the lesser-known contactees of the 1950s was a man called Richard Miller. He had his initial close encounter in 1954, after contacting extraterrestrials on short-wave radio. They instructed him to go to an isolated location near Ann Arbor in Michigan, where after fifteen minutes a disc-shaped object appeared and landed nearby. This, he was to learn, was called *Phoenix*. A doorway opened in the base of the vehicle and a staircase descended. Miller described what happened next. 'There, standing at the head of the stairway, was a young man dressed in a brown one-piece suit. He beckoned me to enter the ship, which I did. I was standing in a large circular hallway which seemed to encircle the whole craft. Although nothing had yet been said, the young man radiated a kind of friendliness which put me at ease.'

Miller was taken to the control room of the ship where he met the alien commander, Soltec, who greeted him in perfect English. He explained that their planet, Centurus of the Alpha Centauri system, belonged to the 'Universal Confederation', a group of over 680 planets which earned the right to membership by their evolutionary progress.

The contactee was told that, before Earth could become a member, mankind would have to awaken to higher spiritual values: 'When love of your fellow man becomes established, then will the Sons of Light appear and the Kingdom of your God will reign on Earth.' The 'Sons of Light', Miller was told, were what the Bible referred to as 'angels'.

Sceptics often ask why intelligent aliens would contact ordinary men and women and not some higher, more influential authority. Through Soltec, Miller provided an answer to this criticism. The extraterrestrials *had* contacted government heads and top scientists, he was told, but they had spurned the aliens, not wanting to give up their power base in the coming New Age; a cover-up had been agreed by the establishment. So Soltec and his friends sought to contact general members of the public, in the hope that they would spread the word and that the resultant pressure would force governments to change their policies.

Soltec went on to describe how the Atlantians had fought a nuclear war with their neighbours, the Lemurians, which was a result of material greed. Referring to modern civilisation, Soltec said: 'There is a much safer way to utilise the power of the atom than by trying to split it or break it up. Do they not realise that by destroying matter, they are opposing the will of the Creator?'

Soltec also explained about the 'Big Bang' theory, which holds that whole galaxies are travelling through space following a central explosion which brought about the creation of the universe. Currently, he said, the Earth was moving through a cloud of radioactive particles. The alien spacecraft, in orbit around the Earth, were reflecting the radiation away before it could pierce our atmosphere.

Richard Miller's contacts continued for over twenty years, all meticulously recorded in a library of writings and tape recordings.

The strange tales of Frank Stranges

Dr Frank Stranges, like Daniel Fry, is academically well qualified, making it hard for sceptics to understand why he should involve himself in 'space age gobbledegook'. An evangelist, he combines the teachings of his faith with the teachings of extraterrestrials gleaned from his various contacts.

Since 1956 Stranges has claimed many encounters with UFOs and their occupants, which are described in three books. One of them, *My Friend from Beyond Earth*, is similar in many particulars to Kenneth Arnold's famous sighting (see Chapter 5). In a later book, *Stranger at* the Pentagon, Stranges describes his meeting with Val Thor, a man from Venus, in the Pentagon Building in Washington.

> I then saw one lone man … It was as though he looked straight through me. With a warm smile, and outstretched hand, he slowly started towards me. I felt strange all over. As I gripped his hand, I was somewhat surprised to feel the soft texture of his hand … like that of a baby. His eyes were brown and his hair wavy brown, also. He was to all appearance like an Earth man, but *he had no fingerprints.*

The Venusian knew Stranges' name, and was there with the knowledge of American officials who were doing some tests on his clothing. 'He produced a one-piece garment that glittered as he brought it towards the sunlight streaming through the window. I asked him how it held together. He demonstrated by holding the front together, passing his hand as though to smooth it out, and I could not even locate the opening. It was held together by an invisible force.'

Val Thor was some sort of interplanetary missionary on behalf of 'the Lord'. He and his kind felt that man had drifted too far away from God and needed some help to get back there. The alien even hinted to Stranges that he might be Jesus Christ.

Truman Bethurum was taken aboard a flying saucer by a platoon of little men. There he was introduced to their female captain, Aura Rhanes, who could pass for human. Bethurum wrote in 1954 that she 'tops in shapeliness and beauty.' He later saw her in a restaurant, sipping orange juice, but she ignored him.

The contactee circus

There were many other contactees, including George Van Tassel, Truman Bethurum, Gabriel Green and Reinhold O. Schmidt. Many modern ufologists, such as Jerome Clark, view the contactee era as an embarrassment, a circus of deluded and perhaps over-imaginative men who preyed on the hopes and fears of others. Certainly they took to the lecture circuit like a duck to water, peddling stories of alien contact to a receptive audience who were willing to pay to hear what they wanted to hear.

This all happened in the immediate post-war era, when the world understood that man now had the power to destroy the entire planet. The aliens who courted the contactees were angelic beings who wanted to help us save ourselves from the holocaust. Many of the contactees were sincere people who brought hope and solace to their audiences and readers. But did the contactees have anything to do with ufology, or was it just a scam riding on the back of genuine UFO reports?

There are some researchers who think the contactee phenomenon was part of the CIA anti-UFO plot (see Chapter 10). What better way

Flying Saucers Have Landed – the book which tells the story of George Adamski's encounters.

of defusing intelligent public interest than by encouraging people to peddle tales so outlandish that they were guaranteed to quieten respectable members of society. In the meantime the authorities could continue their clandestine investigations unimpeded by enquiring busybodies. Even more important, it allowed governments to keep the lid on the pot. This probably contained a stew of potentially damaging ramifications should any government have to admit the reality of UFOs. Such an admission of impotence could bring about sociological and financial chaos around the world.

So what was behind the contactee phenomenon – fraud, delusion, disinformation or genuine contact with 'aliens'? It is quite possible that all of these things played their part. Certainly there were people out to make a fast buck, and there were individuals who wanted to believe they had been chosen as disciples of an intergalactic order. Just as likely is the probability that many were the witting or unwitting puppets of government security agencies. But were there actually any aliens?

Many commentators poured scorn on the names of George Adamski's extraterrestrial brothers – Orthon, Ashtar, Firkon and Kalna. But Adamski claimed they did not have names: they were an invention of his ghost writer to make the story more digestible to the public. One wonders just how much of the original story was sacrificed for commercial reasons. Stripping away some of the layers reveals a darker side not generally acknowledged at the time.

Fundamentally, it seems reasonable to conclude that some of the contactees were dealing with an objective phenomenon – an intelligence. This could have been extraterrestrial, but more likely something masquerading as such.

—— 12 ——

ALIENS OVER EUROPE

In October 1954 Europe experienced its first major UFO wave.

According to Ralph Noyes, then a British diplomat and later head of the Ministry of Defence section that handled UFO data, the Washington flap of 1952 had a profound effect across the Atlantic. RAF intelligence officers flew to the Pentagon to find out what was going on. Ruppelt recalled the visit, referring to a six-page list of questions that they had brought with them!

Recent data obtained by ufologist Gary Taylor from the British Public Record Office gives clear evidence of government activity at the time. Winston Churchill wrote from the Prime Minister's office on 28 July 1952 demanding of his Secretary of State for Air: 'What does all this stuff about flying saucers amount to? What can it mean? What is the truth?' (A copy of the memo is reproduced on page 120.) In response, intelligence staff were sent to the USA and the Prime Minister was advised by the Air Ministry on 9 August that a 'full intelligence study' into UFOs had been carried out in 1951. From this they had concluded that 'all the incidents reported could be explained' (citing astronomical and meteorological phenomena, balloons, birds, optical illusions, psychological delusions and deliberate hoaxes). They added that the Americans had told them that they had found the same in 1949 (Project Grudge, which of course was by no means as straightforward as Churchill was misinformed).

Now, as Britain and America consulted over new developments, the UFOs conspired to establish their global nature. In September 1952 a major NATO exercise was under way in eastern England and the North Sea. Called Operation Mainbrace, it involved aircraft and ships of various Allied powers. But was a third party taking part in these war games?

Subject File B.7 . 6. 8 52   Defence (Research)

PRIME MINISTER'S
PERSONAL MINUTE

SERIAL No. M. 412 /52   5

SECRETARY OF STATE FOR AIR

LORD CHERWELL

What does all this stuff about flying saucers amount to?   What can it mean?   What is the truth?   Let me have a report at your convenience.

W.S.C.

28 July 1952

Playing tag with the RAF

See opposite
Winston Churchill's memo to the Secretary of State for Air, Lord Cherwell.

On three consecutive days – 19, 20 and 21 September – major close encounters took place amidst the exercise. On the 19th, at 10.53am, a 'silver and circular' object was seen following an RAF Meteor jet as it overflew a base near Dishforth in Yorkshire. Five air crew were witness to the event. One of them, Flight Lieutenant John Kilburn, described how it was 'swinging in a pendulum fashion' as it descended. This is an early reference to the so-called 'falling leaf' motion (he even used the term 'similar to a falling sycamore leaf'). UFOs often display this unusual flight pattern, which can be mimicked if you drop a plate into a bowl of water.

The Dishforth UFO then gave up its pursuit of the landing jet, hovered in mid-air, rotating on its axis, and left 'at an incredible speed towards the west, turning on a south-easterly heading before disappearing'. Such changes in direction and speed defy identification as a balloon.

The base commander at RAF Topcliffe received a number of reports from residents in the York and Thirsk area who had evidently also seen the UFO. A man at Easingwold spoke of a bright silver object that kept appearing, then disappearing; it hovered and finally shot away at great speed.

The next day a photographer aboard a US Air Force carrier in the North Sea was taking official film of an aircraft when he saw officers staring at the sky. He looked up and saw another silvery disc, of which he took several photographs. That film has not been released.

Twenty-four hours later no fewer than six RAF jets over the North Sea observed a similar silvery object in daylight. They closed in on the target and it accelerated away. Then it played tag with one Meteor, turning as it turned, before growing tired of the game and streaking away far beyond the capabilities of the RAF. This form of behaviour was becoming repetitive.

Ruppelt says an RAF intelligence officer then based at the Pentagon told him that the Operation Mainbrace reports led to official recognition of UFOs by the British government – especially since it followed swiftly on top of the Washington flap.

Official suppression

RAF encounters became quite common. In many cases the crews were advised to say nothing as the matter was covered by the Official Secrets

Act. Ralph Noyes has confirmed that he has seen gun camera film of UFOs that were captured by pursuing RAF jets. None has been released.

There are various references in the archives of the Public Records Office to letter FC/S.45485/Signals (13 January 1953). This appears to have been about the implementation of new policy arising after the envoys had returned from the Pentagon. Clearly it was decided to upgrade UFO study in Britain considerably.

A restricted memo of 16 December 1953 sent to senior air staff in southern England told how sightings of UFOs by 'Royal Air Force personnel are in future to be reported in writing by officers commanding units immediately and direct to Air Ministry (DDI Tech) with copies to group and command headquarters'. This report also noted that 'the public attach more credence to reports by RAF personnel' and, as such, 'it is essential that the information should be examined at the Air Ministry and that its release should be controlled officially'.

Military personnel who dared tell their story of a close encounter after many years have often referred to the order to remain silent. We now have proof of that order, as this 1953 memo added: 'All reports are, therefore, to be classified "restricted" and personnel are to be warned that they are not to communicate to anyone other than official persons any information about phenomena they have observed.' So, in Britain, an official cover-up of the best-quality UFO evidence had been ordered right from the top and was in force by 1953 as a direct result of the events in Washington and during Operation Mainbrace.

Typical incidents during this intense period include the encounter over Salisbury Plain one winter's day in early 1953. Flight Lieutenant (later Wing Commander and an MoD radar specialist) Cyril Townsend-Withers was at 55,000 feet aboard a Canberra stripped bare to avoid weather effects on the new radar equipment. Suddenly he spotted an object dead ahead – both visually and on radar – which he termed 'a reconnaissance device from somewhere else'. It was a flat silver disc with two small 'fins'. As the jet made a radial turn the object sat there waiting for them to fly straight at it. They closed in and prepared for evasive tactics, but the UFO flipped into a vertical mode and shot skywards at an unbelievable speed.

Townsend-Withers awaited the required expiry of thirty years under the Official Secrets Act before he could talk. The radar system was thoroughly checked and was working perfectly. The RAF told the officer that a top-secret project was investigating the many sightings like his own at RAF Farnborough and was working on the premise that they could be alien craft.

The British magazine Flying Saucer Review *was launched in 1955 in the aftermath of the wave and became the first successful international UFO journal to be published regularly.*

Definitely not a balloon

Then, on 4 April 1957, a spectacular series of radar spottings occurred at RAF West Freugh in south-west Scotland: three separate bases tracked the object as it crossed the region. News was briefly made public, as some of the operators had been civilians. The Civil Defence organisation was put on alert before the subject was quickly hushed up. The commanding officer at West Freugh, Wing Commander Walter Whitworth, merely stated; 'I have been ordered by the Air Ministry to say nothing about the object.' A later press story stated that the UFO could have been a balloon, and this idea was generally accepted by sceptics. Only with the release of the official reports after they had come out of the jurisdiction of the thirty-year rule could it be seen that this theory was never remotely tenable.

The object was at a fantastic height (70,000 feet was recorded by Balscalloch radar, but this information was concealed because it exceeded aircraft capabilities of the day). The UFO changed course when 'it made a very sharp turn . . . to the SE at the same time increasing speed', said a secret Air Ministry report dated 30 April 1957. The UFO moved at 70 mph, then accelerated to 240 mph. As the same report concluded: 'There were not known to be any aircraft in the vicinity nor were there any meteorological balloons. Even if balloons had been in the area these would not account for the sudden change of direction and the movement at high speed against the prevailing wind.' It seems that the Air Ministry were learning well from the 'debunk at all costs' tactics then in use by Project Blue Book in the USA.

Furore in Whitehall

However, by far the most important UK sighting of the decade was never made public – at least, not until the University of Colorado study of UFOs in 1967 found it by accident. The USAF officer who told them assumed that the scientists would already know all about it, because – according to public statements by the White House – the team had complete access to all the US government's UFO data. The USAF officer knew the matter had been investigated eleven years earlier. What he did not know was that this vital case had never become part of the Blue Book or MoD public records.

The events occurred over the night of 13–14 August 1956. Three separate ground radars – at the RAF/USAF bases of Lakenheath and Bentwaters in Suffolk and the RAF command centre in East Anglia at Neatishead – all tracked an object which was seen by ground staff as well as from above (air crew looking down upon it from a USAF transport plane).

Squadron Leader Freddy Wimbledon – in charge of battle alert station that night – has subsequently told how he scrambled two RAF Venom fighters into the area in response to the USAF sightings. The first jet, he alleged, used the correct codes, locked on to the target with its airborne radar and also saw the light – which instantly swept around to the back of the plane and began to follow it. We have also tracked down and talked to civilians in Cambridgeshire who apparently saw the Venom streak overhead with the UFO in hot pursuit near Ely and Lakenheath!

It is hardly surprising that this case created a furore in Whitehall. Ralph Noyes says that the whole place was buzzing with it, and when in 1969 he came to take on the task of heading an MoD department which received UFO data he was fully briefed and shown the gun camera film taken by the Venom. Whilst this apparently only depicts a fuzzy light visible for a few seconds, it is further proof of the value of this most extraordinary encounter – especially as the MoD continue to choose not to release the film.

The scientists at the University of Colorado – whilst rejecting any validity to UFO sightings in general – concluded of this particular case that it was 'the most puzzling and unusual' in their files, adding that 'the apparently rational, intelligent behaviour of the UFO suggests a mechanical device of unknown origin as the most probable explanation'.

Yet the MoD says of this affair that it has 'lost' all record on its files, that it was never among the fifteen thousand cases on the Project Blue Book archives declassified in 1976, and that its gun camera film remains secret forty years later. Indeed, but for a fluke we would not know that this incident had ever occurred. How many others like it are out there somewhere?

Oddly, despite the fact that this classic case must have generated rainforests of paperwork, the Public Record Office files contain only one brief reference which appears to relate to it. This comes in an Air Ministry briefing paper offering assistance to a minister facing questions in the House of Commons. Some of these came from the then MP, NATO defence committee officer and future President of BUF-ORA (British UFO Research Association), Major Sir Patrick Wall. The paper is dated 2 May 1957 and describes radar contacts with UFOs during the past year.

It refers to three radar contacts during 1956. One was picked up on the airborne radar of a Vulcan bomber, but the crew saw nothing

visually. A second involved a radar lock by an aircraft sent to intercept an object tracked by Weathersfield radar. The third was 'an unusual object on Lakenheath radar, which at first moved at a speed of between two and four thousand knots and then remained stationary at a high altitude'. These latter two (whilst undated) may both refer to the night of 13–14 August 1956, as some details do match.

Claims that aircraft were sent in pursuit of UFOs were common during the early 1950s. Some photographs (from then and later) do exist, but sometimes the UFO is suspected to be a defect on the film that was accidentally in shot when the aircraft was being photographed.

18,000 mph!

In 1991, by more good fortune, we discovered that there was a sequel to this 1956 incident which the minister was never briefed about. A retired RAF fighter pilot contacted Jenny Randles and reported an episode which befell him, his navigator and the two-man crew of a similar Javelin fighter during the afternoon of 30 August 1956 – just two weeks after the Lakenheath/Bentwaters affair had rocked Whitehall and Washington.

The pilot again assumed that he was now free to talk about the matter since thirty years had elapsed. Investigations by Paul Fuller and others have uncovered data from official records and other sources that go some way to verifying this story. We even have his duty log book for the day in question, in which he had noted alongside his mission details: 'UFO !' Yet public records contain no reference to this case, despite its obvious importance – suggesting that it may be one of many.

At the time the two Javelins were practising air intercepts: one aircraft was used as a target while the other tried to fly across its path in mid-air. They were just south of the Isle of Wight at 45,000 feet, well above cloud cover and in perfect visibility.

The navigator manning the radar preparing to lock on the target aircraft picked up an object some nineteen miles north-east. Looking visually, the crew saw a glint in the distance as they closed in on their pre-planned position. They requested permission to abandon the exercise and pursue this object, which was granted. The target aircraft caught up with them, to fly alongside. In the meantime the UFO had moved ahead of them to cross their path and had slowed down to a near halt.

By now the crew and both radars had a lock on the object and the jets went into a steep bank to intercept the target. Radar showed it to be almost stationary and they were closing in fast. They obtained a good visual sighting of a grey metal disc.

Then – at eight miles from intercept – the UFO suddenly shot vertically upwards and left the radar scopes at the unbelievable speed of almost 18,000 mph! The four crew members were told to report the matter to the Air Ministry. A secret ground radar station at Sopley near Bournemouth confirmed that it too had tracked the object.

Official excuses, public hysteria

Evidence is overwhelming that there were many dramatic sightings such as these occurring throughout the 1950s – both in the UK and in the USA, and almost certainly high above many other countries too. They must have confirmed to the authorities that UFOs were real phenomena with amazing abilities and utterly inexplicable. Further secrecy was guaranteed by them.

As these cases were influencing judgment in Whitehall, the Pentagon and elsewhere in secret, Blue Book was debunking everything in sight. Governments almost everywhere else were explaining away sightings as fast as they were made or hiding the best data. Contactees created amusing headlines, and hysterical protestations about massive cover-ups kept coming from popular writers and the countless private UFO groups now springing up all over the world.

The official view was always that UFOs were nonsense. The public outcry from the extremists was that aliens had landed and the world governments knew this fact for certain. The truth probably lay somewhere in the middle – that unexplained and baffling UFO events were happening frequently, but nobody really knew what was causing them.

The Nordics and the Greys

Amidst all this, in October 1954, the first major wave outside the continental USA struck in France and Italy, spreading also into other countries, including Britain. For the first time reports of alien entities were coming in. But these were not from contactees meeting friendly space brothers; they were made by highly credible witnesses.

Over two-thirds of the autumn 1954 wave in Europe were focused in France, which subsequently became the leader of European research into the subject.

France took the brunt of these reports. Many involved small figures, under four feet tall, wearing silvery diver's suits. At Quarouble on 10 September 1954 a man was alerted by his dog barking furiously; when he investigated, he found an object that had landed on railway tracks by his house. Heavy indentations in the sleepers were later recorded by the police. Two entities fired a beam of light at the witness, who was endeavouring to chase off what he assumed were vandals. The beam 'froze' him in place until it was turned off.

Several more French cases during September and October included paralysing beams – sometimes fired from small objects like flashlights held by the entities. From this time, too, came the first well-attested reports of the engine and lights of motor vehicles failing in the presence of a UFO.

At Torpo in Norway on 23 November 1954 three witnesses saw a round object with a transparent dome on top. Inside this was a human-like figure operating controls and wearing goggles. The object shot upwards, hitting a power line as it did so and sending a shower of sparks down to Earth.

The most impressive sighting in Britain during this particular wave occurred on 21 October 1954 at an isolated house near Ranton in Staffordshire. Mrs Jessie Roestenberg hid with her children under the table as a large object with a transparent dome circled around, giving off a pulse of ultra-violet light. In the dome, as if curious tourists, were two 'ski-suited' men with blond hair.

The flood of such cases settled into a clear pattern. There were two basic types of entity, and they behaved in a remarkably consistent way.

First there were the tall, or near human height, figures such as at Ranton, often with blond or white hair and blue eyes (sometimes

Photographs of aliens began to appear during the early 1950s – including this image of a landed object and spacesuit-clad figure reportedly taken in July 1952 on the Bernina Mountains of Italy by Giampiero Monguzzi. It is widely believed by ufologists to be a table-top model photographed in close focus.

described as looking oriental or like a cat). In appearance they resembled the popular idea of Norse gods, and were therefore nicknamed 'Nordics' by UFO buffs. These entities tended simply to observe, to be compassionate or even friendly, and to display near-magical powers like wizards (such as walking through walls, possessing ESP, materialising and dematerialising). They became particularly common in Europe.

The other entities were much smaller – usually around three and a half feet tall or slightly more. They often wore silver suits and had large heads and huge round eyes. They behaved with rather less concern for any witnesses than the other group, and not infrequently rendered

victims unconscious with a weapon of some sort. Later they became the kind of entity most frequently involved in alien abduction stories and were given the name 'Greys' because of their greyish skin colour.

The entities issue warnings

A gynaecologist in Venezuela was visited by the Nordics, who arrived in a magical flash of light and professed concern about human progress and our abuse of nuclear power. The doctor was told that these aliens would not interfere but would try to help in subtle ways (genetic engineering was even hinted at).

On the other hand these friendly Nordics knew about the Greys, whom they described clearly and claimed to have come from Orion. They were reputedly up to no good. Earth should guard against them, we were warned!

This photograph is one of the few considered truly impressive by UFO experts. It is one of a series of three taken by a postman at Namur, Belgium, on 5 June 1955. The disc-like object had reportedly ejected a vapour trail into which the object climbed. This image, showing UFO and vapour trail intermixed, is important because a vapour trail cannot form lower than several thousand feet making the size of this object too great for a model as might be used in a hoax.

THE SPACE GENERATION

One of the most significant periods in human history occurred in late October and early November 1957. We became an interplanetary species – perhaps in more ways than one!

In early October the Soviet Union freed mankind from the bonds of Earth by launching Sputnik 1. It was only a tiny capsule which simply went up and down, but it represented the start of a new age. Rather more significant was the mission on 2–3 November of Sputnik 2, which took the first living thing into orbit – a dog called Laika. This historic event made headlines around the world over the next few days.

Did man's space missions create UFO response?

Throughout this four-week period, and especially the key night of 2–3 November, UFO activity was enormous. If UFOs are in any way connected with intelligent beings observing humanity, then they must have noted the importance of this time. Either what took place during that period is an extraordinary coincidence, or it is strong evidence that UFOs are being intelligently controlled and made a direct response to these shattering events.

On the night that Laika (see opposite) became our first space traveller, fantastic things were afoot. The most astonishing set of close encounters struck the USA in what appears to be a blatant demonstration of superior technology.

The wave focused on New Mexico and Texas, the area where dramas had already unfolded the decade before. It was here that the Roswell events had occurred (the supposed UFO crash in 1947). The region contained sites, such as Vaughn and White Sands/Alamogordo, where the green fireballs had baffled top scientists. And in this same

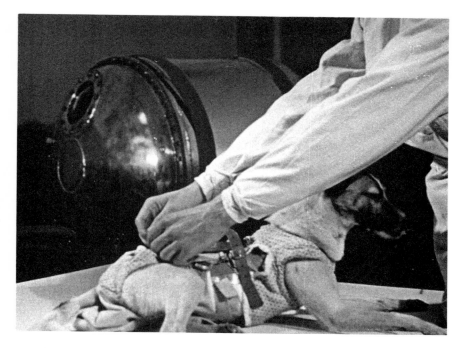

A technician prepares Laika, the bitch who became the first animal in space, for her launch aboard Sputnik 2 on November 3, 1957.

scrub desert location was Las Cruces, where the only twentieth-century scientist to discover a new planet (Professor Clyde Tombaugh, who discovered Pluto) had experienced his own UFO sighting.

The scene of this eminently topical UFO wave could also hardly have been more appropriate for other reasons. Here the first atomic weapons were detonated. Here missile and rocket technology was under intense development. There could have been no more likely place for any intelligence worried by our first foray into space to take a personal and very specific interest.

Electrical systems put out

Between 31 October and 6 November no fewer than thirty-six cases were reported of vehicles experiencing close encounters with glowing objects that impeded or destroyed their electrical systems. This was unprecedented. Undoubtedly the most astonishing came as a series of independent events that occurred between 10.40 pm on 2 November and 1.30 early the following morning – directly before the Laika mission. As many as twenty sightings occurred within a ten-mile radius of the border town of Levelland, and half of them involved physical effects created by the UFO.

Pedro Saucedo and Joe Salaz were driving a truck when four miles outside town they spotted a flying object heading straight for them.

Saucedo reported: 'When it got nearer the lights of my truck went out and the motor died. I jumped out and hit the deck as the thing passed directly over.'

There was a huge blast of wind and a wave of heat. Then the object shot into the sky, looking like a torpedo. In a semi-hysterical state the two men drove into the nearby town of Whiteface and called the sheriff's office at Levelland. The officer who took their call assumed they were drunk, but he was very soon to realise his mistake.

Under an hour later another call came in and by midnight there had been several. Soon half the town was seeing these oval balls of light roaming around the sky. Virtually every vehicle that came near one – as it sat on the road blocking the path or lay in wait by the sidewalk – was stopped dead in its tracks by some mystery force.

The sightings were unusually consistent. As soon as the object shot into the air, the ignition and lighting systems on the vehicle involved were said to have returned to normal.

By now Sheriff Weir Clem had set off with two deputies to find the intruder. At 12.15 Frank Williams, driving near Witharall, saw a yellow-red ball dead ahead and felt the power drain from his engine and lights. The object pulsated in rhythmic fashion, like lights in a disco accompanying the music. Williams's car headlights faded in and out. Then there was a terrific roar and the object shot skyward. The car now worked perfectly once more.

As each case was radioed through, Sheriff Clem sped off to the location to try to find the UFO. He failed, until at 1.30 he reached the spot where a few minutes before truck driver James Long had become the latest victim of the power-sucking UFO. Here Clem found a 'brilliant red sunset' across the highway. He drove towards it but could not catch up, and the police car suffered no interference. The object just ahead of him creating the glow was 'like a huge football', Clem reports, and shot away at great speed.

At the time Clem was in a convoy of three vehicles. Another police car with his deputies inside was behind him and saw the whole thing; they too suffered no ill effects. Ahead of Clem was fire marshal Ray James, whose truck suffered partial loss of power and lighting, but quickly returned to normal as the object streaked away. These were to be the final encounters of the night.

After the local media reported the matter, the sheriff's office received over a hundred calls from local residents who had seen the object during that three-hour spell. Newell Wright, on the road east of Levelland at 12.05, had noticed how his ammeter jumped to 'discharge', as if suddenly overloaded, then fell back to normal, taking with it all the car's power and lighting. Real, hard, scientific evidence about the power source was being gathered at last. Wright had inspected his engine but could find no fault. As he was doing so he noticed a green, oval mass dead ahead. As soon as the object vanished the car returned to normal as with all the others.

Ball lightning: another theory

Project Blue Book sent an investigator to the town three days later. He spoke with only two witnesses and quickly decided that because it had rained on the night *after* the events the UFO was sheet lightning exaggerated by hysteria. Later an idea grew that the UFOs were ball lightning – a rare form. At first this theory was supported by Allen Hynek, who later said he was ashamed of doing so – adding that, had he made any investigation, he would have discovered that specialists in this field knew that car stoppages do not result from ball lightning, and that this phenomenon is always isolated and extreme, never repeating on a regular basis.

Sadly, had anyone even checked the weather records – as Dr James McDonald, atmospheric physicist at the University of Arizona, did – they would have found that there was no storm nor any possibility of lightning anywhere near Levelland that night. Indeed, the conditions were mild and 'completely antithetical to conductive activity and lightning of any sort'.

Sheriff Clem says his investigation did what Blue Book failed to do and asked a local meteorologist about the lightning theory. The weather man said it was ludicrous. Of course, in 1957 Blue Book were aiming to debunk: they just needed an answer to this case that could superficially fool the public, not one that had any proper scientific credibility.

The Levelland events might have been a strange atmospheric phenomenon; but if so, it was one that science knows little about. Indeed, were the Levelland incidents seen in isolation (as Blue Book saw them) then the concept of such a phenomenon appears sensible. Yet there must still be disquiet about how the UFO 'showed off', almost acting like a naughty child playing with cars on a road. This sequence of events has a real hint of an intelligence behind it – as if it were a form of UFO poltergeist.

Indeed, hundreds more similar car-stop cases have occurred since 1957 all around the world, and that same feeling recurs with many of them. They seem to single out cars, toy with them, never provoke a serious accident, and then disappear rapidly. Lightning, on the other hand, avoids cars due to a physical law called the Faraday cage effect.

Car-stop cases in Britain

Exactly ten years after the Levelland events – in late October and early November 1967 – Britain suffered a major wave, with police cars chasing UFOs. Questions were asked in Parliament. Two classic car-stop cases occurred during the wave. The most impressive was at Sopley, right beside the secret MoD radar base involved in the August 1956 jet fighter chase (see page 123).

At 1.30am on 6 November a Leyland Comet diesel truck and a Jaguar car (driven by a local vet who had been out on a call) were both affected by a purple-red 'rugby ball' that hovered in front of the two of them and above a phone booth as they waited either side of a road junction. The Jaguar lost power to both its engine and lights, while the Comet truck only lost electrical power and its diesel engine continued to tick over. The object gave off a pungent odour (seemingly ozone from ionised gases in the atmosphere) and emitted a high-pitched humming noise.

The police were called to the scene immediately, and the witnesses claim the MoD sent investigators to follow up this case. Next day the road surface at the location was covered with fresh bitumen, the phone booth was repainted and scientists with geiger counters pored over the scorched grass on the embankment. Yet the MoD claim to have no record of any of this.

The truck driver was taken by police to collect his lorry from a compound in Christchurch. It had to be towed out to get it started. All the electrical circuits had burnt through and it required a new dynamo, starter motor, regulator, ammeter, batteries and bulbs.

Cases like this offer the strongest possible evidence for the physical reality behind some UFO events and tell us a great deal about the science that makes these UFOs real. It is scandalous that the University of Colorado team completely ignored the Levelland events in their two-year study project of 1967–9 (see page 174).

A UFO demo?

In early November 1957, even as Blue Book prevaricated, the Texas/New Mexico triangle was alive with more car-stop incidents. In daylight on 4 November there was a repeat run of the Levelland events, which seems to rule out any chance of their being a freak of nature. Ten different cars and pick-ups were stopped on a remote desert road between Orogrande and Alamogordo, New Mexico by a very similar-looking oval object.

Alamogordo is where the atom bomb was first exploded in 1945. White Sands, adjacent to it, is where rockets and missiles were being secretly developed. Indeed, one of the victims of this latest episode was James Stokes, an engineer working on the science of the upper atmosphere with the US government at the nearby missile development centre.

He was driving along when his radio faded and then his engine cut out after spotting a 'light colored egg-shaped object making a shallow dive across the sky'. As the thing passed at its closest Stokes could feel a kind of heat wave that made his skin tingle and hair stand on end, but, he added, 'There was no sound ... When I got back in my car and checked the engine I found it intact but the battery was steaming.' The UFO flew into clouds, causing them to disperse like Moses parting the Red Sea! Presumably the electrostatic force associated with this object was causing the particles of cloud vapour to become charged and repel one another like tiny magnets. When he got home Stokes found that his skin was badly sunburnt.

The most famous fictional space traveller, Captain James T. Kirk, alias William Shatner of Star Trek, *claims to have seen a UFO in the Californian desert.*

The focus on such a strategically sensitive area has the hallmarks of a demonstration. Indeed, at 3am on 3 November 1957, just an hour and a half after the Levelland affair, a huge oval had been spotted descending on to the desert floor by two military policemen. They called in reinforcements, who also watched as the object pulsed in and out before departing. In this case the UFO seemed to be goading the military by its presence – right next to the disused bunkers at the Alamogordo range where the first atomic bomb had been detonated some twelve years before!

A further extraordinary coincidence

If coincidence has not already been stretched to breaking point by all these independent reports, the strangest is yet to come. There were no atomic explosions at the Alamogordo site in autumn 1957, but there had just been a new series of tests elsewhere in the world.

At the western Australian desert site of Maralinga, three atomic weapons were fired during September and October 1957 by the British military authorities. Derek Murray, now working as a photographer for the Home Office, was at the time a member of the RAF crew that ran these experiments.

We do not know the exact date (again the MoD claim to have no records of this incident), but it was during the last couple of days before the RAF team left the outback after their final test. They departed on 4 November, so the UFO event was very closely (possibly even exactly) coincident with the amazing episodes in the Texas/New Mexico triangle. The Maralinga event occurred at four o'clock on a hot afternoon, which equates to the middle of the night in New Mexico. They may even have occurred simultaneously!

Derek Murray was playing cards with some fellow officers when a man came rushing in to say that there was a UFO hovering over the site where the bombs had been exploded. Everyone laughed, until they saw that he meant it. Out they went, and found a flat metal disc with a dome on top, which had a clearly visible row of windows in it. It was 'perched there like a king sitting on his high throne looking down on his subjects . . . it was a magnificent sight,' Murray confessed.

The thing hovered at a 45 degree angle in an aerodynamically impossible manner, as if daring somebody to do something about its audacious presence. The air traffic controller looked at it completely stunned, then dashed off to call Alice Springs. Nobody had any air traffic in this area of the Nullarbor Plains, hundreds of miles from civilisation.

Derek Murray says that the object was so real, so blatantly there and undeniable, that trained military personnel stood watching open-mouthed. It then shot silently upwards and disappeared at the sort of astonishing speed that many pilots have reported during aerial encounters down the years.

The still stunned witness says of all this many years later; 'I swear to you as a practising Christian this was no dream, no illusion, no fairy story – but a solid craft of metallic construction.'

The abductions begin

Within days of the launch of Sputnik 1 in mid-October that year the first alien abduction had occurred in Brazil (see page 141). The UFO phenomenon had entered a new phase and set in motion a programme that may still be going on today. According to testimony, it involves the taking of genetic samples from humans for what is reputedly the creation of a hybrid space baby. Absurd as this is, some consistent threads do weave many of these early alien contact cases together, as you will discover later in this book.

The genesis of this bizarre story occurred right in the middle of the four-week spell between the two Sputnik launches. It adds more intrigue to the news of the reaction shown by UFOs in New Mexico and western Australia.

Although the Villas Boas story in Brazil was not investigated until January 1958 and not published in UFO records for five years, only days after Laika had breathed her last in Earth orbit there was another extraordinary alien contact case that seems to have had remarkable and related features.

The Nordic and the suburban housewife

It began in a suburban house in Fentham Road, Aston, Birmingham, on 16 November 1957. Twenty-seven-year-old Cynthia Appleton, mother of two daughters aged three and one, experienced what we would now call a 'time lapse'. She lost all memory for about an hour and was later told that there had been a failed attempt to contact her by some visiting aliens.

The failure lasted only two days. For at 3pm on the 18th, a strange 'atmosphere like a storm' filled the air with charged electricity and a rose-pink hue filled the air (all of this is very similar to what was reported at Levelland). Then there was a high-pitched whistling noise. A smell like ozone filled the room and a figure materialised inside Mrs Appleton's lounge on top of a discarded newspaper left scorched black by the electrical discharge.

The lighting conditions returned to normal and the young mother found herself staring at a tall humanoid creature with elongated eyes, pale skin and long blond hair (a classic Nordic-type entity). He wore a silver one-piece suit with a covered helmet. In Cynthia's own words, the figure looked like 'a Greek athlete'.

She was stunned at first, but then he began to communicate with her by telepathy, saying 'Do not be afraid', and a long conversation resulted. The gist of this was that he came from a planet they called Gharnasvarn (but which she thought was Venus) and wanted to interact peacefully, but could not do so because of our atomic weapons and earthly aggression.

The entity opened its arms wide and created what seems to have been a hologram in mid-air. In 1958, when this was first documented by Mrs Appleton to psychologist Dr John Dale, holograms had not been invented, but that seems to be what she was describing. Three-dimensional images of UFOs and atomic explosions appeared in this space.

This was simply the first of what turned out to be fourteen months of visits – a total of eight up to his final one on 17 January 1959. Only on the first two did the alien arrive in the pyrotechnic haze. On the others he came through the front door (having reputedly driven there!) wearing an old-fashioned suit and, on one occasion, even a homburg hat!

During these visits masses of information was conveyed to the woman. She was told that she had a brain which they could 'tune into' that allowed them to communicate better than with other people. She was given lectures about the structure of the atom, how to cure cancer by realigning the vibrational rates of sub-atomic matter, how time was an artificial concept, and even news of the development of a laser beam (documented with Dr Dale before such a discovery was made on Earth). Most of this was way above her head, and Mrs Appleton could never understand why such information was conveyed to her. She had no desire to become a media star or to set up a cult as the contactees had done; in fact she seemed rather embarrassed by the whole thing, but accepted what had occurred.

Dr Dale was very impressed and visited her several times. So did a clergyman, the Reverend G. Tiley, who said that he went out of spiritual curiosity and concluded that she was 'a very trustworthy woman. I believe her story from beginning to end.'

Her husband Ronald Appleton, a metal welder, was never present during any of these visits but stood by his wife's sincerity. On the other hand, a rather condescending doctor had suggested to her that she was suffering post-natal depression and fantasising the whole thing.

Even though Ronald saw nothing, Cynthia's older daughter, Susan, did. She was four at the time of the last visit and recalled being present when the entity arrived and said he had burnt his hand. Her mother put some jelly on to it that the man gave her, and then bathed it in water.

After the entity departed, a large piece of skin was left in the water and taken away for analysis. Birmingham University studied a sample, but failed to identify its nature. Dr Dale took some home to Manchester, where university scientists examined it under an electron microscope. They concluded that it was more like animal skin than human, but its exact form remained unidentifiable.

A twentieth-century Immaculate Conception?

The most extraordinary visit was the penultimate one, in September 1958. Mrs Appleton was doing the washing when the alien arrived at her door and calmly announced that she was going to have a cosmic child! He added: 'The baby's father will be your husband but the child will belong to the race on Gharnasvarn.' He did not specify how any of this was to come about, but told her that they knew all the details of the forthcoming baby. He (for it would be a boy) would be born in late May 1959, would weigh in at 7lb 3oz, and would have fair hair. They told her what name to give him. He would grow to become a powerful world figure.

There was one problem with this diagnosis. So far as Cynthia knew, she was not pregnant. However, she went to the doctor for a test and soon discovered that the alien was right – even though she had been less than a month into the pregnancy when he had called.

All of this was unequivocally documented before the baby was born. Ron Appleton, perhaps a little perturbed about any possible intergalactic paternity suit, stuck admirably by his wife – even when the baby was born. It was a boy, did have fair hair, was the right weight (within an ounce) and was born within a few days of the predicted date.

Ron Appleton said after the birth (naturally called what the aliens had suggested!) that Cynthia should ask the folk on Venus to cough up some money to help raise the child. In response (by a telepathic message) she was informed that they do not use money on Gharnasvarn. Ronald was quoted in *The People* newspaper as saying about the alien: 'If he shows up I'm going to tell him I'm [the boy's] father.'

Several times since its foundation, NASA (the American space agency), has been asked to mount a UFO study programme. It has always said no.

Towards a better human race

So what are we to make of any of this? Throughout the 1950s the first alien contact stories warned witnesses that the earth's misuse of atomic weapons was causing great concern, especially as we were taking our first tentative steps towards exporting deadly technology into outer space. Our visitors claimed to have superior powers, but could not (or would not) use them to stop us. We had to learn by our own actions what was right and what was wrong.

Within days of the first-ever projectile leaving Earth and entering outer space a systematic programme was reportedly set in motion, in places as diverse as a Brazilian ranch and a Birmingham street. This offers the first signs of an alien plan to improve humanity genetically – to hoist us up by our own bootstraps towards becoming a better race.

They were allegedly taking samples to try to create an alien—human hybrid and they told an English woman who would later gave birth to a perfectly normal child that she was somehow being used by them. We do not know how.

Sputnik 2 carried the first-ever living thing into Earth orbit and suddenly UFOs demonstrated their superior technology in a huge way, showing how our electrical systems can be rendered useless with ease. This demonstration focused on the centre of our missile and atomic weapons technology – the cutting edge of Western space and atomic science at that time. Indeed, to further emphasise the point dramatic appearances were set up – possibly at exactly the same time on the same day, and certainly just as Laika floated in orbit as a symbol of our earthly threat. These demonstrations were at the precise locations where the world's very first and the world's most recent atomic detonations had taken place.

Maybe this was all just a coincidence, but it certainly has the ring of something far more remarkable than that.

—14—

VILLAS BOAS AND THE ALIEN SEDUCTRESS

The night of 5 October 1957 saw a sinister shift in the alien contact phenomenon of the 1950s.

The tail end of the 1950s saw the alien contact phenomenon shift gear from an innocuous persona into a more sinister phase. It is significant, perhaps, that the flood of abduction reports in the 1980s are rooted in a case that seemed to bridge the gap between contactee stories and modern tales of alien genetic experimentation. In 1957 a Brazilian was relieved of sperm through forced copulation with a 'space woman'. Today, the aliens use more sophisticated means to remove sperm and ova from the men and women they have 'borrowed'. In the closing years of the twentieth century we would expect nothing less.

The story of the kidnapped Brazilian farmer was first brought to the attention of the English-speaking world in a 1965 issue of the magazine *Flying Saucer Review*. It was based on a report by Dr Walter Buhler of Rio de Janeiro, who had interviewed the percipient in 1961. Dr Buhler supplied to editor Gordon Creighton a full transcript of the man's declaration and a medical report compiled by Dr Olavo Fontes. These documents were dated 22 February – just a few months after the encounter.

Arrival of the intruders

Antonio Villas Boas (pictured on page 145) helped manage the family farm near the town of Francisco de Sales, in the state of Minas Gerais. Of mixed Portuguese and Amerindian origin, the twenty-three-year-old man possessed little formal education but was taking a correspondence course around the time of the incident. He was later evaluated as an intelligent individual.

Two months before the Villas Boas abduction, USA Senator Barry Goldwater wrote to a constituent regarding UFOs: 'I, frankly, feel there is a great deal to this.'

A silvery fluorescence

There had been a family celebration on the night of 5 October 1957, after which Antonio and his brother João, with whom he shared a room, went to bed at 11pm. Antonio decided to open a window because the night was so warm, and on doing so observed that the yard outside was lit with a silvery fluorescence. At first the brothers decided to ignore it, but eventually Antonio's curiosity got the better of him and he went to the window again. As he watched, the light moved towards the farmhouse. He slammed the shutters to, which woke up his brother, and the two young men watched the light penetrating the wooden slats before moving over the roof, shining down between the tiles.

Nine days later between 9.30 and 10pm, the brothers were using a tractor to plough a field. Suddenly they saw an intensely bright red light at the northern end of the field, hovering about 300 feet above the ground. Antonio's brother stayed put while he went over to investigate. As he drew near, the light suddenly moved to the southern end of the field. Antonio followed it there, and the light skipped back to its original position. It did this twenty times in all. Antonio gave up and returned to João. The light remained where it was for some time, occasionally giving off rays and bright flashes, before disappearing.

Seized by aliens

The following night, Antonio was out on the tractor alone. At exactly 1am he observed a large red 'star' in the sky. Suddenly the light grew larger as it swooped down towards him. An object now hovered above him, emitting a light so bright that it swamped the tractor's headlights. This was from a red 'headlight' set at the front of the craft. The farmer thought of escape, but realised that the low speed of the tractor would make this futile. Escape on foot was similarly out of the question on the muddy, churned up soil. As he remained on the tractor in a state of terror, the craft dropped to the ground a few feet in front of him. Now the farmer was able to see it in detail, as he told Buhler.

> I could see the shape of the machine clearly, which was like a large elongated egg with three metal spurs in front (one in the middle and one on each side). They were three metal shafts, thick at the bases and pointed at the tips. I could not distinguish their colour, for they were enveloped by a powerful reddish phosphorescence (or fluorescent light, like that of a luminous sign) of the same shade as the front headlight.
>
> On the upper part of the machine there was something which was

revolving at great speed and also giving off a powerful fluorescent reddish light. At the moment when the machine reduced speed to land, this light changed to a greenish colour, which corresponded – such was my impression – to a diminution in the speed of rotation of that revolving part, which at this point seemed to be taking on the shape of a round dish or a flattened cupola.

I saw three metal supports (forming a tripod) emerge beneath the machine when it was at only a few metres from the ground. I totally lost the little self-control that I had left. Those metal legs were obviously meant to take the weight of the craft when it touched the ground on landing. I started up the tractor (its engine had still been running all this time) and shifted it round to one side, trying to open out a route of escape. But I had only travelled a few metres when the engine suddenly died and, simultaneously, the tractor lights went out. I tried to get the engine to start again, but the starter was isolated and gave no sign of life.

Antonio opened the tractor door and started to run when 'someone' grabbed his arm. In his desperation the farmer swung round and managed to throw his pursuer off balance, but three more caught up with him and hoisted him into the air. The creatures were shoulder height to him, and dressed in grey, tight-fitting coveralls with a helmet that obscured all their facial characteristics except the eyes, which were visible through lenses. They wore boots and gloves, and three tubes ran from the back of the head to the body. Antonio was carried struggling up a ramp and into the craft.

Inside, he found himself in a small square room lit as bright as day by square lamps set in the metal ceiling. The door closed so completely that there was not even a seam in the wall where it had been. One of his kidnappers indicated for him to follow into another room, which he did, not having any real choice.

We left the little room and entered a much larger one, semi-oval in shape. I believe this room was in the centre of the machine for, in the middle, there was a metal column running from ceiling to floor, wide at the top and bottom and quite a bit narrower in the middle. It was round and seemed solid. The only furniture that I could see was a strangely shaped table that stood on one side of the room, surrounded by several backless swivel chairs. They were all made of the same white metal.

Preparation for sexual intercourse

The young man was held in the room while the beings observed him and talked in a series of barks similar to a dog's. Then they forcibly undressed him and spread over his body a thick liquid which quickly dried. Two of the beings escorted Antonio into another room where blood was taken from him through a long tube. They then left him alone, and he lay down on a grey couch to rest. Suddenly he began to feel nauseous, and noticed a vapour coming out of some tubes in one of the walls. Antonio went into a corner where he was violently sick.

After a further period, the Brazilian was surprised by the entrance of a 'beautiful' naked female entity. She had blonde hair and a wide face, which came to a point at the chin. Her blue eyes were elongated and her lips quite thin. She had a slim waist, but broad hips and large thighs. Her breasts were high and well separated.

The 'woman' moved towards Antonio and rubbed herself against him. The farmer became aroused and sexual intercourse took place twice. Antonio enjoyed the experience, although it was almost spoilt when the 'woman' started grunting, 'giving the disagreeable impression that I was with an animal'. Shortly afterwards the door opened, and one of the 'men' appeared on the threshhold and indicated for the female to leave: 'But, before going out, she turned to me, pointed at her belly and then pointed towards me and with a smile, she finally pointed towards the sky.'

This indicated to investigators that she was telling him she was going to bear their child on her home planet. The female left and the other entity carried Antonio's clothes over to him, gesturing him to dress. He was taken back into the central room where several of the creatures were now seated. Antonio was left standing while they grunted amongst themselves. He decided to take an instrument, resembling a clock, to present as proof of his adventure. But no sooner had he picked it up when it was angrily snatched away from him.

Eventually the abductee was taken outside, along a catwalk, and given a conducted tour around the craft where certain features were pointed out to him. Afterwards he was allowed back into the field and the object took off. He had been on board the craft for four hours and fifteen minutes. The young man told his mother of the event – but no one else until he contacted journalist Señor João Martins, who had published an article about UFOs.

Evaluation by the investigators

Dr Fontes commented on the farmer's account:

Right from the outset it was obvious he presented no psychopathic traits. Calm, talking freely, revealing no nervous tics or signs of emotional instability, all his reactions to the questions put to him were perfectly normal. At no moment did he ever falter or lose control of his narrative. His tendencies corresponded precisely to what could be predicted in an individual who, in a strange situation, could find no explanation for certain facts. At such moments, even though he knew that the doubts expressed by him on certain questions might lead us to disbelieve him, he answered quite simply: 'I don't know about that', or, 'I can't explain that.'

Symptoms of radiation poisoning

In his medical report, Dr Fontes records that Villas Boas arrived home exhausted and slept for most of the day. For the next two nights he could not sleep and was plagued by a dreadful headache and nausea, causing him to lose his appetite. During the second sleepless night he felt a burning sensation in his eyes, followed by continual watering. From the third night Villas Boas experienced excessive lethargy for about a month, which caused him to keep nodding off. Small wounds appeared on his arms and legs which left scars, and two yellowish patches manifested on his face. It was speculated that these were symptomatic of radiation poisoning. If they were, they did not lead to any long-term health problems.

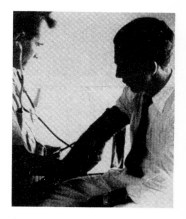

Antonio Villas Boas being examined after his abduction.

This case, and others which later emerged, were met with extreme scepticism at the time. Up until then people's experiences had been limited to objects sighted from a distance, or contacts with human-like extraterrestrials possessing the most gentlemanly manners. Antonio Villas Boas helped introduce terror and a new scenario where contactees became victims, not the chosen few.

As remarked earlier, the case bridged contactee claims and modern abduction accounts; but it was not a straight precursor for what was subsequently reported. Villas Boas remembered vividly being carried up a ramp and into the craft, while modern abductees suffer 'doorway amnesia' and have no recollection, even under hypnosis, of how they got inside.

The medical examination is central to most accounts. In many contemporary American cases, however, sperm and ova are taken from victims using medical procedures, where Villas Boas was relieved of sperm in a more natural way. Most American investigators believe the material is used to breed hybrid beings, to help reconstitute an alien race which is dying due to a reduced genetic pool. In the 1960s, investigators postulated that the female who copulated with the Brazilian farmer was such a hybrid. It is interesting that the broad face, pointed chin and thin lips exactly describe modern alien entities. However, the detailed description of the ramp and the copulation seem to have more in common with the technological and sociological expectations of the 1950s than with a hypothetical visiting extraterrestrial spaceship.

Villas Boas update

In 1978 Antonio Villas Boas broke twenty-one years' silence and was interviewed for a Brazilian television show. His private studying had evidently paid off because he was now Dr Villas Boas – a respectable lawyer living near Brasilia, married with four children. He had decided to break his silence because he was annoyed at the way his case had been treated over the years. He reaffirmed the experience with no contradictions, but added that, after having intercourse with the 'woman' for the second time, she had used a container to collect a sperm sample. Before his recent death, Villas Boas also confirmed that in the 1960s he was also invited to the USA by 'security forces' to view wreckage of a UFO. He constantly declined to discuss this further, even with his family.

Part Six

1960s:
COSMIC WATERSHEDS

THE HILL ABDUCTION

The Betty and Barney Hill UFO abduction was the first case of its kind to be thoroughly investigated by ufologists and medical professionals. It set a precedent for the use of hypnotic regression as a valid tool for exploring periods of 'missing time' and laid down arguments still with us more than thirty years later.

'They're going to capture us!'

The Hills, a mixed race couple (pictured opposite), were returning to New Hampshire from holiday in Niagara Falls on the night of 19 September 1961. As Barney drove through the White Mountains on Route 3, traffic was sparse. Close to midnight the couple noticed a peculiar light in the sky which began to move. Barney stopped the car and Betty exercised their dog, Delsey, while he observed the object through binoculars. He told his wife it was probably just an aircraft heading towards Montreal.

As they continued, the object seemed to remain with the car, causing them to speculate afresh at what it might be. It was definitely moving, so that ruled out a star or bright planet, and if it was an aircraft or even a satellite it should have slipped over the horizon long before.

Then the light suddenly changed direction and drew closer. Betty picked up the binoculars and saw it was a disc-shaped object with a band of light around its circumference. They stopped the car once more and Barney climbed out for a better view. He was still trying to rationalise it, thinking at this point it might be a military helicopter having fun by scaring them, but he could not understand why it was completely silent. Then his wife heard him repeating over and over: 'I don't believe it! This is ridiculous!'

The object was now so close that he was able to see several figures staring down at him through lighted windows. One in particular made him very afraid. Suddenly he lost control and panicked. He cried out: 'They're going to capture us!' Barney raced back to the car and put his foot down hard on the accelerator. The next thing the couple were aware of were several 'bleeps' like the sound made by a microwave oven.

Betty and Barney Hill had an abduction experience while driving through the White Mountains on 19 September 1961.

Stress and nightmares

The following day Barney noticed some unexplained blotches on the body work of his car. There was also a soreness at the back of his neck and his shoes were badly scuffed. Some time later the Hills realised they could not account for two hours and thirty-five miles of their journey. They began to suffer from stress, but had no idea why. Betty experienced horrible nightmares in which she was taken into a room and examined by strange beings.

Hypnotic revelations

They sought medical expertise and saw two doctors in the space of more than a year. Finally they were passed on to Dr Benjamin Simon, a prominent Boston psychiatrist specialising in hypnotic therapy. In an effort to explore their anxieties, Dr Benjamin used hypnosis, regressing them separately so that neither would know what the other had said. However, so much time had passed since the event that it was never clear to what extent their stories were intertwined. They had discussed the sighting and Betty's dreams between themselves, and with others, long before they saw Dr Simon.

A terrifying story emerged that filled in the period of amnesia. Over several months an account was pieced together which told how their car was stopped by a group of strange-looking 'men' with pear-shaped heads and large wrap-around eyes. These beings forcibly carried the couple into the lighted object, where they were taken into separate rooms. Was this how Barney's shoes had become scuffed? After the 'men' had stopped his car, they 'assisted' him out of the vehicle and he suddenly felt very weak and cooperative: 'I can't even think of questioning what is happening to me. And I am thinking of a picture I saw many years ago, and this man is being carried to the electric chair. And I think of this, and I think I am in this man's position. But I'm not, but I think my feet are dragging, and I think of this picture.'

During their separation the couple underwent various tests by the entities, which included the taking of hair and skin samples. Under hypnosis, Barney described how a device was put on his genitals to extract semen. He developed a ring of warts around that area, and these became inflamed during the hypnosis sessions.

Betty claimed that a needle was inserted through her navel – this, according to her abductors, was a 'pregnancy test'. This detail caused Dr Simon to comment to investigator John Fuller: 'There's no such medical procedure. This is the sort of thing that makes me doubt the

A year before Betty and Barney Hill were abducted, a memo was sent out by the Secretary of the USAF to all base commanders. It contained these words: 'There is a relationship between the Air Force's interest in space surveillance and its continuous surveillance of the atmosphere near Earth for Unidentified Flying Objects – UFOs.'

story of the abduction.' But in later years a similar procedure was used to test the amniotic fluid cells in pregnant women for chromosomal aberrations – Down's Syndrome. Although the test had been developed in the 1950s, it was not in use until the mid–to late 1960s.

Certainly the extraction of reproduction material was the forerunner to countless similar abduction cases which surfaced strongly in the mid-1980s. They went one step further than either the Villas Boas or Hill cases. More recent abduction victims are shown their hybrid offspring by entities who had reabducted them and removed the foetuses for development 'elsewhere'.

The Hill story was very effectively presented by Fuller in his book *The Interrupted Journey*. Dr Simon concluded that the Hills were not lying, hallucinating nor suffering from any detectable psychosis. He told Fuller during their first meeting: 'You are going to have your hands full with this story. There are many things that are unexplainable in this case. I threw many kinds of tests at them during the months of therapy. I couldn't shake their stories, and they were definitely not malingering.' However, Dr Simon was later to conclude that the incident was an unconscious fantasy.

Barney Hill became so emotional under hypnosis when he was 'reliving' certain episodes that he had to be held down by several people. The authors have witnessed similar distressing abreactions with modern abductees. It seems hard to imagine an internal fantasy causing such emotional trauma in people who are not particularly interested in 'aliens' or unidentified flying objects.

A TV film was made of the Hill case. Entitled The UFO Incident, *it was shown in several countries during the mid 1970s.*

Betty Hill's 'star map'

One of the pieces of tangible evidence was a 'star map' that Betty Hill recalled seeing inside the craft.

There were all these dots on it. And they were scattered all over it. Some were little, just pin-points, and others were as big as a nickel. And there were lines, they were on some of the dots, there were curved lines going from one dot to another. And there was one big circle, and it had a lot of lines coming from it. A lot of lines going to another circle quite close, but not as big. And these were heavy lines. And I asked him what they meant, and he said that the heavy lines were trade routes. And then the other lines, the solid lines, were places they went occasionally. And he said the broken lines were expeditions.

Later, under post-hypnotic suggestion she was able to reproduce the map. In 1974 Ohio schoolteacher and amateur astronomer Marjorie Fish published the results of her studies of the map, which Betty Hill had said was three-dimensional.

Ms Fish wondered if the map might correspond to a star system. She restricted her search to a thousand stars situated within fifty-five light

The front cover of *UFO Review*, issue 9, which featured Betty Hill.

years of our sun. Next she concentrated on those stars which astronomers thought might have planets capable of nurturing intelligent life. After five years Ms Fish thought she had a match. Indeed, one of the stars was the sun, and the alien's home planet appeared to be Zeta Reticuli.

However, she could not match up all the dots on Betty Hill's map. Meanwhile another astronomer came up with an even better match. But when noted astrophysicist Carl Sagan compared the Fish map using a more accurate computer program, he found there was little similarity.

Mixed marriage anxieties

Much has been said of Barney Hill's general anxieties due in part to his colour and marriage to a white woman. Indeed, Barney was referred to by his wife as a natural worrier. On the journey home, before the abduction, the Hills stopped at a restaurant. These were his feelings about that visit, as expressed during hypnosis:

> There is a dark-skinned woman in there, dark by Caucasian standards, and I wonder – is she a light-skinned Negro, or is she Indian, or is she white? – and she waits on us, and she is not very friendly, and others are there and they are looking at me and Betty, and they seem to be friendly or pleased, but this dark-skinned woman doesn't. I wonder then more so – is she Negro and wonder if I – if she is wondering if I know she is Negro and is passing for white.

The fact that the abduction 'memories' matched Betty's nightmares has been used to support the theory that there was nothing to the experience but dreams which she communicated to Barney while in a state of anxiety, resurfacing later through the medium of hypnosis. Others believe that the nightmares were a leaching through of repressed memories, later more fully released with the aid of hypnosis. But Betty did herself no favours in the years that followed Barney's death in 1969: she started seeing UFOs behind every tree and in every cloud.

Conclusions

Because of this, sceptics reasoned that the original encounter was also a misidentification of a bright star or planet, even though a nearby Air Force base had tracked an unknown object on radar that night. Perhaps

Betty's later bogus sightings are not surprising. A victim of any major trauma will find their life permanently affected by it. The victim of a knife attack will see knife men hiding around every corner, but no one ever questions the reality of the original crime.

The Hill abduction contains elements to be found in both later and contemporary cases. Apart from the medical examination and extraction of genetic material there is the common description of the entities, a floating, almost out-of-the-body sensation experienced by the couple, and of course the period of amnesia. Some ufologists have tried to separate the Hill case from other abductions, but there are too many common factors. If one falls, they all fall. Ironically, even though Betty Hill is adamant that her own experience was real, she believes that some of the contemporary cases are purely psychological.

— 16 —

MEN IN BLACK

In 1964 the concept of Men in Black entered the harsher reality of the UFO debate.

The concept of Men in Black (or MIBs as they are abbreviated) began as murky folklore, but in 1964 entered the harsher reality of UFO data. Although some suspect links with demonic forces far into the past, the real basis of the MIB legend began in April 1952 when a horror and science fiction buff, Albert K. Bender, latched on to the new UFO craze and created the 'International Flying Saucer Bureau' in Connecticut. It quickly spread to the rest of the world – indeed, the Bristol-based British Bureau still exists, as the world's oldest UFO group.

Broken promises

Bender's pioneer group was short-lived. After recruiting a gaggle of acolytes such as Gray Barker (who went on to become a witty writer on weird ufology), he announced the break-up of the team in September 1953. Bender confided 'the truth' to a few close friends. He said he had been visited by three men in dark suits driving a Cadillac and who had warned him to cease ufology. They explained that the US government had known about the alien origin of UFOs since 1951 and knew all of the reasons behind it. They would reveal these within five years, and civilian UFO study was dangerous.

In the coming months a few other figures associated with the old UFO group quit suddenly, and rumours spread about these mysterious 'men in black'. The legend took firm hold. In 1956 Barker gathered it together in an entertaining – if poorly documented – book entitled *They Knew Too Much about Flying Saucers*.

That might have been the end of the matter, except that in 1962 Bender finally broke his silence. The UFO truth had not been revealed.

The promises made had not been kept. Now he came out with a startling treatise entitled *Flying Saucers and the Three Men*. In this he told how the MIBs were really monstrous aliens in human disguise, on Earth to extract sea water; they had flown him to the Antarctic and scared him into submission. But in 1960 they left Earth, leaving the ufologist free to talk.

Even Gray Barker said he found it hard to believe Bender's second version of 'the truth'. To some it reinforced the mythology but Bender's book firmly ensured that an already dubious side alley of the subject was effectively rebuked by sceptics and ufologists alike.

The intruder in the photograph

But then, on 24 May 1964, Jim Templeton, a fireman from Carlisle in the North of England, took his young daughter out to the marshes overlooking the Solway Firth to take some photographs. Nothing untoward happened, although both he and his wife noticed an unusual aura in the atmosphere (seemingly reminiscent of that described by Cynthia Appleton before her 1957 encounter). There was a kind of electric charge in the air, though no storm came. Even nearby cows seemed upset by it.

Some days later Mr Templeton got his photographs processed by the chemist, who said that it was a pity that the man who walked past had spoilt the best shot of Elizabeth holding a bunch of flowers. Jim was puzzled. There had been nobody else on the marshes nearby at the time. But sure enough, on the picture in question (see opposite) there was a figure in a silvery white space suit projecting at an odd angle into the air behind the girl's back, as if an unwanted snooper had wrecked the shot.

The case was reported to the police and taken up by Kodak, the film manufacturers, who offered free film for life to anyone who could solve the mystery when their experts failed. It was not, as the police at first guessed, a simple double exposure with one negative accidentally printed on top of another during processing. It was, as Chief Superintendent Oldcorn quickly concluded, just 'one of those things . . . a freak picture'.

A few weeks later Jim Templeton received two mysterious visitors. He had never heard of MIBs: the subject was almost unknown in Britain then. But the two men who came to his house in a large Jaguar car wore dark suits and otherwise looked normal. The weird thing about them was their behaviour. They only referred to one another by numbers and asked the most unusual questions as they drove Jim out to the marshes. They wanted to know in minute detail about the weather on the day of the photograph, the activities of local bird life and odd asides like that. Then they tried to make him admit that he had just photographed an ordinary man walking past. Jim responded politely, but nevertheless rejected their idea, at which they became irrationally angry and hustled themselves into the car, driving off and leaving him. The fire officer had to hike five miles across country to get home.

A section of the photograph taken by Jim Templeton showing the mysterious figure standing behind his daughter Elizabeth.

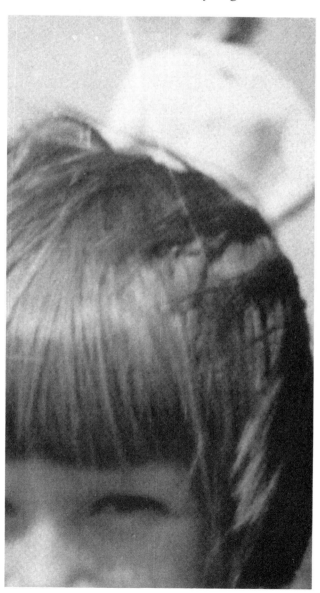

The MIB evidence

Men in Black are common in Britain and America but almost unknown in the UFO records anywhere else.

In fact, this little-known (and long unpublicised) version of the MIB story is far more the stereotype than the Bender saga. There are rarely three visitors – two is much more common. They often look very normal, except for their dark clothing. Their car, if they have one, whilst usually large and imposing, is rarely the black Cadillac so beloved of the apocryphal tales.

By far the most notable feature that singles these visitors out as more than just members of a UFO group or curiosity seekers is their irrational and eccentric behaviour. They seem uncomfortable with the English language, use strange grammar, ask bizarre questions, know a considerable amount about the background of the witness and frequently attempt to argue them into accepting a mundane solution. When they fail (usually because the theory they offer is highly improbable) they tend to respond in an unexpected manner – either leaving in a huff or getting up and walking away without another word. They seem part of the mystery, not apart from it. The fact that the real MIB scenario is less known than the early 1950s' version that gets most publicity (even in UFO books) tends to suggest that there is some substance to it.

It is certainly worth noting that, in the Appleton case, Cynthia said that after the first two visits (when her visitor was clearly identified as an alien in strange clothing) the remainder occurred in true MIB style: the being wore ordinary clothing, came in a car and sometimes brought a colleague. Had it not been for the first two visits, when the alien origin of the encounter was expressed directly to Mrs Appleton, this 1957 case would itself be better described as a typical MIB episode.

Demonic manifestations and other theories

Between 1965 and 1967 there was a new spate of MIB activity in the USA. John Keel wrote about much of this in his books *Operation Trojan Horse* and *The Mothman Prophecies*. Indeed, towns in Ohio and West Virginia where strange lights and alien entities were being seen in alarming numbers had almost as many visits from MIBs. Keel himself professed some experience of nocturnal meetings with these entities.

It was from such a maelstrom that he developed the then heretical view that no aliens were visiting us in spaceships, but that an almost demonic or interdimensional manifestation was occurring, using the extrasensory perception of witnesses. This view, whilst still very unpopular in the USA, gained ground elsewhere and now has many adherents in Europe.

Another view is that the MIBs are, like alien contacts, an act for the benefit of witnesses. What if, for example, UFOs were flown by time travellers from the future observing our society? Perhaps in cases where hard evidence of their presence is obtained, such as a photograph, they later return disguised as MIBs to try to retrieve it or to learn more about the mistakes they made.

Jim Templeton made a common assumption: that his visitors were Ministry of Defence investigators. In the USA rational witnesses presumed that MIBs who called on them were US Air Force intelligence staff. Indeed, in about half the MIB cases in both the USA and UK proof of identity claiming governmental allegiance has reputedly been shown. Names and identities have even been proffered. Unfortunately, on no occasion has any organisation who were named confirmed that these visitors are their agents. Indeed, when checks are made firm assurances to the contrary are usually issued.

On 1 March 1967 Lieutenant General Hewitt Wheless, assistant vice chief of staff to the US Air Force, even issued a secret memorandum (see page 160) to all senior personnel and divisions. It was headed 'Impersonations of Air Force Officers' and shows that the USAF were as concerned as ufologists about the matter. It cites how:

> In one reported case an individual in civilian clothes, who represented himself as a member of NORAD (the North America Radar Defence Network), demanded and received photographs belonging to a private citizen. In another, a person in an Air Force uniform approached local police and other citizens who had sighted a UFO, assembled them in a school room and told them that they did not see what they thought they saw and that they should not talk to anyone about the sighting. All military and civilian personnel and particularly information officers and UFO investigating officers who hear of such reports should immediately notify their local OSI offices.

American MIB cases tend to stress the 'alienness' of the visitor, whereas British reports of the MIB almost invariably describe them as being ordinary humans supposedly from the MoD or RAF.

What, if anything, the Air Force's intelligence unit (the OSI) found out about these matters has never been made public.

Threats, hoaxes and deceptions

Further extraordinary cases have continued to occur. Indeed, in Britain they seem more common than ever. In August 1972 a landed object

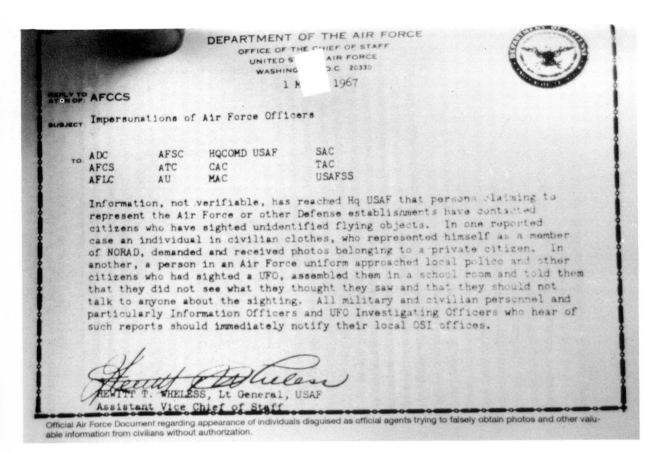

Official Air Force Document regarding appearance of individuals disguised as official agents trying to falsely obtain photos and other valuable information from civilians without authorization.

During the 1960s 'Men in Black' came to be reported in connection with UFO sightings. Witnesses would allege being visited by mysterious strangers who knew a great deal about their (often unpublished) story and would ask them bizarre questions. For a time the US Air Force became concerned as these visitors often claimed a military origin. This memo warning air bases about the 'impersonations' by men in black was circulated in March 1967.

was seen by two witnesses beside the top-secret National Security Agency telecommunications base at Menwith Hill in Yorkshire. The local police investigated right away, then called a press conference. But it never even started, because two men arrived in a large car, flashed identification that claimed they were from the MoD, told the journalists present to leave and then interrogated one of the witnesses on just one very minor aspect of the case (the method by which the UFO door opened). They had no interest in any other part of the story. The MoD deny that the visitors were anything to do with them.

Then in January 1976 a young woman in Lancashire had a terrifying encounter. After strange phone calls to her unpublicised address two men arrived and gave her a grilling in the presence of her parents (who claim they felt strangely powerless to act, as if they were 'under a spell'). The men were typically bizarre. One sat and said nothing, simply holding a strange black box close to his person. The other had only one arm, merely called himself 'The Commander', and asked peculiar questions of oblique relevance to the sighting. As in other cases they tried to get the witness to accept a mundane solution, and grew angry when she stubbornly refused to change her view of what she had seen.

In September 1976 a doctor who had been called in to consult and hypnotise a UFO witness in Maine, USA, found himself visited by two strange MIBs (actually one was a WIB – a woman in black). The man had lip gloss on his mouth and lipstick smears; he also wore ill-fitting clothes. The woman was physically lopsided. At the conclusion of the by now routine sequence of inane questions this far from UFO-obsessed witness, Dr Herbert Hopkins, was told by the MIBs that they had to go as they were running low on energy!

The extent to which witnesses report the MIBs possessing secret personal knowledge is illustrated by a former police officer who took a photograph of an entity over Ilkley Moor (see page 243). In January 1988 only about four people, two of whom were the present authors, knew about this case, let alone had the confidential witness's address or unlisted phone number. But then the MIBs arrived.

The two men wore business suits, professed to be with the MoD (and showed photo identity cards to confirm this). They gave their names as 'Jefferson' and 'Davies' (*sic!*). The witness's wife was present and confirmed the meeting. The men then asked him to tell his story, which the witness did – but without mentioning the photograph. The men asked for the negative. Fortunately Peter Hough had this, as investigation was under way. The men left without any attempt to find out where the photograph was.

The following morning the witness received a phone call professing to be from a national newspaper which knew all about his case and was going to publish it. This terrified him so much that he almost abandoned the investigation on the spot, only being reassured when Jenny Randles spoke discreetly to both the London and Manchester offices of the paper in question (which never did feature the story). It was clear that they had not made any phone calls about a UFO story that morning.

Was this whole business a complex attempt by the MIBs to silence the witness, playing on his fear of publicity by making a bogus phone call? The MoD will not admit responsibility for Jefferson and Davies; and even so, how was the witness traced when his story was then secret? As with all of this accumulating evidence, if this MIB story is true then we still must ask major questions about the true origins of these mysterious visitors.

The selectivity with which MIBs are supposedly involved is curious.

The film Hanger 18 *mystified many viewers by listing actors in its credits under the designation MIB-1, MIB-2, etc!*

An artist's impression of a 'man in black'.

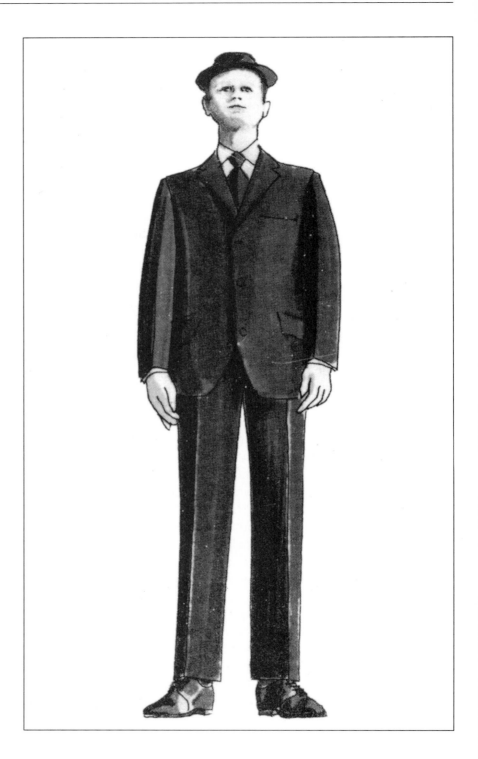

Only a handful of cases feature such visits, and they tend to be those with something unusual about them. A very credible abduction, for example, might not attract a visit. A close encounter with a small feature never reported before, such as a door that opens like a letter 'T', will . Photographic evidence seems a particular lure to such visitors, reinforcing the thought before that they mean to try to stifle new evidence.

Of course, a government investigation team might keep a look-out for cases with unusual features. If you know a lot about UFOs already, these may be just the ones to provide valuable clues. We may also understand the concern when events occur near sensitive sites, such as the 1967 event by the Sopley radar site and the 1972 landing at Menwith Hill.

There are a few occasions where MIB stories have simple explanations. In 1982 a UFO group in Swindon were given warnings to stop their investigations. Using a clever system with an automatic camera they baited a trap and photographed the MIB in live action. It was a rival ufologist!

In 1989 a series of lights were witnessed by police officers and an ambulance crew at Heywood in Lancashire. Police called in the local UFO team within minutes, and a few hours later Peter Hough and two other men from the group visited the site to interview the officers involved.

This case was, in fact, a result of rare atmospheric conditions, but a UFO magazine later published the amazing claim that another investigator had tried to interview the officers and suspected that they had been 'got at'. When he arrived at the scene three MIBs in smart suits left hurriedly. Unfortunately, the said MIBs were neither from the government nor from Mars but from the group MUFORA, suitably business-like and professionally dressed for their on-site investigation!

On the other hand, in July 1993 a man who took film of some lights of a UFO on his camcorder from an east coast town loaned it, on their request, to a UFO group. They provided no identification or a receipt (as all reputable groups will do), and the film disappeared without trace. That UFO group, as later enquiries established, does not exist.

There are countless stories of films disappearing in this manner, which is why bona fide ufologists have set up procedures to avoid them. In 1989 even Jenny Randles fell victim when a journalist arrived to make a radio programme for the BBC. At his insistence she gave him an important tape recording of an encounter at a military base. He refused to take a good-quality copy instead of the original. In fact, luckily, he was given another better-quality copy – not the original, as he believed. The programme never appeared, and extensive checks with the BBC could identify neither him nor his work.

Glasnost at the MoD

However, there are certainly times when legitimate activity by the defence authorities can be misconstrued. In October 1993 a man in a remote croft near Lockerbie in Scotland observed some lights and filmed them with his camcorder. He reported the matter to Prestwick Airport. Then a call came to his home from a man who claimed to be investigating UFOs at the MoD. He requested a copy of the tape, but suggested that if the witness was interested in a fuller investigation he should also contact a UFO group. Within the hour the witness was talking to Jenny Randles and an investigation had begun.

In the past the MoD would almost certainly have denied that they would display such overt interest or offer cooperation with a UFO group, such as giving out unlisted phone numbers. Another legend about an MIB impersonating an MoD officer could easily have been born from this simple story.

In fact there was no mystery here. A new policy at the MoD has ensured that actions like this are becoming commonplace. Indeed, in this new era of ufological glasnost the name of the MoD official involved was quickly and freely given by him – and he does exist!

—— 17 ——

ALIEN MUTILATORS

Even on a good day the UFO phenomenon barely manages to hide its dark, sinister side. When the sugar-coated candy of the contactee and channeller messages are digested, what remains is a bitter pill. At least the Men in Black display a farcical face to soften their threats and intimidation. But what of the mutilation of animals, claimed by many ufologists to be the work of aliens – where is the humour there?

In the late 1960s animal mutilations hit the headlines in America. In succeeding years the body count soared and the phenomenon spread into Canada and across to Europe – albeit in a variation of the American experience. By the close of the 1970s it was estimated that around ten thousand head of cattle had fallen victim to a methodical, skilled, cold, intelligent and unknown predator. Animals were found drained of blood, with their organs surgically removed. No one saw or heard this butchery, but UFOs were connected with it by many witnesses who observed strange lights hovering over paddocks just before the discovery of dead animals.

Yet the precursor to all of this was not a cow, but a horse – an Appaloosa saddle horse belonging to a Mrs Berle Lewis on a ranch in a remote area of Colorado's San Luis Valley.

The Lady killers

Lady – erroneously called Snippy by reporters and in several books – was given the run of the ranch in Alamosa to wander through miles of chico bush. On the evening of 7 September 1967, she arrived as usual at the ranch house for a dole of grain and a drink. She seemed in good health, but it was the last time Lady was seen alive.

The following evening she failed to turn up, and when dawn came

Memorándum

TO : Mr. Adams

FROM : R. J. Gallagher

Miscellaneous - Non-Subversive

SUBJECT: MUTILATION OF LIVESTOCK
STATE OF COLORADO
INFORMATION CONCERNING

DATE: September 12, 1975

1 - Mr. Adams
1 - Mr. Gallagher
1 - Mr. O'Connell
1 - Mr. Cooke
1 - Mr. Sheer
1 - Mr. Bowers

In response to a telephone call from Honorable Floyd K. Haskell, United States Senator from Colorado, to the Director 9/11/75, I contacted Senator Haskell telephonically today, 9/12/75.

Senator Haskell indicated his concern for a situation occurring in the western states where cattle have been discovered mutilated. The bizarre mutilations involve loss of left ear, left eye, sex organ, and the blood drained from the carcass with no traces of blood left on the ground and no footprints.

Senator Haskell repeated his request that the FBI enter the investigation. The provisions of the Interstate Transportation of Stolen Cattle Statute, Title 18, U. S. Code, Section 2311, were explained to him. It was po... ...ere must be an interstate ... Senator "

Part of an official memo concerning mutilation of livestock in Colorado in 1975. What could have caused such bizarre injuries?

Ben King, Mrs Lewis's brother, called his sister and they went in search of the horse. When they discovered the carcass they could not believe their eyes: the neck and head had been completely stripped of flesh, but there was not a drop of blood on the ground. More than a month later, a Denver pathologist carried out an autopsy on the animal. He was shocked to discover that the abdominal, brain and spinal cavities were empty. The killers had removed the internal organs with surgical precision.

Mrs Lewis's husband arrived not long after the animal was discovered and noticed a strange, medicinal smell and a substance resembling tar around the body. They noted a lack of hoofprints, footprints and tyre tracks. Nearby chico bushes had been flattened to just ten inches high, and there were several circular 'exhaust' marks and six identical holes in the ground. Ben King, an expert tracker, found the hoofprints of three horses which showed that the animals were in a headlong flight towards the ranch. The tracks split, with one set heading away. These stopped abruptly and mysteriously 100 feet away from where Lady's body now lay.

On 16 September, Mrs Lewis and some friends discovered in a bush a piece of flesh with horse hairs hanging to it. When it was prodded, the skin split and a green viscous matter spilled on to her hand, causing it to burn.

The macabre death was picked up by the media and eventually spread through the global wire services. Sheriff Ben Phillips, who declined to examine the remains, declared that Lady 'was probably killed by lightning'. A veterinary surgeon who did examine the carcass declared that the horse had collapsed due to a leg infection. He speculated that a passing Samaritan must have found Lady suffering and had put her out of her misery by cutting her throat. Natural predators had then moved in and stripped the neck of flesh and eaten away the internal organs.

Duane Martin of the Forestry Service arrived on 23 September with a geiger counter. The carcass showed normal background radiation, but some distance away, and around the 'exhaust' marks, the readings were higher. The mutilation of Lady was not as mundane as the sceptics reported, but was it as bizarre as many believed?

The UFO connection

Prior to Lady's death there had been a spate of unidentified lights over the area. It was these that caused Mrs Lewis to comment: 'I really believe that a flying saucer had something to do with Lady's death.' Her eighty-seven-year-old mother reinforced the belief when she was interviewed. Mrs Agnes King lived in a cabin just a quarter of a mile from where the horse was found. She told reporters that a large unidentified object passed over the cabin on the evening Lady did not show up for her feed. Mrs King was judged to be remarkably alert for her age.

However, most ufologists were cautious. As late as 1980 the Aerial Phenomena Research Organization (APRO) reiterated: 'APRO does not claim that Lady was killed by "flying saucer people", rather that she died in a very strange manner and that her death has yet to be satisfactorily explained.' Others, though, are more convinced of the UFO connection. The Doraty abduction case is a CE4 (close encounter of the fourth kind, see page 183) with an added dimension.

Judy Doraty, her daughter Cindy, and her sister-in-law were driving back home from Houston, Texas after an evening out in May 1973.

Charles Fort, a collector of curiosities, recorded the slaughter of sheep during May 1810 at a farm in Ennerdale, Yorkshire. No bodily parts were missing, just blood, which apparently had been sucked out through a wound in the jugular vein.

The night was clearly illuminated by a full moon. Suddenly they were aware of a strange light in the sky. At some point Judy stopped the car and climbed out for a better view, although the family were not unduly concerned about it.

Afterwards, however, Judy suffered headaches and feelings of extreme anxiety. In the award-winning documentary *Strange Harvest* produced by Linda Moulton Howe (pictured below), psychiatrist Professor Leo Sprinkle hypnotises Judy and takes her back to 'relive' the journey. Under hypnosis she describes a scenario that apparently has been edited from her conscious recollection. She starts with a description of the light and then comes a surprise: 'It's like a spotlight shining down on the back of my car. And it's like it has substance to it. I can see an animal being taken up in this. I can see it squirming and trying to get free. And it's like it's being sucked up.'

Then she feels she is in two places at once – still standing beside the car, yet now also in a strange room. 'It's taken into some sort of chamber. And I get nauseated at watching how they excise parts. It's done very quickly, but the calf doesn't die immediately.'

She then describes how the excised organs have needles, or 'probes', pushed into them. Two small entities with large eyes explain to her that the work is necessary 'for our betterment'. Then horror is heaped on horror when she sees her daughter placed on a slab and the beings examine her. She begs them to stop, convinced they are going to mutilate the child too, but they only take samples from her.

Linda Moulton Howe produced the award-winning documentary *Strange Harvest* on animal mutilations in the USA. She believes they are being carried out by extraterrestrials. The documentary drew the largest audience for a locally produced programme in the history of Denver. Demand was so great it was repeated just four months after its original broadcast.

It was not until 1990 that Cindy Doraty was regressed. The hypnosis was carried out by a psychiatrist called John Carpenter in Springfield, Missouri. Cindy confirmed, for what it's worth, her mother's testimony of seeing the calf rising up into the craft in a beam of yellow light.

There have been other cases where people have apparently observed UFO entities in connection with the procurement or mutilation of animals. In 1989 Linda Moulton Howe was contacted by a security guard in Denver, Colorado, who claimed to have observed from his truck a large circle of lights over a pasture. He kept silent because he did not want to lose his job. The following day he saw a farmer gather up two dead and mutilated cows from the same pasture. Linda also investigated the case of Myra Hansen and her young son, who in 1980 had observed two white-suited beings mutilating a cow which was bellowing with pain. When she tried to interfere, she and her son were abducted for a while.

During January 1978, four poachers received a shock on the banks of the River Weaver in Frodsham, Cheshire. They were chasing pheasants when one of them noticed a silver balloon-like object floating on the water. As they watched, it took off and landed in a nearby meadow where some cows were grazing. Shocked, they watched several figures emerge from the object; they were dressed in silver suits and wearing headgear which included what looked like miners' lamps. They approached one of the cows, which seemed to become paralysed. A 'cage' was then constructed around it, and the entities seemed to be measuring the animal.

The men had seen enough and started to run, but their escape was impeded by a force which tugged painfully at their genitals. Afterwards, one of them had a mark on his leg similar to strong sunburn.

In Japan at a farm near Saga prefecture, the mutilated corpse of a cow was discovered on 29 December 1990. It lay in the cowshed, half its tongue missing, teats cored out from the udder. On 4 January 1992, the same farmer was alerted by the furious barking of his dogs. He ran to the cowshed and saw a small white object, similar in appearance to a jellyfish, suspended in the air. It flew outside and vanished. A cow was discovered on the floor with a badly broken leg.

In more recent years, Linda Moulton Howe created the popular TV series Sightings.

The killing fields

The publicity surrounding Lady's macabre demise opened the flood gates to a wave of reports by other pet owners and farmers previously too embarrassed to say anything. In some cases the organ removal was so good that veterinarians at Oklahoma State University said they were unable to produce students capable of duplicating such expertise.

Mutilated animals were turning up in Brazil, Puerto Rico and Spain as well as the USA and Canada. They included horses, cats, dogs and sheep. Cows were the predominant victims in the southern states of America. As the 1970s rushed towards a conclusion, the human players in this affair became polarised in their views. On the one side were the ranchers and local sheriff's departments who were convinced there was no rational explanation, and on the other were the sceptics and government departments like the Colorado Bureau of Investigation. The latter claimed that the animals had died of natural causes, and then been mutilated by coyotes and magpies. But ranchers, who had been around animals for many years, knew this could not be the explanation; yet when the CBI took away tissue samples for analysis, the conclusion 'done by predators' invariably came back.

Elbert County Sheriff George Yarnell, suspicious of this, cut off a piece of hide with a sharp knife and sent it to the CBI for analysis. As he predicted, the subsequent report said the cut was the work of natural predators . . .

Another explanation was that Satanists were removing bodily parts for use in rituals. However, no one has been convicted of mutilating, and for the scenario to be viable, a whole army of occultists would have to be involved to account for all the killings. Even Carl Whiteside, Director of the CBI, did not think this could be the explanation when he commented in 1979: 'The thing which has always bothered me is the absence of any physical evidence. In my experience of cult type organizations, whether it be occult, organized narcotics trafficking, or anything which involves groups of people, sooner or later you will have someone who is a member of that group who will come forward and provide information. That hasn't happened.'

A number of cases included the sighting of unidentified helicopters. It was speculated that the mutilations were carried out by a secret government department testing for pollution and radioactive contamination. Other commentators think the helicopters are disguised UFOs. Whatever the explanation, the mutilations go on unabated.

The spread of mutilation

Since the beginning of the 1980s hundreds of horses have been found mutilated in southern England and Sweden. Is this an old song set to a new tune, because the injuries are much cruder than those inflicted across the Atlantic? Or is the 'obvious' explanation the real answer – that the injuries are carried out by individuals with a psychopathic hatred of horses?

Approximately half of the animals have died, or had to be destroyed because of their injuries. These consisted mainly of cuts around the sexual organs, causing some people to resurrect the spectre of Satanic cults. Apart from a couple of arrests, the attacks remain an enigma and continue at an increasing rate. A mainstay of this mystery is that, despite guard dogs and alarm systems, horses are still mutilated. Owners wonder how someone can avoid detection and then attack a horse which apparently does not struggle or make a noise.

In August 1993, a horse was found in Oxfordshire with its hide cut from its body in squares. Sixties' pop star David Jones discovered two mutilated horses on his farm in the Meon Valley in Hampshire during July 1992. One of them had suffered an object being forced up its vagina. In response to horse mutilation, the Automobile Association brought out a special insurance policy in 1993. Stan Forbes, Regional Manager for AA Insurance, said: 'There is a sickening trend for mutilation, yet most policies don't cover it.'

Other animals, too, have been discovered mutilated in recent years. Thirty seals, were found on a beach in the Orkneys in 1991. Someone – or something – had removed their heads. According to Mike Lynch, an inspector with the Scottish Society for the Prevention of Cruelty to Animals, the heads had been removed with surgical precision.

In January 1985, forty-four ewes were slaughtered at a farm near Ballymoney in Northern Ireland. They had not been mauled, but all of them had puncture marks on the neck. Collector of curious stories Charles Fort recorded several similar cases from the nineteenth and early twentieth centuries – sheep with puncture marks through which the blood had been extracted. Peter Hough investigated a case at a farm near Rhayader, mid-Wales, where thirty-five sheep were attacked in August and October 1988. Farmer's son Charles Pugh said: 'This has been happening just three hundred yards from us, but no one has seen or heard anything. It's the strangest thing we've encountered in forty years of sheep farming.'

Are UFO entities responsible for these bizarre killings? If so, is it to extract genetic material, as some ufologists have suggested, in order to manufacture biological entities – flesh and blood robots? If so, why leave the evidence behind? Is it because they do not care, and know that no one will accept the evidence left right under their noses?

THE END OF THE ROAD

Throughout the first twenty years of UFO study there was a twin-edged attack from disparate groups with very different, even incompatible, aims.

Private UFO organisations obtained much publicity, but in the main they were believers – not investigating what UFOs might be, because they already 'knew' that they were alien spacecraft. They collected UFO reports just as others might collect stamps, and attacked the authorities because of a perceived cover-up of the truth. Ufology had become a political football, not a scientific endeavour.

The military, on the other hand, had grown weary of UFOs. In 1947 they had been charged with the secret responsibility out of fear of a threat that had never materialised. Yet some UFO sightings puzzled their scientific experts and, try as they might to squirm free, they were ordered to maintain a vigil on the data – just in case. Scientific input was minimal – Allen Hynek in the USA (by now a convert to the view that some UFOs were real, but being discreet so as to retain access to the secret data) or the occasional intelligence staff expert called upon to write a position paper in other countries such as Australia and Britain.

Attempts to pass the buck

During the early 1960s the US Air Force tried to dump the problem on to somebody else (hardly a sign that they considered an alien invasion to be imminent). Their primary target was the newly created NASA, set up to coordinate US space activity. NASA were not to be snared. But this does show the mind-set that perceived UFOs as alien or nothing. NASA became the chosen ones because their expertise was space flight.

Fortunately, as the evidence grew in stature during the 1960s with some quietly impressive cases, aided by the decreasing levels of media hysteria, the need to transfer UFO study to scientific research was gradually realised.

In late 1965 the US Air Force convened an independent review body, headed by optical physicist Dr Brian O'Brien, to assess its work. For the first time it comprised a respectable array of physical and non-physical scientists, including psychologists. One member was cosmologist Dr Carl Sagan, whose later TV spectaculars made him a household name.

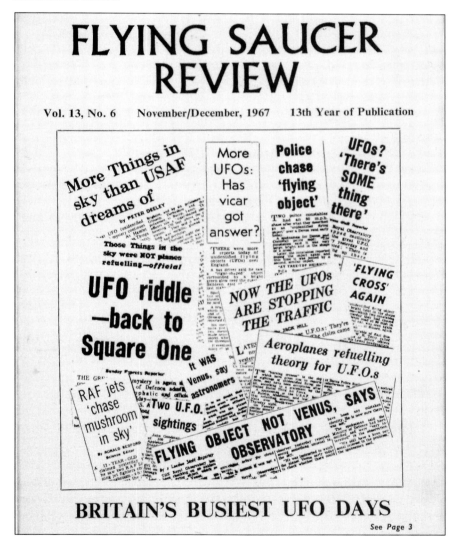

The O'Brien commission met for just one day in February 1966 and came out with a host of excellent proposals. They urged that, to defuse public outcries of 'cover-up', all official UFO files should be declassified and handed over to scientists. Further, they suggested that several teams be set up at universities around the USA, with at least one psychologist and one physical scientist at each to review the best of the incoming data. In this way UFOs would finally get the sort of objective appraisal required.

Whilst this was being digested by the government, a major outcry occurred when a series of sightings hit the state of Michigan. Allen Hynek, following typical Blue Book orders to debunk on sight, suggested that swamp gas (floating pockets of glowing methane) might have been responsible for some sightings. He was probably right, but the media exaggerated this into an attempt to explain everything away. The row spread to Congress.

The most influential figure in this debate was then US Congressman and future President Gerald Ford. His insistence ensured that some of the O'Brien panel ideas were taken up, but sadly in a limited form.

Just one man was put in charge. Universities were invited to tender to do the job professionally, but only one would be selected. It was stated that the chosen university would be given full access to all government records. However, that was clearly untrue. We have already seen how one of the most impressive cases – the Lakenheath/Bentwaters radar/visual from August 1956 – was not handed over (see page 123). There are also good grounds for arguing that other major cases never were.

Colorado project

The Condon Report is the most widely quoted UFO book ever published.

A number of scientific establishments were on the government shortlist during 1966, but the job went to the University of Colorado in Boulder. Given the task of coordinating the project was Dr Edward Condon, a quantum physicist who was a member of the team that built the atom bomb. He had high security clearance and was to some degree 'the government's man', but he had earlier challenged government sources over a toxic poisoning scare, which gave him the credibility that the project needed to gain public acceptance. Condon built his team with a hefty grant from taxpayers' money. Indeed the Condon project, which began work in October 1966 in a blaze of publicity, was extended well into the summer of 1968, with a total budget of half a million dollars, then a good deal of money. Its members then sat down to prepare its final report, which was to be released to worldwide anticipation in January 1969. But major traumas were to split the Condon team apart before then, which left the project irrevocably tarnished.

It later emerged that many more prestigious scientific bodies, such as the famous MIT (Massachusetts Institute of Technology) all turned down the chance to participate before Colorado got the contract. Unfortunately, just a few weeks into the project Condon was quoted as saying: 'It is my inclination right now to recommend that the government get out of this business. My attitude right now is that there is nothing to it.' He added with a smile; 'But I'm not supposed to reach a conclusion for another year.' His views on UFOs were thus never in much doubt.

Equally, the selection of cases to be studied by the scientists left a lot to be desired. Only fifty-nine were researched in depth for the final report. These excluded much impressive data such as the phenomena at Levelland in 1957, and included personal choices from Condon such as a ridiculous story about aliens from a universe populated by bears.

The problem, clear to some rapidly disillusioned scientists who were involved, but not obvious to others until the final report was issued, is that Condon focused on the wrong questions. The report asked if UFOs offered evidence of an alien visit to Earth. It concluded, not unreasonably from the evidence then, that the answer was no. But the real issue is whether any UFO sightings represent unexplained phenomena. The answer to that proved much more open. Of course, because most people continued to equate UFOs with alien spacecraft they assumed that the report's negative findings about their extraterrestrial origin translated into a debunking of the entire phenomenon.

The 'trick memorandum'

Matters took a catastrophic turn when a group of renegade scientists within the project discovered lurking in the files, a memo written two months before the contract was awarded. Written by the university administrator Robert Low, and entitled 'Some thoughts on the UFO project', it was instrumental in persuading Colorado to go for the contract. In this devastating document Low had justified taking on the work by saying that the study 'would be conducted almost exclusively by non-believers' who 'could and probably would add an impressive body of evidence that there is no reality to the observations. The trick would be, I think, to describe the project so that, to the public, it would appear a totally objective study...'

The so-called 'trick memorandum' was leaked to scientists within UFO groups to prove that there was honour left within the Condon ranks. So certain were the disillusioned project members that the final report would recommend deeper analysis that they agreed not to make this memo public. To everyone's credit, it was withheld, and known only to a select few. However, in January 1968 an atmospheric physicist at the University of Arizona, Dr James McDonald (one ufologist who was shown the memo), mentioned it in passing in a letter he sent to Low and Condon. They hit the roof.

The scientists who had leaked it to McDonald, Hynek and others were fired from the project forthwith under accusations of treachery. Others walked out in sympathy and disgust. This team, led by mathematician and psychologist Dr David Saunders, gave the memo to the prestigious magazine *Look*, who featured it strongly. They also set about writing their own rival report to challenge the official version about to be edited by Condon!

There is clear evidence that the Low memorandum did form the basis of the project. He went on to become its administrator. His memo recommended that the work should stress the psychology of UFO witnesses rather than 'the old question of the physical reality of the saucer' and that, if this were done, 'the scientific community would quickly get the message.' The university psychology department were given the casting vote in whether to take on the project, and a questionnaire issued to witnesses by the team was twenty-two pages long – just one page discussing the sighting, and twenty-one asking about the psychological and social background of the witness!

In 1967, the only full year of project operation, the main thrust of UFO activity was not in the USA but centred on Europe, especially in Britain, including a debate in the Houses of Parliament because of the many high-quality sightings. Low, soon after publicly dismissing UFOs as 'nonsense', went to Europe on project business but refused to look at any British cases, talk to leading researchers or chase up data on events being studied. Instead Low visited Loch Ness and justified this decision by saying that the monster did not exist and neither did UFOs, so he needed to examine how people in Scotland were trying to research a non-existent phenomenon.

Rival reports with ironical results

The Saunders alternative project report (*UFOs? Yes!*) was first out by three months. It took a devastating view of how evidence was squandered and opportunities lost. Jenny Randles has visited Boulder in the company of Allen Hynek and his wife Mimi, where she met one of the scientists who had assisted Saunders, Dr Richard Sigismund. He affirmed much inside information about how the Colorado University team went about their task. Like many others, he had become convinced that UFOs were a real mystery.

Condon wrote the conclusions to the thousand-page official report by himself. These were cleverly put at the front, and the entire bulky text then given to the press only hours before release. Most reporters only had time to read the summary rather than the densely argued evidence (which lacked even basic facts and figures).

Whilst this all put over a very negative view, the report itself is in fact, one of the most important documents about UFOs ever produced. Most people who have read it through have reached entirely the opposite conclusions to those that Condon himself seems to have done.

Almost a quarter of the cases are considered unexplained, often in very direct terms. Typical phrases from these conclusions are 'the probability that at least one genuine UFO was involved appears to be

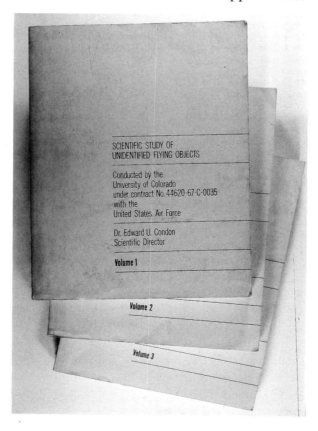

The original Condon report.

fairly high', or 'this unusual sighting should therefore be assigned to the category of some almost certainly natural phenomenon, which is so rare that it apparently has never been reported before or since' (which seems a near-perfect description of a genuine UFO), or the quite explicit 'all factors investigated, geometric, psychological and physical, appear to be consistent with the assertion that an extraordinary flying object, silvery, metallic, disk-shaped, tens of metres in diameter, and evidently artificial, flew within sight of two witnesses'.

Quite how Condon could argue, after evaluations like this, that there was nothing to the UFO mystery is rather difficult to grasp. Yet Condon even urged that children should have marks deducted if they mentioned UFOs in their school work. Later he was quoted as saying that authors of UFO books should be publicly horse-whipped!

Until his dying day, Dr Edward Condon did not publicly accept that there was anything of scientific value in the UFO mystery.

Jenny Randles has taught the subject in schools to the benefit of young children. Finding out how UFOs interact with meteorology and astronomy is a positive step for many of them, who learn through a topic that interests them. This illustrates the narrow-mindedness of Condon's approach.

Fortunately many scientists saw through the façade to the heart of the report. The American Institute for Aeronautics and Astronautics formed a sub-committee of eleven scientists and challenged its findings. Then, in December 1969, the American Association for the Advancement of Science (the AAAS) gave it the ultimate thumbs down by staging a UFO seminar in Boston.

Condon was distraught. Indeed he tried desperately to stop it, even appealing to a personal friend (the then Vice-President Spiro Agnew). Agnew politely refused for the White House to interfere. Figures like Hynek and Sagan were lecturing. Thornton Page, who had been one of the CIA's Robertson Panel debunkers sixteen years earlier but had made a reassessment after seeing the full evidence, was also taking part. So were the chief analyst for photographic evidence in the Condon team, William Hartmann, and a host of scientists including atmospheric physicist James McDonald from Arizona. His brilliant in-depth and independent reinvestigation of the Lakenheath/Bentwaters case put the Condon project into sharp perspective.

A very fine, well-balanced book entitled *UFOs: A Scientific Debate*, edited by Sagan and Page, emerged from the proceedings in 1972. It was everything that the half-million-dollar Condon report should have been. A vital outcome was a declaration signed by thirteen top scientists, including all those who participated in the Boston meeting. It urged the US government to preserve the UFO archives and hand them over to a recognised scientific institute for open assessment by any qualified researcher.

Sadly, this wish was completely ignored. Indeed, as recently as 1993 Barry Greenwood located some files that had been retained by a Condon report archivist.

The US government fought back. Days after the Condon report was published, Allen Hynek was notified that his twenty-one-year tenure was over. Blue Book was closing down following the recommendations of the Colorado report. But the news was withheld from the public for the moment.

Years later, under the US Freedom of Information Act, documents about this closure process surfaced. An Air Force memo signed by Brigadier General C.H. Bolender discussing the procedure and dated 20 October 1969 gives some devastating news which was long suspected but never before confirmed in writing. The closure of Blue Book was the termination of a sham operation. Indeed, the closure itself was a sham!

Bolender reported that, even with the termination of Blue Book, 'reports of UFOs' would still 'continue to be handled through the standard Air Force procedure designed for this purpose'. And, affirming that this meant what it seems to mean, he noted that 'Reports of unidentified flying objects which could affect national security' (citing the appropriate coding procedure) 'are not part of the Blue Book system.'

In other words, all the hot cases between 1947 and 1969 – those, like the Lakenheath/Bentwaters affair, with serious implications – bypassed Blue Book altogether, were handled in other ways and (as of 1994) have still never been declassified. Furthermore, despite the alleged shutdown of any Air Force interest, all important UFO data was still to be collected by whatever department seemingly did the really significant work in secret. Blue Book had for a long time been just a public relations exercise.

Interestingly enough, after sitting on the closure for some months the US government chose to call a press conference and describe their alleged termination of all UFO interest immediately prior to the start of the AAA symposium in Boston. It seemed calculated to achieve indirectly what the Vice-President had refused to do for Condon – defuse the gathering.

If that was the plan, it failed miserably. The cessation of Air Force investigation work freed many scientists, like Hynek, finally to go public. The Condon report worked in the opposite direction to that which was anticipated. The AAAS symposium built a platform on which serious, scientific study could at last be searched.

Thornton Page reports that, a few years after the AAAS debacle, he called Condon for help when he (Page) was asked to write the entry on UFOs for the *Encyclopedia Britannica*. The ex-CIA scientific adviser and one-time UFO debunker was now writing an objective appraisal, and says in a 1984 letter that Condon's response to his telephoned request was very explicit: 'He shouted at me . . . then there was a bang, and silence. I am told that he threw the phone on the floor with such violence that it broke.'

Part Seven

1970s:
UFOs TOP SECRET

THE WALTON STORY

The rehabilitation of Hynek

Following the closure of Project Blue Book and the new wave of scientific interest, Dr J. Allen Hynek was quick to launch his own organisation. CUFOS – now named the J. Allen Hynek Center for UFO Studies in honour of the late ufological pioneer, who died in 1986 – began as Hynek's definitive book *The UFO Experience* hit the book-stands in 1974.

The private groups now had a virtual monopoly on the public relations front, but the internal squabbles that rent the Condon report apart have since been duplicated within many UFO organisations, and these battles have seriously distracted from the work in hand. Mindful of this, Hynek built the group around scientists from an underground movement (the 'invisible college', as it was termed).

Close encounters with Spielberg

Hynek became the guru to whom the media would automatically turn. The astronomer never shirked that responsibility, but it was sometimes difficult to match it with his wider ambitions. He turned down offers to appear in TV commercials advertising beer, but let Steven Spielberg use his book to develop the multi-million-dollar 1977 movie *Close Encounters of the Third Kind*. This weird title comes from the classifi-cation scheme adopted by Hynek in *The UFO Experience*, and is still largely used today in expanded form. (Hynek defined three types of encounter. Later, working with Jenny Randles, these were slightly modified and the fourth category was added. *Close encounters of the first kind* are close up visual observations of UFOs where the object inter-acts with the witness or environment in some way. *Close encounters of the second kind* further involve the leaving of some physical evidence after the sighting, i.e. landing traces. *Close encounters of the third kind* not only provide sightings of a UFO but also of their crew, e.g. alien occupants. *Close encounters of the fourth kind* are alien abductions in which the entities interact with the witness and take them into the UFO or another dimension.) Hynek even appeared in cinema trailers explaining what close encounters were and had a cameo role in the movie itself, where the ufologist is seen watching in awe as the aliens land.

Hynek was a thoroughly honest and cautious man, which meant that even after forty years he was still struggling to accommodate the wilder shores of ufology, and he made these moves because he believed the time was right. Spielberg was personally interested and did make an excellent UFO movie, with many of its scenes based upon real cases. The director also indirectly aided the launch of the Center; although Hynek later suffered through arguments about whether he had given away the movie rights to his non-fiction book.

Despite the fine intentions, Spielberg's strange combination of science and showbiz had an uncertain effect on the blossoming UFO subject. In particular, the public presentation of a close encounter in such blatant fashion to an audience of millions around the world was bound to affect the data coming in.

Movies: the damaging effects

However, Spielberg's *Close Encounters* was not the first UFO movie. That distinction probably goes to the American low-budget TV feature *The UFO Incident*, a plodding but accurate portrayal of the Betty and Barney Hill abduction from September 1961. The movie premiered on US television in late October 1975 and reached much of the rest of the world just before Spielberg's incredible big-budget epic knocked them for six.

The entities in both these movies are quite similar, as they were based on the real reports gradually coming in from the USA. Witnesses spoke of small humanoids with large domed heads, huge dark eyes and white or pasty skins. The impact of screening to such vast audiences what 'real' aliens looked like began to ensure that even hoaxers described them like this, which removed an important control test. Reports began to even out after this time – worldwide, more and more took on the form of the American prototype, whereas before these movies there had been considerable variety. It is difficult to imagine this as mere coincidence.

By the time that *The UFO Incident* hit American TV screens there were perhaps a dozen well-attested abduction cases that had been studied by ufologists – including one (that of police officer Herb Schirmer at Ashland, Nebraska) which had been explored by the Condon team in December 1967. This was the day before the dam broke. Within five years there would be two hundred. By 1993 that number was in four figures and rising so fast it was termed an epidemic.

The Travis Walton affair

Probably the final case to occur before things became irrevocably altered through these movie images was the unparalleled incident of 5 November 1975. It came a couple of weeks after the Betty and Barney Hill story had aired on local Arizona TV, and included features otherwise rare in the UFO archives. However, the main protagonists of the Arizona abduction claim not to have seen *The UFO Incident* beforehand.

At the time the case was a minor sensation because of its unusual features. But in 1993 Tracy Torme, a former scriptwriter with *Star Trek: The Next Generation*, convinced Paramount Pictures to finance a movie about this old case, called *Fire in the Sky*.

Travis Walton had been a member of a seven-man logging crew working on a contract in the Sitgreaves National Forest near the small town of Snowflake. Leading the gang was Mike Rogers, whose sister would later marry Travis. Rogers was struggling to complete this major contract for which the crew had been paid some cash up front. They had missed one deadline, partly through work with other contractors and partly through unavoidable problems.

As darkness fell on 5 November they left the forest in their large truck, bouncing along the rough tracks. Suddenly they saw a glow in the sky and rounded a corner to confront a strange blue diamond shape hovering above a clearing. Most of the men were terrified, but young Travis Walton was not. He leaped out and stumbled towards it, staring upwards. Then, as he stood beneath the huge mass, fixed within its spotlight beam and trapped like a rabbit by hunters, a ray of light shot from the object's base. The woodsman was hit in the midriff and thrown several feet into the air. He crashed on to the ground as if he had been struck by lightning.

Walton lay motionless and his colleagues believed him dead. The UFO was still there and unsurprisingly they panicked, quickly fleeing the scene. Only some minutes later did Mike Rogers realise it had been

A promotional poster from the 1993 film based on the story of Travis Walton.

wrong to leave their friend and turned the truck around. But there was no sign of the UFO or of Travis Walton.

Lie detector tests

This part of the story and its aftermath is handled exceptionally well by the Paramount movie. Back in town the shocked men came under suspicion that they were covering up a murder, and next day a major search was mounted to find Walton's body. Protesting their innocence, the men eventually took lie detector tests. All bar one (who had a past record and was nervous) convinced the operator that they did not know where their colleague was.

Never before or since has an abduction begun in this overtly hostile manner or has the victim vanished for days on end with police squads out searching. Of course, that is what gives the case its Hollywood edge, but, paradoxically, it is also what creates difficulties from a UFO perspective. It is an atypical CE4 (close encounter of the fourth kind) which bucks the trend so much that it worries some investigators; although others defend it staunchly.

Rival ufologists

A few hours after Walton returned, a UFO was recorded visually and on radar at the Canadian Forces installation at Falconbridge, Ontario. NORAD informed the media that two F-106 jets were scrambled but no contact was made with the object.

Travis Walton was missing for five days and then telephoned from a nearby town where he 'awoke' with no memory of what had taken place. The police remained unhappy, still thinking that a crime might have been committed. They considered taking action but were unable to come up with any hard evidence to support the idea that Walton, Rogers and the other men were not simply telling the truth as they had seen it.

After the police released Walton, Rogers and their families, the UFO groups moved in. Two in particular fought a war of attrition. Walton chose to cooperate with one but not the other, who were rather more sceptical. So that team set about reporting evidence that might discredit the case. They found, for example, that Walton had taken (and failed) a lie detector test soon after his return. It was paid for by a national tabloid who were promoting his story. The paper decided not to make this public and asked the supporting UFO group not to do so either. Later they gave Walton a second test, which he passed, and publicised that outcome instead.

Walton, not unreasonably, pointed out that he was heavily stressed in the immediate aftermath of his experience and that this could easily have affected him during the first test. Lie detector experts and psychologists who talked to the witnesses disagreed on the credibility of the story, and it eventually just fizzled out as something that you could either believe or not.

UFO debunker Philip Klass fought very hard over the years to prove that this case was just a hoax. He suggested that the men knew they could never finish the logging contract before the extended deadline and so invented the story to get them out of the deal. An 'act of God' clause gave them the right to quit if there was something unforeseen that prevented them returning to the forest; otherwise they might forfeit money owed. The crew never did finish the job. Klass also noted that the foresters received a considerable cash sum from the media source which bought their story.

How you evaluate any such facts is another matter, of course. One cannot blame anybody for accepting sums proffered by the media if their story is true, nor for cashing in via book and movie deals after-wards. This may offer a possible hoax motive in the first place, but it is also a natural consequence of any case like this even if the story were true. In addition, Arizona ufologist Jim Speiser conducted an impress-ive follow-through in 1993 after the movie's release, and sceptics tried to prevent the use of the term 'a true story' in advertising campaigns.

Speiser not only spoke at length with Mike Rogers about the logging deal but also talked to the then contractor and his successor in the Sitgreaves Forest. Most of what he found seems to support the Rogers and Walton story. Indeed, Rogers and the then contractor, Maurice Marchbanks, both confirmed that the 'act of God' clause was never actually enforced in 1975, nor was this invocation requested by Walton and Rogers – which makes it unlikely that this was part of a plan concocted to get out of the logging contract. Of course, it might be argued that under the circumstances nobody from the logging com-pany was going to press the issue. The crew were simply allowed to walk away from the deal, and so may never have needed to invoke any clause within the contract. Either way it was not a major factor.

After his return Travis Walton did get a few flash memories about what had happened to him during those missing five days. Hypnotic regression later plugged a few more gaps. Again these images were curious – including being taken to a giant hangar with lots of UFOs and being probed by odd looking aliens in unusual clothing. But these images were very confused.

Fact and fiction part company
This is less of a problem than it seems. The recall of abductees is often cloudy and filled with what are called 'screen memories' that appear to

be cover stories or even fantasies masking deeper, more painful thoughts which they repress into their subconscious. However, in the movie *Fire in the Sky* these patchy and rather weak memories were considered inappropriate. So Tracy Torme found it necessary to write a letter to fellow ufologists, apologising for having to go along with a directive to alter this part of the script. The final sequence in the film is more like a fantasy, rather than Travis Walton's memory of what took place inside the UFO. When the woodsman visited Britain in June 1993 he said that these scenes made a point, but were not meant to be accurate. However, the horror-inspired images of needles being stuck into eyeballs and giant cocoons trapping his body do detract from this otherwise sensible account of the case.

The affair will probably always be shrouded in controversy, but if it did happen – as a quite unassuming Travis Walton and Mike Rogers unflappably insist that it did – then it forms a watershed. It links the scattered and rather limited abduction cases of the later 1960s and early 1970s with the nightmare invasion of alien kidnappers who seemed bent on widescale medical experimentation. This latter scenario was about to become the terrifying norm.

—20—

MILITARY ENCOUNTER OVER IRAN

On 19 September 1976 the Imperial Iranian Air Force command post received four telephone calls from people saying that they had seen strange objects in the sky.

One of the most dramatic cases to come to light through the Freedom of Information Act in America contained details of an air confrontation between military jets and possibly several UFOs. The theatre was the air space over Tehran in September 1976, not long before the Shah was deposed. A report of the incident was sent by the Defence Attaché at the US Embassy to the Defence Intelligence Agency (DIA). Here are some direct quotes from the report:

A. At about 12.30am on 19 Sep 76 the Imperial Iranian Air Force (IIAF) command post received four telephone calls from citizens living in the Shemiran area of Tehran saying that they had seen strange objects in the sky. Some reported a kind of bird-like object while others reported a helicopter with a light on. There were no helicopters airborne at that time. The command post called B.G. Yousefi, assistant deputy commander of operations. After he told the citizens it was only stars and had talked to Mehrabad Tower he decided to look for himself. He noticed an object in the sky similar to a star bigger and brighter. He decided to scramble an F-4 from Shahrokhi AFB to investigate.

B. At 0130 hrs on the 19th the F-4 took off and proceeded to a point about 40nm north over Tehran. Due to its brilliance the object was easily visible from 70 miles away. As the F-4 approached a range of 25nm he lost all instrumentation and communications (UHF and Intercom). He broke off the intercept and headed back to Shahrokhi. When the F-4 turned away from the object and apparently was no longer a threat to it the aircraft regained all instrumentation and communications. At 0140 hrs a second F-4 was launched. The backseater acquired a radar lock on at 27nm, 12 o'clock high position with the vc [rate of closure] at 150 nmph. As the range decreased to 25nm the object moved away at a speed that was visible on the radar scope and stayed at 25nm.

C.   The size of the radar return was comparable to that of a 707 tanker. The visual size of the object was difficult to discern because of its intense brilliance. The light it gave off was that of flashing strobe lights arranged in a rectangular pattern and alternating blue, green, red and orange in color. The sequence of the lights was so fast that all the colors could be seen at once. The object and the pursuing F-4 continued on a course to the south of Tehran when another brightly lighted object, estimated to be one half to one third the apparent size of the moon, came out of the original object. This second object headed straight toward the F-4 at a very fast rate of speed. The pilot attempted to fire an AIM-9 missile at the object but at that instant his weapons control panel went off and he lost all communications (UHF and Interphone). At this point the pilot initiated a turn and negative G Dive to get away. As he turned the object fell in trail at what appeared to be about 3–4nm. As he continued in his turn away from the primary object the second object went to the inside of his turn then returned to the primary object for a perfect rejoin.

D.   Shortly after the second object joined up with the primary object another object appeared to come out of the other side of the primary object going straight down, at a great rate of speed. The F-4 crew had regained communications and the weapons control panel and watched the object approach the ground anticipating a large explosion. This object appeared to come to rest gently on the earth and cast a very bright light over an area of about 2–3 kilometers. The crew descended from their altitude of 26 m to 15 m and continued to observe and mark the object's position. They had some difficulty in adjusting their night visibility for landing so after orbiting Mehrabad a few times they went out for a straight in landing. There was a lot of interference on the UHF and each time they passed through a mag. bearing of 150 degrees from Mehrabad they lost their communications (UHF and Interphone) and the ins fluctuated from 30 degrees – 50 degrees. The one civil airliner that was approaching Mehrabad during this same time experienced communications failure in the same vicinity (Kilo Zulu) but did not report seeing anything. While the F-4 was on a long final approach the crew noticed another cylinder shaped object (about the size of a T-Bird at 10 m) with bright steady lights on each end and a flasher in the middle. When queried the tower stated there was no other known traffic in the area. During the time the object passed over the F-4 the tower did not have a visual on it but picked it up after the pilot told them to look between the mountains and the refinery.

E.   During daylight the F-4 crew was taken out to the area in a helicopter where the object apparently had landed. Nothing was noticed at the spot where they thought the object landed (a dry lake bed) but as they circled off to the west of the area they picked up a very noticeable beeper signal. At the point where the return was the loudest was a small house with a garden. They landed and asked the people within if they had noticed anything strange last night. The people talked about a loud noise and a very bright light like lightning. The aircraft and area where the object is believed to have landed are being checked for possible radiation.

A classic case

The White House, Secretary of State, National Security Agency and CIA were sent copies of this remarkable report. Additional to the report was a DIA Defence Information Report Evaluation, which concluded that the case was 'outstanding'. The evaluator wrote that it was a 'classic', meeting 'all the criteria necessary for a valid study of the UFO phenomenon'. The criteria included multiple witness sighting from various locations and viewpoints, highly credible observers, confirmation of sightings by radar, electromagnetic interference with three aircraft, physiological effects, and outstanding manoeuvrability exhibited by the objects.

The report was originally released by the DIA to a Berlin ufologist and American High School teacher in Germany named Charles Huffer. When Ray Boeche, an American UFO investigator, also requested the document, it was (perhaps significantly) missing the evaluation report.

Almost two weeks after the aerial encounter, the *Iran Times* ran a story based, they claimed, on recorded communications between the first pilot and ground control. His name was Lieutenant Jafari and he was twenty-three years old. The article fleshed out the official report by describing, first, how Jafari attempted to catch the object, breaking the sound barrier in hot pursuit, but failing. When ground control suggested he abandon the mission, he agreed, then radioed: 'Something is coming at me from behind. It is fifteen miles away . . . now ten miles away . . . now five miles . . . it is level now. I think it's going to crash into me. It has just passed by, missing me narrowly.' Lieutenant Jafari was so shaken by the near miss that he had to be guided back to Shahrokhi Air Base.

This is a significant case in our official history of the UFO phenomenon. Psychological and sociological theorists need not apply here. The objects exhibited intelligence and a technology superior to our own. Yet this demonstration of an apparent nuts and bolts phenomenon only serves to muddy the water of the ufological pond.

—21—

FREEDOM OF INFORMATION

From late 1976, as a result of the Freedom of Information Act, *previously secret UFO files began to pour out.*

Despite the appeals of scientists after the AAAS symposium, seven years elapsed before their cries were heard. The UFO data in the government archives remained locked away until the introduction of a Freedom of Information (FOI) Act gave the authorities little choice. From late 1976 the ex-secret UFO files began to pour out.

The FOI Act assured citizens access to all data unless national security would be compromised by its release. Since the government's public stance for many years had been that there was nothing sensitive (indeed nothing much at all) to the subject of UFOs, there would appear to have been little room for argument if they had tried to withhold many of these files.

The secrets of declassification

The Blue Book data was declassified on many reels of microfilm – allowing sight of fifteen thousand UFO cases collated between 1947 and 1969, and the varying degrees to which these had been pursued. Much valuable material came forth in that way, showing the inadequacy of early methods. Photographs now so obviously dubious had not been rejected – indeed, sometimes they were endorsed. But conversely, promising cases had been left dangling through lack of time and money.

The Ruppelt era shone like a beacon of sober investigation. For the rest of the time, disgruntled officers with no scientific training were doing a job that most seemed to regard as the military equivalent of being sent to Siberia.

It was not long before the files of other secret organisations were being sought. The FBI, CIA and other authorities were petitioned.

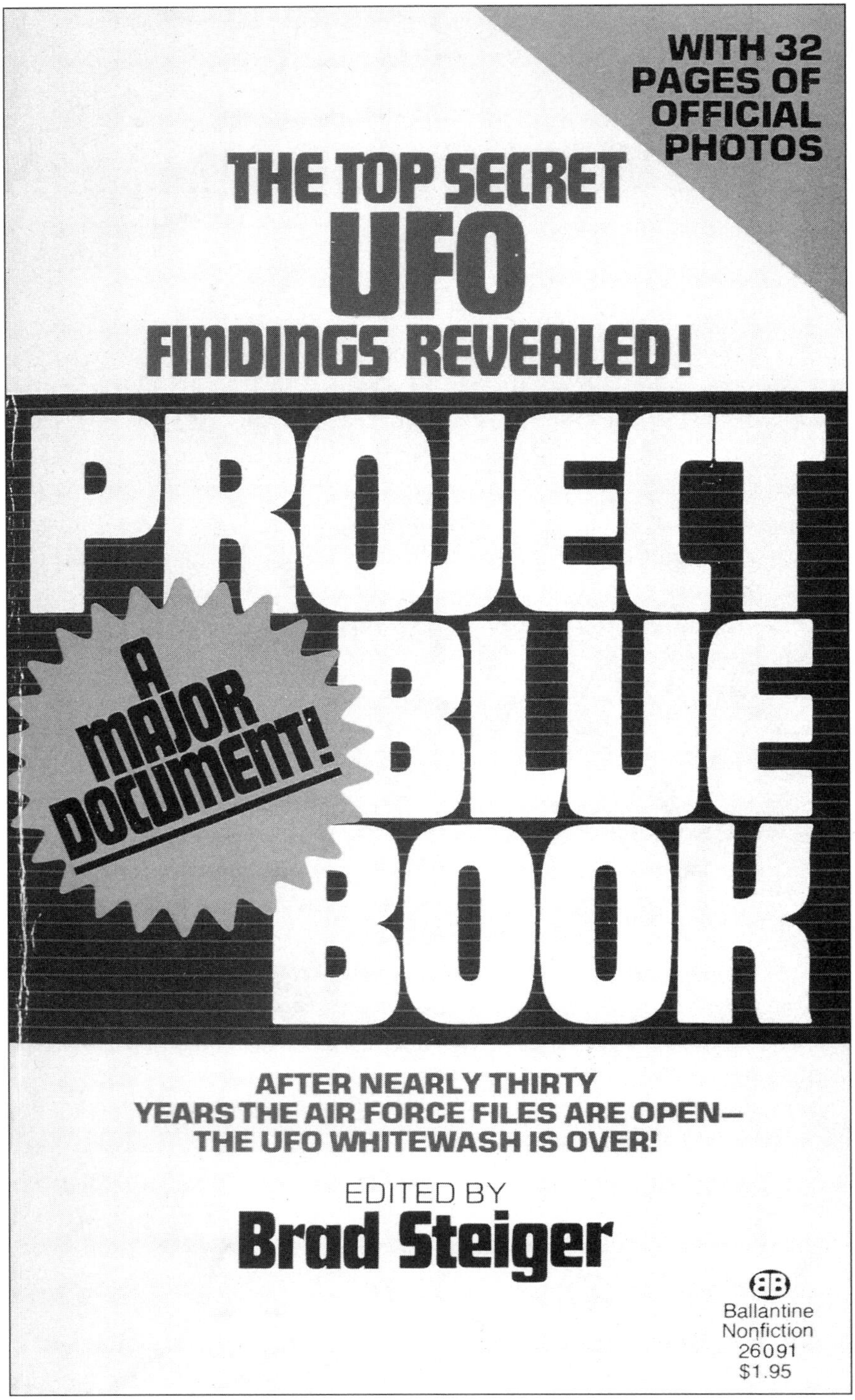

WITH 32
PAGES OF
OFFICIAL
PHOTOS

THE TOP SECRET
UFO
FINDINGS REVEALED!

A MAJOR
DOCUMENT!

PROJECT
BLUE
BOOK

AFTER NEARLY THIRTY
YEARS THE AIR FORCE FILES ARE OPEN—
THE UFO WHITEWASH IS OVER!

EDITED BY
Brad Steiger

Ballantine
Nonfiction
26091
$1.95

Sometimes they would deny having data, then succumb when ufologists were persistent. But many obstacles were placed in their way. For a time the battle for FOI documents became the focal point of ufology, but it should have been obvious that nothing of any real importance would be released, even if it had ever existed. If it did, it was clearly going to be subject to the national security codicil applied to all FOI releases.

Doing battle with the NSA

The big fight was with the NSA – the super-secret National Security Agency. They employ satellites to intercept phone calls and have the most sensitive operation in the USA, with outposts all over the world. In Britain a base at Menwith Hill near Harrogate was and still is NSA-operated. As their job was to bug the world for sensitive data, this meant two things: first, that anything they had about UFOs was likely to be fascinating, but second, that the chances of very much being releasable without compromising the NSA's procedures were slim.

Initially the NSA denied having any files about UFOs. Then, after much pressure, they agreed that they had a few. A figure of several hundred eventually emerged, but the request for access was refused. As a sort of sop a document entitled 'UFO hypotheses and survival questions' was released – its relevance to the NSA UFO data seems curious, and it poses many questions about what the actual data might contain. The document effectively surveys key options for what UFOs might be and seems to favour the view that some objects are extraterrestrial.

Despite many appeals, the NSA files themselves were still kept secret. The FOI Act allows protests all the way up to the US Supreme Court, however, and many ufologists backed a fighting fund to pay for the costs of doing just that. But even the top security-cleared judge who presided over the case was not allowed to see the files. Instead, the NSA issued a twenty-one-page statement for his eyes only, explaining why their UFO data had to be kept secret.

One assumes that this document went beyond the publicly presented reasoning that the data is unimportant but the methods used by the NSA to collect it have to be secret. Sadly, we do not know what else it said, as the judge rapidly agreed that to release the files would 'seriously jeopardise the work of the agency'. That effectively was that.

The document that the judge saw was then appealed for by an inspired FOI fighter. After much hassle, on 27 April 1982 it was made

After the introduction of the Freedom of Information Bill there were so many requests for UFO data that the US government began to charge serious sums for the work involved in the hope that it might deter people!

public – or rather a sanitised version of it was released. This is one of the most astonishing UFO files ever revealed. Eleven of the twenty-one pages were totally blacked out by the censor's pen, and most of another six were similarly treated. Only four pages still contained any moderate-sized sections which were readable – principally the opening paragraphs of the document.

We learned that one of the denied files concerned an NSA agent's secret visit to a UFO conference (unreleased as it was said to be 'irrelevant'!). Typical of what *is* visible through the sea of black ink is reference to a file by the author of the 'Survival Questions' paper. He penned another of the 239 secret documents entitled 'UFOs . . .' (the title goes on for a line and a half, but the rest of what it was called is rated as unreleasable!). We are told that 'In this document the author discusses what he . . .' (three inches of missing text follow).

It seems clear that in both these instances the denial of the material is unconnected with the methods used by the NSA to gain access to it. The title of the paper and a summary of its overview appear to be considered too sensitive because of what they say – not because of the means by which what they say was accrued. The same may be true in many other cases, for all we know.

'Surprise material'

After a further struggle to get access to minor snippets, such as the dates and locations of intercepted UFO messages without any reference to how these messages were intercepted, just a few extra words in the affadavit were freed for public scrutiny. In these we discover that the NSA use an odd term for UFO data – 'surprise material', which suggests that they have made unexpected discoveries as a result of their access to it. What a pity the rest of the world is being denied a sight of the sort of surprise that these NSA agents have had.

Although the search for FOI files has abated, except in connection with specific cases, the belief in a 'smoking gun' to prove alien reality still persists. No smoking gun has appeared, despite the desperation, but there are hints that someone on the fringes of the UFO movement may have felt the need to invent one. Bogus documents have begun to flood American ufology.

The search for the missing link

American researchers seek the file that will prove there was a secret investigation team with access to all the better evidence – up to and including alien spacecraft wreckage and the captured bodies of their alien crew. The belief that such things do exist remains undented in American culture; although it is far less accepted outside that country, where UFOs and spaceships are not viewed as automatically synonymous terms.

The Bolender memo from 1969 proved that there were other procedures by which UFO data was processed. Who handled these cases, and where are their files? More important, who decides which cases threatened national security and should be routed past the USAF?

We knew that a case like the Lakenheath/Bentwaters 1956 radar-visual was one such example from the time when Blue Book operated and which seems to have gone through the national security channels. From the lack of data supposedly available on the equally extraordinary Rendlesham Forest saga in 1980 (see page 212) it seems that, even long after Blue Book's closure, this is the type of case which qualifies for exclusive handling.

The big question is this. How many other files are out there somewhere, and what degree of material evidence do they possess?

In 1992 Dr Jacques Vallée published the so-called 'Pentacle' memo, written in January 1953 by a source at the Battelle Institute during the time they were doing lengthy top-secret research on UFOs. This seems important because it refers to thousands of cases under investigation. Where are those files? However, it might just be a minor dispute over semantics, as Battelle had over four thousand USAF files to select from even in 1953.

This urgency is typical of the desperate search in the USA to find that missing link which so many ufologists believe must exist. That belief stems from the fact that the FOI files which have been released are on the whole very disappointing to them.

Of course, disappointment rather depends upon what you expect to find within these files in the first place. They seem to reflect a puzzled administration with little clue as to what is happening and not much idea of how to deal with it. Might that not be exactly what was happening?

Australia introduced a similar FOI Act soon after the USA, and ufologist Bill Chalker was one of the first to make use of it. Learning from the American experience, the Australian government in Canberra invited Chalker to access all their records and extract and copy whatever he wanted. If they let him report all of this to the UFO world it would save them the effort of fielding hundreds of individual requests.

Chalker did an excellent job, but the same pattern emerged – many

UFO researcher Jacques Vallée.

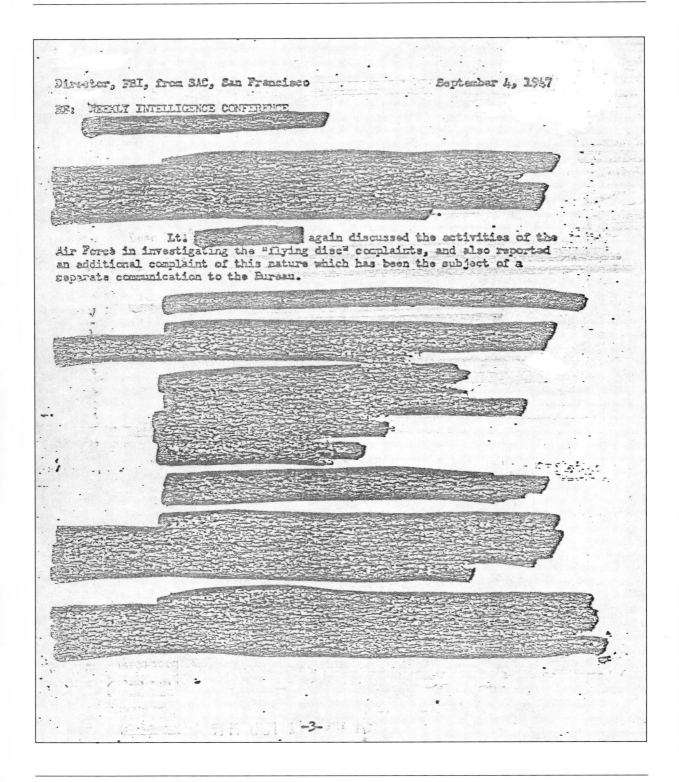

Director, FBI, from SAC, San Francisco   September 4, 1947

RE: WEEKLY INTELLIGENCE CONFERENCE

        Lt. ________ again discussed the activities of the
Air Force in investigating the "flying disc" complaints, and also reported
an additional complaint of this nature which has been the subject of a
separate communication to the Bureau.

odd cases, inadequate investigations, occasional memos from baffled experts speculating on wild theories of origin, vain attempts to make cases disappear by explaining them away, but ultimately a continuing series of reports that defied resolution. This all remained undented by changes in public mood or UFO credibility. The essence of the UFO phenomenon shines through, just as it does in the databases of private UFO groups all over the world.

Everything we know, from BUFORA and CUFOS to the CIA and Canberra, tells us that most UFO sightings are readily explained, but just a few are not. With these unsolved cases, nobody has a monopoly on truth and hard answers are much thinner on the ground than endless speculation. This covers many theories from alien spaceships to altered states of consciousness.

Of course, there are those who can say, and have said, that Chalker was only shown what the Australian government wanted him to see and that the real 'hot stuff' was held back. But he was satisfied with the assistance that he received and appears to believe that the authorities played fair. If there was a smoking gun or a secret cache of Australian files, these were outside the province of the bureaucrats and administrators who are charged with the responsibility of collating UFO data. These people, on the whole, seem as puzzled, confused and full of curiosity as are most responsible ufologists.

Confusion in Europe too

As we shall see, the French data reveals a very similar picture, as do sporadic releases from other countries – such as Spain, where military files about radar trackings, air force jet chases and unsolved sightings have been released from time to time over the past fifteen years. These all establish the same level of mystification. But it adds no great new insights. There seems precious little evidence about some massive global conspiracy to withhold vital solid evidence that would prove alien reality to the world.

Indeed, in December 1993, when the energy commission of the EC passed a proposal by an Italian delegate to request funding for a European UFO commission, there was an outcry. Yet the idea was a sensible one. Most people saw this in terms of a search for 'little green men'. What they did not see was that, if some UFOs are natural physical phenomena (and there is strong evidence that they are), then energy and power might be harnessed if we can investigate them properly. The funding requested makes sound economic sense.

See opposite
This memo is typical of the data revealed under *Freedom of Information Act* requests – showing the sea of censorship. This particular memo dates from before the US government were even officially investigating UFOs (ie four months before Project Sign began). But it's clear to see how little they are prepared to release even half a century later!

In 1976 the Spanish Government invited journalist Jose Benitez to Madrid. Benitez was introduced to an Air Force Lieutenant-General who was Chief of Staff of the Air Ministry. The journalist was handed documentation on twelve of their best cases. This included film taken by Spanish Air Force pilots.

In strict terms, government investigations are as hamstrung as private ones by lack of money and insoluble questions about UFO origin. Yes, there is a cover-up, but it hides a lack of certainty and much confusion as to what UFOs might be. There is no sign of any desperate rearguard action to prevent the world from learning incredible secrets about an alien invasion.

──22──

THE FRENCH CONNECTION

In 1977 France became the first world government to create a full-time, permanent team of scientific ufologists.

Although many of the major historical developments took place in the United States, one of the most important did not. In 1977 France became the first world government to create a full-time, permanent team of scientific ufologists, and in the mid-1990s it is still operating.

Its origin goes back to March 1974 when the then Minister of Defence, Robert Galley, went on French national radio with an interview that should have provoked global headlines, yet oddly did nothing of the sort. Galley assured the French people that his Ministry took UFOs very seriously and was studying them. He reported that there had been radar trackings and that French Air Force jets had chased these objects. Whilst many sightings could be accounted for, others could not. He added that, if people were able to see the extent and quality of the data that was coming in to the authorities, they would be properly disturbed.

It was an astonishing admission and probably represents the honest views of most nations. But France, not tied to the USA by the NATO defence treaty, had simply chosen to be the first to speak out.

Galley seems to have taken advice from scientific staff, notably Dr Claude Poher from the French Space Agency at Toulouse. He and another colleague, astronomer Dr Pierre Guerin, had evidently been impressed by the Condon data, the AAAS symposium, Hynek's appearance in the public arena and first-hand observation of cases being channelled through to them for evaluation by the French Defence Ministry.

Soon after Galley's speech Poher completed a major statistical analysis of UFOs and Guerin wrote a position paper. These scientists published their work in English in the then prestigious journal *Flying Saucer Review*.

A scientific riddle acknowledged at last

On 1 May 1977 the French government created GEPAN, which translates as Study Group into Unidentified Aerospatial Phenomena. It was placed under the directorship of Poher with the collaboration of others who included Guerin.

Coming as it did when Spielberg and Hynek's movie *Close Encounters of the Third Kind* was starting its journey around the world, and just as the US government had finally begun to release once secret UFO files through the new Freedom of Information Act, it was perceived as a very important step forward. Ufology had come visibly further in the few years post-Condon than it had done in the previous quarter-century. The main reason was that at last it was being treated as a scientific riddle and not as a military headache.

In the early days GEPAN was very interactive with the UFO world. Sadly, most English-speaking ufologists were ignorant of this data and mainstream science journals never mentioned it. However, for those who took the trouble to access GEPAN reports their significance was obvious.

The *gendarmerie* were specially trained to deploy units to follow up cases and call in GEPAN if it felt necessary. A number of scientific laboratories were on standby to handle samples or other physical evidence. Everything was extremely efficient and open.

Confirming the Battelle results

During 1978 354 reports were sent to GEPAN (by 1985 the total was over 1,600) and of these more than half represented close encounters rather than just lights in the sky. This was partly because less productive cases had been filtered out by the police.

A quarter of the cases were evaluated by GEPAN as genuine UFOs. As their first status report, published in 1979, pointed out, 'these reports . . . pose a real question'. Even more important than this honest admission was the fact that GEPAN duplicated the Battelle research from twenty-five years before and made the same finding: the more data made available on any case, and the better the calibre of the reporting witnesses, then the *more* likely it was that the event would remain unexplained.

But there was more still. For example, they found that puzzling UFOs were more prevalent given better atmospheric clarity. This is significant because if UFOs were simply misperceptions then the opposite would be true. Equally, if UFOs are hallucinations or fantasies they would have no correlation with the quality of the atmosphere. That the incidence of unidentified UFOs increased in better viewing conditions was strong support for their physical reality.

Based on this evidence, two years into their project GEPAN sought more funding and expressed the view that their work was proving that witnesses were really seeing UFOs. However, there was a price to pay for the upgrading of the project: increased secrecy. One of the last published GEPAN reports about internal discussions with the French government noted that the results were proving disconcerting and that presidential scientific advisers were recommending 'great vigilance' in publication.

This advice seems to have been enforced from about 1980. Dr Poher 'retired to sail around the world' and a new young astronomer, Dr Alain Esterle, took command. He was far more circumspect, but still retained some links with the UFO world. Jenny Randles met him in London in May 1981 and he intimated that scientists on the project were starting to think that some evidence might actually support the alien nature behind some cases.

In early 1983 Jenny went to France and was able to get hold of some new GEPAN data. They were publishing limited-edition 'Technical Notes' in a regular series (each one was stamped with an individual identifying number under 100). These incredibly detailed documents, which included photographs, site measurements, laboratory data and so on, consisted of almost book-length treatments each focusing on a single investigation. The cases were classic encounters such as an incident of 26 January 1981 when an object with portholes hovered over a farmer's car, caused its engine to fail and then damaged its electrical circuits. GEPAN's conclusion was that this case was 'in the proper sense, an unidentified aerial phenomenon'.

In 1983 British and French ufologists tried to initiate an annual series of entente-cordiale *joint meetings. So few British ufologists could understand French that this laudable move soon failed.*

GEPAN goes underground

Ironically, on the very day that Jenny went to France, 21 February 1983, the *Sunday Times* (which had mentioned none of GEPAN's positive research) carried a small item quipping 'Flying saucers sought no more'. It claimed that as an economy measure the Mitterrand government was closing down GEPAN because the group was viewed as 'an expensive folly'. French ufologists, Jenny found, generally believed that GEPAN was merely going underground and had stopped all cooperation with the public. However, GEPAN was far from on the point of extinction. It was revamped in 1983, but retained its status in

Toulouse. The *Sunday Times* never seem to have corrected their earlier claim that it was completely dead and buried.

Later in 1983 Pierre Guerin issued another position statement. In it he argued that the powers-that-be used various tactics to try to 'put it into the minds of the scientists to deny the existence of UFOs' – or at least, he added, the majority of scientists 'who are not sufficiently interested in the matter to search through the records for themselves'.

From what we have seen of the history of UFOs throughout this book, such an assessment has merit. Science has been manipulated into discounting UFO evidence by a host of reasons, ranging from the ufologists' own sad obsession with extraterrestrial invasions to governmental desire to restrict research to a few militarily controlled appraisals. Of course, if you are interested in UFOs not for what they are, but rather for how you can use them to build some sort of weapon, then the very last thing you want is for scientists all over the world who have not signed allegiance to the MoD or NSA to think there is something worthwhile connected with the data.

The landing at Trans-en-Provence

A truly dramatic case that GEPAN came across was the landing at Trans-en-Provence; it was certainly subjected to one of their most intensive investigations. In June 1987 Jenny met, in Washington, engineer Jean Jacques Velasco, the new head of GEPAN. Velasco was very impressed by the calibre of the Provence case (which Alain Esterle, GEPAN director at the time, had also enthused about, saying: 'We have a combination of factors which induce us to accept that something akin to what the witness described actually did take place.')

It seems that on 9 January 1981 police at Draguinan, a town in south-eastern France long plagued with UFO sightings, received a new report. It came from a farmer called Renato Nicolai in the nearby village of Trans-en-Provence. The man's house sat astride a slope built into a series of terraced orchards in the valley of the River Nartuby. The police visited Nicolai and he showed them the site.

At 5pm the previous day he had been working outside on the terraces when he had heard a 'faint whistling'. He turned to see 'a device in the air at the height of a big pine tree ... not spinning, coming lower towards the ground'. It was like a slightly elongated egg with four circular openings on the base. As he walked towards it he saw that it had touched down on the slope. It was there for a very short time and 'right away it lifted off, still emitting a slight whistling sound'. It 'kicked off a

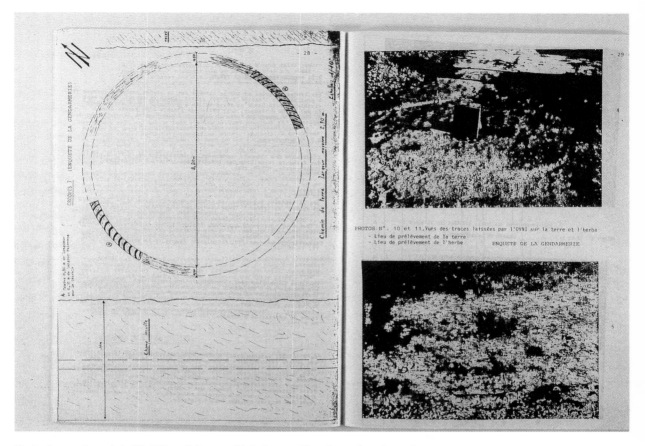

PHOTOS N°. 10 et 11.Vues des traces laissées par l'OVNI sur la terre et l'herbe
- Lieu de prélèvement de la terre
- Lieu de prélèvement de l'herbe   ENQUETE DE LA GENDARMERIE

little dust when it left'. The object – slightly smaller than the size of a car – climbed about twenty feet up and then sped away to the north-east.

Nicolai said it was 'the colour of lead. The device had a ridge all the way around its circumference.' Two of the holes 'could be reactors or feet. There were also two other circles which looked like trapdoors.' There were two small legs at one point on the base. He had no doubt that it was a constructed machine.

A near-identical object had landed on the snowy slopes of a hillside at Meanwood, West Yorkshire, in February 1979 amidst a major two-day flap. That weekend a UFO also landed at a quarry in nearby Bacup and US Air Force jets chased an object out to sea between Southport and Blackpool. Blackpool pier shook (according to reports from a security guard), and a caravan park at Scarisbrick was damaged by the noise. This led to questions in the house by then MP (and future TV celebrity) Robert Kilroy Silk. The parallels between these two cases are quite strong.

Part of the GEPAN report detailing the Trans-en-Provence case.

Back at Trans-en-Provence the police did not merely have Nicolai's story but also physical evidence. For there was a curious ring in the earth where the object had landed. It was several inches wide and over six feet in diameter. They took samples.

GEPAN were contacted three days later and the *gendarmerie* were instructed to take further, more specific samples, including controls from outside the ring area. Scientists from GEPAN then made their own study.

A leading expert in plant damage, Michael Bounais, supervised the analysis work at the National Institute for Agronomy Research. Many major findings appeared. The chlorophyll content of the plants in the landing zone had altered markedly. The leaves on the grass had aged 'in some way that neither natural processes nor laboratory experiments could duplicate'. There were also major deformations of the ground which could not be explained. GEPAN said in conclusion; 'We cannot give any precise or specific interpretation for this remarkable set of results . . . But we can state that there is nevertheless confirmation from them that a very sigificant incident took place on this spot.'

It was soon after the completion of the research on this case that GEPAN went underground. In Washington, Velasco reported that the Trans-en-Provence landing was very important. He suggested that an electromagnetic field, rather than an irradiating energy source, was more likely to have caused the plant and soil changes.

In a paper written for the *Journal of Scientific Exploration* in 1990 Bounais himself also had his say about these effects. He was baffled, he said, because; no normal method such as ionising, thermal or hydro factors could explain the changes that he had found.

In November 1988, ufologist Dr Jacques Vallée visited the site and interviewed Nicolai in the company of plant specialist Bounais. Samples were taken back to California where a prestigious scientific institute conducted further tests on Vallée's behalf. The institute wished to remain anonymous because it preferred not to be publicly associated with UFOs (which is, sadly, still a common problem). It could offer no mundane explanation, even after bombarding the material with X-rays and testing it under an electron microscope.

GEPAN/SEPRA discredited?

On 15 July 1991 Robert Galley, now retired from government duties, gave a new interview to the respected journal *OVNI Presence*. He explained how in his 1974 interview he was not proclaiming a belief in little green men, simply that 'There certainly are, even now, within the atmosphere luminous phenomena which do not have an immediate explanation.'

Galley was also questioned about the wave of triangular objects sighted in Belgium between 1989 and 1991 (see page 268) and about the idea that these may have been American stealth aircraft. He seemed very open-minded on the possibility, citing an instance in which an American spy plane flew over French territory to photograph a uranium enrichment plant at Pierrelatte. Galley intercepted the mission and sent a French Air Force colonel to Ramstein Air Force Base, where the jet landed, and had the negatives promptly confiscated! They had not publicly accused the Americans of this, but, Galley implied, if it could happen once then it might have happened above Belgium with a new type of aircraft that resembled UFOs.

Another responsible French journal, *Phenomena*, published a devastating appraisal of GEPAN (or SEPRA as it has been retitled to take account of a newly expanded role that includes orbital space re-entry investigations). This journal, unlike much of French ufology, had been restrained in criticism. Whilst Velasco and others had attended overseas UFO conferences, GEPAN seemed reluctant to support events closer to home. Quite a few researchers were openly accusing them of being closet debunkers. Physicist Jean-Pierre Petit had said in 1988, for example, that GEPAN had been set up after a wave of sightings and the impact of Galley's public endorsements not to research the UFO matter but rather to 'extinguish the problem'.

Now Perry Petrakis, a moderate French ufologist, was saying that after giving GEPAN/SEPRA the benefit of the doubt they had to face the truth. He cited various impressive cases where the scientists seem to have been either reluctant to get involved or disinclined to speak out.

On 2 September 1990 a Boeing 727 heading from Strasbourg to Algeria picked up a UFO on radar. The crew tracked it for three minutes, travelling at around 5,000 mph! As it flew over Algeria, ground radar was temporarily jammed. Despite access to military sources, SEPRA were silent on the case.

Then on 3 October 1991 the Dordogne region was hit by a major wave of reports of a weird 'cloud' which created electromagnetic disturbances, affecting TV transmissions for instance. Strange lights were also seen. The following morning police were called by residents because a white, filament-like material had been sown over power lines and trees. This so-called 'angel's hair' was common in sightings during the 1950s and emitted by mysterious clouds; it had not been reported

SEPRA officially gets funding to study unusual atmospheric phenomena, which includes UFOs. This avoids the scientific row that would develop if government money from a science budget was allotted to UFO study.

In October 1954 Europe was subjected to a major UFO wave. In France there were several cases involving a rare type of physical evidence – so-called Angel's Hair. This white fibrous material fell from the sky after the passage of a UFO and has appeared only in a very few cases since. It is variously argued to be either spiders' webs or some kind of meteorological residue.

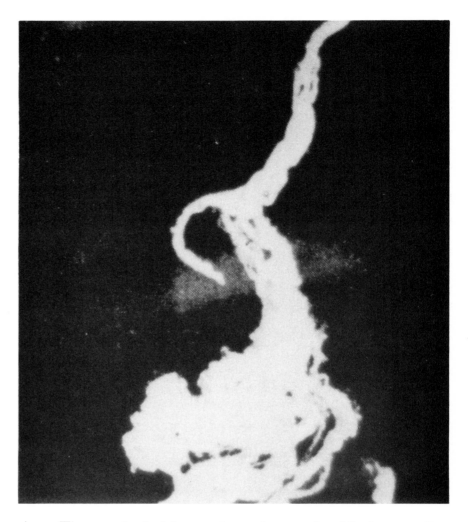

since. The case looked impressive and created public interest. But SEPRA fell silent. It took many months of investigation by the ufologists to establish that a military exercise had deployed the fibrous material as a form of electromagnetic decoy, and this was the source of the angel's hair and the reported odd effects. SEPRA could have prevented wasted effort had it used its internal contacts to dispel public concern from the start.

Then, on 8 July 1992, a military helicopter flying from Le Luc to Aurillac had a close encounter in daylight with a black diamond or lozenge shape. It was crossing at 6,000 feet above the town of Brignoles. This case is remarkably similar to a series of mid-air encounters over southern England involving commercial jets coming into close proximity with dark cylinder shapes. More than half a dozen are known since April 1991 (see Chapter 34).

The military allowed ufologists on base to interview personnel. The object was about fifteen feet long, moving at about 300 knots towards the south-east. The group sent a fax to SEPRA, but nothing emerged. They also claim that, when they tried to report the case on TV, SEPRA expressed concern, saying that they could not approve discussion of a military matter in public. These, of course, are the personal opinions of some French researchers. We can only note from our experience – particularly during its days at GEPAN – that SEPRA officials were helpful and provided us with useful data on their work. Now, sadly, but perhaps not altogether surprisingly, they seem more constrained.

Petrakis closed his report on the world's only official UFO team by asking of GEPAN/SEPRA; 'What are their results ... other than the Trans-en-Provence case which is twelve years old? Can one accept that a public service such as SEPRA, funded by public money, be such a secretive or inefficient group? We do not think so and no longer trust it.'

During February 1994 outraged reaction by British MEPs and a hostile media temporarily blocked EEC plans to fund an expansion of SEPRA into a 'common market' wide European UFO research centre.

Part Eight

1980s: GLOBAL PENETRATION

THE RENDLESHAM FOREST AFFAIR

During the last few days in December 1980 an English pine forest was host to an amazing case. It was either 'one of the most important in world history', as one researcher termed it, or 'a ghastly embarrassment to ufology' as a leading astronomer and sceptic has claimed.

Rendlesham Forest is a large woodland area on the quiet, sandy coastland of East Anglia eight miles north-east of Ipswich. The Forestry Commission 'farms' it for its hardwood and it is home to wildlife such as deer and rabbits. But equally it has a rather sinister aspect.

To the north is Sizewell, with several controversial nuclear power stations. A coastal spit called Orford Ness runs along its eastern rim. Apart from a lighthouse this has housed secret American research units linked to the super-sensitive NSA (National Security Agency). Officially this is home for new 'Over the Horizon Radar'. However, the locals are more suspicious about possible electronics experiments. South of the forest, at Martlesham Heath, is a communications HQ, and at RAF Bawdsey radar was first developed during the mid-1930s and secret research continues. There are tales of strange lights in the sky, mystery hummings and explosions, and weird effects on house lighting and other power sources such as cars.

However, right in the heart of the forest itself are two air bases – RAF Bentwaters and the smaller RAF Woodbridge. Until the end of the cold war these were leased to the Americans for NATO defensive duties. Staffed by hundreds of American personnel as a rearward maintenance site for any possible war in Europe, they had a token RAF 'caretaker' but were otherwise like small American towns transported across the Atlantic.

- **Colonel's top secret report tells the facts**
- **Mystery craft in exploding wall of colour**
- **Animals flee from strange glowing object**

UFO LANDS IN SUFFOLK

And that's OFFICIAL

A UFO has landed in Britain— and that staggering fact has been officially confirmed.

Despite a massive cover-up, News of the World investigators have proof that the mysterious craft came to earth in a red ball of light at 3 a.m. on December 27, 1980.

toward the depressions.

3. Later in the night a red sun-like light was seen through the trees. It moved about and pulsed. At one point it appeared to throw off glowing particles and then broke into five separate white objects and then disappeared. Immediately thereafter, three star-like objects were noticed in the sky, two objects to the north and one to the south, all of which were about 10° off the horizon. The objects moved rapidly in sharp angular movements and displayed red, green and blue lights. The objects to the north appeared to be elliptical through an 8-12 power lens. They then turned to full circles. The objects to the north remained in the sky for an hour or more. The object to the south was visible for two or three hours and beamed down a stream of light from time to time. Numerous indivi-

There are some fascinating similarities between the strategic importance and wealth of modern technology at this particular location and the area surrounding Roswell, Alamogordo and White Sands in New Mexico, where the infamous Roswell 'crash' occurred in 1947.

The Roswell incident was followed by the green fireball and car-stop events that struck the area between 1949 and 1957. Rendlesham Forest is a mere ten miles across but in recent years has also generated both car-stop cases and green fireball events. In 1980 it was the scene of Britain's only 'UFO crash' and the main rival of Roswell in terms of credibility and support.

So much has been pieced together about this affair from many years of research that several full-length books have appeared. But the main interest has been outside of Britain – where the public know little.

Headlines from the *News of the World*.

Mysterious warnings

Jenny Randles (who has written two books and been involved almost from the start) can personally attest that several planned documentaries – including one where a transmission date had been scheduled – were mysteriously cancelled at the last minute. It is also the only case over which she has had to risk prosecution under the Official Secrets Act by using Whitehall documents to which she and colleagues were denied access by the MoD but which were secured under FOI rules in the USA. She was even 'warned off' (Man in Black-style) by a government scientist who told her how dangerous he believed this type of investigation to be and how he, personally, would not follow it up any more. He claimed she was 'messing with something for which you can end up at the bottom of the Thames'.

At times the investigation of the matter was more like a James Bond movie script than a UFO case. Anonymous phone calls came in the night. Top-secret documents and tape recordings were leaked to investigators. Exchanges between senior political figures included US Senators and British MPs such as David Alton, Michael Heseltine, Merlyn Rees and Lord Trefgarne. Secret documents were claimed stolen during a robbery, meetings with 'spies' were set up in country parks and deserted railway stations, and claims about the 'truth' behind the incident abounded, ranging from captured satellite engines to a stray nuclear missile, and an alleged mind-scrambling experiment using a new 'psychotronic weapon' (a combination of electronics with a brain-affecting psychological warfare beam).

Sightings over southern England

We do know that late on the evening of 25 December 1980 many strange objects, which resembled comets breaking up or bright fireballs, appeared in the sky over south-eastern England. Civilian aircraft saw and reported them. The main activity was blamed on the re-entry of a Soviet satellite, but the British Astronomical Association list other events between 9pm and 3am which constitute a sequence of less than fully understood phenomena.

At Sudborne a man putting his dog into the outhouse for the night saw a huge glowing mass pass over, hover briefly, then vanish into the forest. On a small road through the woods between Orford and Woodbridge a courting couple saw the sky light up as an object plunged from the heavens into the trees. Other travellers saw it, too. Moments later

When the British public first heard about the events in Rendlesham Forest, via the News of the World *in October 1983, the story was so big that it even relegated top-rated soap opera* Coronation Street *to a support story on the front page.*

HANSARD EXTRACT

24 OCTOBER 1983

Col. 62

RAF Woodbridge (Alleged Incident)

Sir Patrick Wall asked the Secretary of State for Defence (1) if he has seen the United States Air Force memo dated 13 January 1981 concerning unexplained lights near RAF Woodbridge;
(2) whether, in view of the fact that the United States Air Force memo of 13 January 1981 on the incident at RAF Woodbridge has been released under the Freedom of Information Act, he will now release reports and documents concerning similar incidents in the United Kingdom;
(3) how many unexplained sightings or radar intercepts have taken place since 1980.

Mr. Stanley: I have seen the memorandum of 13 January 1981 to which my Hon. Friend refers. Since 1980 the Department has received 1,400 reports of sightings of flying objects which the observers have been unable to identify. There were no corresponding unexplained radar contacts. Subject to normal security constraints, I am ready to give information about any such reported sightings that are found to be a matter of concern from a defence standpoint, but there have been none to date.

An excerpt from *Hansard* regarding the House of Commons' debate on UFOs and the Rendlesham case raised by MP and NATO defence committee member Major Sir Patrick Wall and responded to by armed forces minister, John Stanley.

Woodbridge base sprang into full alert, with jeeps and trucks running everywhere.

A farmer was also alerted by this incident when some of his cows were sent rushing into the road. A taxi returning from a Christmas party hit them, and he and another farmer had to herd up the injured animals and get them away. Next day he complained to the base that a huge white light that he had seen must have been an aircraft. He demanded compensation, but they claimed no aircraft were flying. Days later he heard the UFO rumours, went back to the base and said it was still their fault because the Air Force should have protected him from the UFO. Soon afterwards the farmer had moved hundreds of miles away and was allegedly paid compensation. When traced two years later he would only say about this claim of being 'paid off' (which the USAF deny) that he did get money and (in his own words) 'whatever it were, it weren't enough!'

The Air Force communicates with UFO entities

Fifty miles away the object had been tracked on radar at RAF Watton as it cut the coast and vanished towards the ground. The matter would have been forgotten had it not been that a few days later US Air Force intelligence officers took the radar film for scrutiny and explained that Watton might have tracked a UFO that landed in the forest. It was confronted by senior officers from Woodbridge – one of whom communicated with small beings floating underneath. The event had been taped live by a senior commander.

Local ufologists Brenda Butler and Dot Street were contacted within days by one of the USAF security police on the base. He explained how he had been in a party of men sent out to the site in response to a report made from the perimeter fence. In the woods they found a landed object about the size of a car; small creatures with domed heads were suspended inside a beam of light underneath. Senior officers had come out and communicated using sign language. The UFO had been damaged by impact as it fell through the trees, but the aliens repaired it and left. It was as if the UFO was expected.

All of these stories, and many others, were offered independently. There was no publicity (not even in the local press). The MoD denied everything until 13 April 1983 when the British caretaker – Squadron Leader Donald Moreland – admitted that the stories were correct (except for the involvement of aliens). Without warning, the MoD confirmed in writing to Jenny Randles that the case was genuine and said they had no explanation for what had happened.

See opposite
In December 1980 a mysterious object crashed into woodland outside a USAF base in Suffolk, England. After three years of denials by the British government the official report about this incident, which had been submitted days later to the British Ministry of Defence, surfaced under the US Freedom of Information laws. The British government then confirmed its accuracy and that no explanation had been forthcoming. Speculation rose as to how many other significant cases it was keeping from the public.

DEPARTMENT OF THE AIR FORCE
HEADQUARTERS 81ST COMBAT SUPPORT GROUP (USAFE)
APO NEW YORK 04755

REPLY TO
ATTN OF: CD   13 Jan 81

SUBJECT: Unexplained Lights

TO: RAF/CC

1. Early in the morning of 27 Dec 80 (approximately 0300L), two USAF
security police patrolmen saw unusual lights outside the back gate at
RAF Woodbridge. Thinking an aircraft might have crashed or been forced
down, they called for permission to go outside the gate to investigate.
The on-duty flight chief responded and allowed three patrolmen to pro-
ceed on foot. The individuals reported seeing a strange glowing object
in the forest. The object was described as being metalic in appearance
and triangular in shape, approximately two to three meters across the
base and approximately two meters high. It illuminated the entire forest
with a white light. The object itself had a pulsing red light on top and
a bank(s) of blue lights underneath. The object was hovering or on legs.
As the patrolmen approached the object, it maneuvered through the trees
and disappeared. At this time the animals on a nearby farm went into a
frenzy. The object was briefly sighted approximately an hour later near
the back gate.

2. The next day, three depressions 1 1/2" deep and 7" in diameter were
found where the object had been sighted on the ground. The following
night (29 Dec 80) the area was checked for radiation. Beta/gamma readings
of 0.1 milliroentgens were recorded with peak readings in the three depressions and near the center of the triangle formed by the depressions.
A nearby tree had moderate (.05-.07) readings on the side of the tree
toward the depressions.

3. Later in the night a red sun-like light was seen through the trees.
It moved about and pulsed. At one point it appeared to throw off glowing
particles and then broke into five separate white objects and then disappeared. Immediately thereafter, three star-like objects were noticed
in the sky, two objects to the north and one to the south, all of which
were about 10° off the horizon. The objects moved rapidly in sharp angular
movements and displayed red, green and blue lights. The objects to the
north appeared to be elliptical through an 8-12 power lens. They then
turned to full circles. The objects to the north remained in the sky for
an hour or more. The object to the south was visible for two or three
hours and beamed down a stream of light from time to time. Numerous individuals, including the undersigned, witnessed the activities in paragraphs
2 and 3.

CHARLES I. HALT, Lt Col, USAF
Deputy Base Commander

Within days the USAF affirmed this to American ufologists and by June had released the official report submitted to the MoD by the deputy base commander, Colonel Charles Halt. This explained that the crashing object had left a gaping hole in the pine tree canopy (already described to us by a forestry worker who had found it a few days later) and three indentations in a triangle formation where the legs of the landed object had been. Radiation of two to three times the normal background count was recorded here. As these marks were being explored by base personnel, further UFOs returned and were seen by many officers including Halt. It was astonishing testament.

Despite further denials, the tape made during this site investigation was released a year later direct to British researchers. It told how photographs and samples were taken (none of which has ever been released) and how during the second encounter beams of light had been fired from the UFO towards the airmen as they chased it through the woods. At the end their voices broke up in terror and they headed back towards the base.

Much later, on interviewing some of those involved in the tape (who had been reluctant to talk until the story went public), it became clear that there was time missing from their full recall. At least one man may even have been abducted.

The sceptics allege that the UFO was a meteor, that the object in the forest the Orford Ness lighthouse beam, and that the physical traces were left by scratching rabbits. Most ufologists and all the witnesses find this idea absurd.

A 1993 documentary about the UFO cover up and the Rendlesham Forest case was made by SKY TV. This programme, No Defence Significance, *scored ratings so high that it beat many popular dramas such as* LA Law.

—— 24 ——

DEADLY RENDEZVOUS

Some cases seem to indicate that UFOs can seriously damage your health. A number of incidents have occurred, after which the witness is left with clear physical ailments. Such cases seem to provide strong evidence of UFO reality. Few were better in this respect, or received a bigger public profile, than the Cash/Landrum encounter.

Restaurant owner Betty Cash heard that a competitor was opening up in her area, so on the night of 29 December 1980 she decided to check them out. With Betty was her friend and senior staff member, Vickie Landrum, who brought along her seven-year-old grandson, Colby. They were driving towards Dayton, Texas, through a pine forest at around 9pm when they noticed a fiery object in the sky. It quickly descended to treetop height and hovered menacingly over the road ahead, forcing the car to a halt just 135 feet away.

Descriptions varied. Betty described it as a very bright light with no distinct shape, but her friend thought it was elongated with a rounded top and pointed lower half. Colby went one step further and said it was diamond-shaped. The witnesses climbed out of the car for a better look, even though they were very afraid. Bursts of flame, accompanied by sounds similar to a flame thrower, jetted down from beneath the object. There was also a roaring and bleeping noise that lasted throughout the encounter.

The whole thing was too much for the little boy, who pleaded with the women to get back in the car with him. He was very distressed, so Vickie got inside with him. Betty remained looking at the object for a little longer. When she took hold of the door handle, it was so hot it was difficult to grasp. The heat from the UFO was fierce and burned her wedding ring into her finger. Inside the car the little boy was hysterical and his grandmother thought it was the end of the world.

The object began to move off and the witnesses decided to follow it. As they did so they noticed around twenty-three twin-rotor helicopters, later identified as Chinooks, which were following the object. The helicopters never got closer than three-quarters of a mile. After stopping a few more times to observe the spectacle, the two women and the child went home. Betty arrived at 9.50pm after dropping the other two off.

Radiation symptoms and cancer

Within hours horrific symptoms similar to radiation poisoning manifested in all three of them. Young Colby suffered 'sunburn' on his face and eye inflammation. His grandmother also had inflammation of the eyes, plus some odd indentations across her fingernails and temporary hair loss. Betty, who had been exposed longest, suffered the most.

In the first four days she complained of blinding headaches, nausea, vomiting and diarrhoea. She also experienced neck pains, swollen eyes and blisters on her scalp, which burst releasing a clear liquid. At the end of this period she was admitted to Parkway General Hospital in Houston as a burn victim. Specialists who were called in to examine her were unable to diagnose her complaints. After leaving hospital she soon returned, as she was no better: now her hair was falling out in clumps. In just two months her medical bill amounted to $10,000. But that was not all. Betty developed breast cancer and was forced to have a mastectomy.

The photographs released by MUFON showing the extent of the injuries are shocking. There is absolutely no doubt that the women and the little boy were confronted by something which resembled nothing within the framework of their previous experience. It was unrecognisable as an aircraft, or as a permutation of any conventional terrestrial flying machine. When the victims of this potentially lethal object learned that the American government did not recognise the UFO phenomenon (at least publicly), they decided that the object which had caused them so much physical damage must belong to that government and decided to sue for $20 million.

The case dragged on for several years in the US District Court in Houston. During this time the story generated numerous newspaper articles and television documentaries. Incredibly, despite its high profile in America, the case was totally ignored by the British media.

In court were representatives of NASA, the Air Force, Army and Navy. The judge dismissed the case in August 1986 on the grounds

Incidents like the Cash/Landrum affair and Michalak's encounter illustrate the deadly potential of the phenomenon. There is a growing body of cases in which victims are damaged psychologically and physically, perhaps even killed. If abductions also turn out to be real, we are looking at a phenomenon which controls, takes, abuses and damages humans without conscience or regret. Angelic beings from outer space these are not...

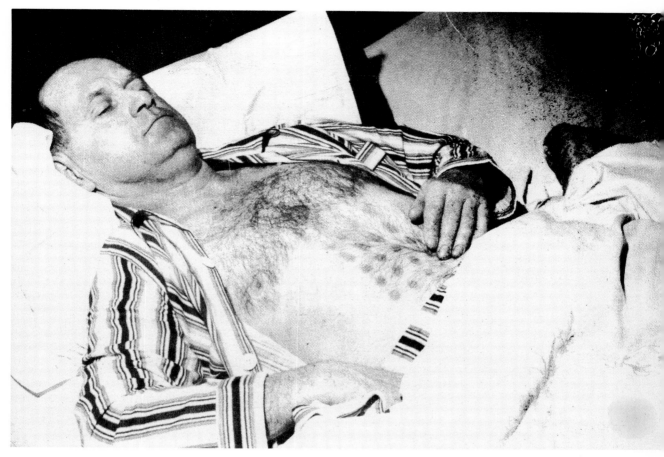

that no such device was owned, operated or listed by any branch of the American government. The case was investigated in their part-time capacities as UFO researchers by NASA scientists John Shuessler and Dr Alan Holt. Schuessler told British ufologist Timothy Good: 'Judge Ross Sterling considered the expert testimony to be sufficient reason to dismiss the case. That means he will not meet Betty Cash, Vickie and Colby Landrum, and he will not hear evidence they wanted their attorneys to present.' Schuessler also pointed out that the evidence regarding the helicopters was virtually ignored. Despite the statements of additional witnesses in the area, no agency would accept liability for the Chinooks!

What are we to conclude about this? Is it significant that the encounter occurred at about the same time events were unfolding across the Atlantic in Rendlesham Forest? Was it a cover-up of some very sensitive prototype vehicle? Rumours abounded that the object was an

This photograph remains one of the best examples of injury caused by a UFO. Canadian prospector Steve Michalak was in a remote location near Falcon Lake, Ontario, in May 1967 when he says that he inspected a landed UFO. This let out a blast of hot air which burnt a checker pattern into his skin. Michalak was treated in hospital and his story is one of the most graphic pieces of physical evidence for the reality of UFOs.

experimental nuclear-powered space shuttle which was experiencing difficulties, or that it was a retrieved alien craft which was being test-flown. It is now several years since the incident happened. If it was a new fledgeling Earth technology, why have we seen nothing more of it? Surely it would have been refined by now?

The military helicopters provide a new twist to an old dilemma. There is a painting of a man swimming in the sea. He has one arm outstretched to attract the attention of people on the beach. The title of the picture is *Drowning not Waving*. On that night of 29 December, were the helicopters 'Escorting not Chasing' or 'Chasing not Escorting'? Either way, three victims bear the physical and mental scars which prove they were escorting, or chasing, *something*.

——25——

ABDUCTION MANIA

Abduction mania was rife by 1982.

By the early 1980s there had been over a hundred cases of alleged alien abduction and a pattern was forming. To some extent that was because 90 per cent of these cases were from the USA and so were very consistent in outline.

Overseas there were far fewer cases. Many countries, such as Australia, had had none at all even by the mid-1980s. In places like Britain the trend was different from the USA. The entities tended to be tall, blond-haired, and blue-eyed – similar to those relatively friendly Nordics which featured in non-abduction cases from Europe throughout the 1950s.

However, this discrepancy went largely unnoticed, as did other patterns that were turning up. In the Far East, for instance Malaysia, entities were only a few inches in height, while South America had a plethora of cases where the aliens were said to be dwarf-like and covered in hair.

The American experience

Ufologists readily ignored this, because the American abduction cases received most publicity. All the movies made about the subject were based on American cases, and it was in the USA that most of the serious abduction research was being conducted. This created an illusion that the type of abduction story emerging from America was identical with what was occurring worldwide. It was not, although there were broad similarities in the scenario reported.

A typical American abduction case would involve a witness (usually alone, although occasionally as part of a couple or rarer still in a family group) who was driving on a lonely road late at night when a strange light was spotted in the sky. There were problems with their engine or lights, and they may then have heard odd noises or felt peculiar sensations in their mind. Then they would 'come to' at a different location and suddenly discover that a period of time (perhaps fifteen minutes, or even up to a couple of hours) had simply vanished from their recall.

During the course of days and weeks dreams or flashback images might hint to the witness about a hidden memory of alien contact. A ufologist would probably suggest they underwent regression hypnosis, using the methods already explored through the Hills' 1961 encounter and various successors.

This hypnosis almost always uncovered 'memories', or rather what were interpreted to be memories by the investigator (and therefore the witness). A story of an apparent abduction by strange creatures crystallised. This tended to involve a medical examination, increasing claims that genetic samples such as blood and tissue were being taken, and other common patterns such as being shown three-dimensional films about the fate of the Earth.

Of course, almost all of these features of the American abductions had already been well publicised after the emergence of the Hills case in 1966. The aliens were a slightly evolved variant of a four-feet-tall figure with a large domed head, pasty skin and huge dark eyes – a type known as the Greys.

A little-known film gem touches on UFO abductions and focuses on the military response to UFO activity. The Disappearance of Flight 419 is arguably the most intelligent film drama about UFOs yet made.

Sprinkle and Hopkins

The first abduction researcher was psychologist Dr Leo Sprinkle, who carried out the hypnosis on officer Herb Schirmer for Condon's team at the University of Colorado in 1968. Sprinkle was ensnared by the phenomenon and has conducted many experiments. He was reaching intriguing conclusions.

He hosts annual gatherings of abductees and feels they are somehow undergoing a spiritual progression. The ethos of the cases that he was uncovering was very positive, as if aliens were giving us a hand up the ladder of evolution. Many witnesses had psychic backgrounds, experienced other strange phenomena and took an active interest in the environment.

Budd Hopkins followed in Sprinkle's footsteps. He was neither a scientist nor a psychologist – in fact a celebrated New York artist. Unlike Sprinkle he went public in a very big way. His first book, summarising a dozen cases from 1975 onwards, was entitled *Missing*

Time. It appeared from a small publisher in 1982 and had minimal impact outside the UFO world; but within ufology, especially in the USA, its effect was tremendous.

The problems of hypnosis

Hopkins worked with a psychologist at first but has since done his own regressions; some people have been critical of this because he lacks a medical background. In 1982 the British UFO Research Association imposed a code of practice on all members, banning hypnosis without medical supervision, and in 1987 it introduced a voluntary moratorium on all use. It never received any credit from the sceptics for this act, even though they were vociferous about the abuse of hypnosis as a tool in abduction research.

The problem with hypnosis was recognised by Dr Benjamin Simon, who had first used it within ufology on Betty and Barney Hill. He showed that it was not 'a royal road to truth' but could reveal fantasy as easily as hidden memory. Experiments by countless psychologists (and some work since in UFO situations) have readily proven that about 50 per cent of checkable 'facts' retrieved from regression hypnosis are imagination: they never really happened. Witnesses can be subtly coerced into thinking something is a memory when it was implanted by suggestion under hypnosis in an unconscious way. Because of this, hypnosis is rarely used in criminal prosecutions.

Alien contact is a subject for which you can never check the facts since nobody knows what they are! So the value of hypnosis is diminished further. At least one sincere abductee (police officer Alan Godfrey, abducted in Todmorden in West Yorkshire in November 1980) has admitted that, whilst he did see a real UFO, his subsequent alien kidnap story retold under hypnosis is, he feels, far less reliable. It could be a fantasy based on books he had read. This kind of contamination is so serious that hypnosis cannot be trusted.

Hopkins is undoubtedly sincere and widely considered to be a researcher with the best of motives, keen to assist witnesses who approach him, but there are some who have expressed concern about his use of regression hypnosis, particularly given his lack of medical background. Hypnotic regression back to alien abduction is a deeply contentious issue. Some people feel that we must draw back from what can fairly be termed an 'abduction mania' that has swept through much of world ufology since the early 1980s.

Clearly something puzzling is going on in these cases. The question is whether widespread hypnosis illuminates the way towards a solution or shrouds the evidence in a blanket of fog.

Budd Hopkins's second book was published in 1987, by which time he was well known through the media and as a lecturer around the world. This book, *Intruders*, had huge sales and discussed one particular case from Indiana. A TV mini-series based upon it was made in 1992 and has been shown all over the world, ensuring that the American stereotype image is deeply engrained in the minds of billions. It has gradually killed off nearly all other variants on the theme.

The 'goodies' and the 'baddies'

It is interesting that Hopkins's witnesses more frequently report 'Greys' than do Sprinkle's. The pattern of medical examination and genetic adaptation is there, but his cases are generally more terrifying. He claims to find little sign of psychic overlap and his witnesses seem more like victims with negative after-effects. They have been likened by psychologists to women who have been raped, with similar post-traumatic stress symptoms. The scenario that emerges from Hopkins's cases is of a group of alien scientists involved in a secret invasion and out to create some kind of genetic hybrid baby via their (mostly female) crop of abused abductees.

The comparison between these two sub-groups of data can be likened in fiction to a 'war of the worlds' scenario (Hopkins) versus the far more pleasant theme of Spielberg's 'close encounters of the third kind' (in Sprinkle's cases). Since Hopkins's version has had far more media attention in the past decade, it has become almost irrepressibly dominant worldwide.

However, these differences cannot be ignored. The fact that since 1987, when Greys were popularised on a global scale by people like Hopkins and Strieber, the data outside the USA has adapted to this pattern is clear evidence of a human dimension behind the reports. The way in which the form and behaviour of the entities previously tied in with the culture from which they emerged was another clue, as was cultural tracking – meaning that cases never display technology in advance of our own, but just at the very edge of it.

American abductees see domineering scientists who want to change the world to conform with their own concept of it. South Americans encounter mythological figures who are hirsute and aggressive. British and other European witnesses have tended to meet genteel, civilised but rather wishy-washy aliens who seemed afraid to do too much because it might upset the universal balance.

It was left to non-American abduction researchers to point out such problems. In 1980, before Australia was swamped with a run of 'Grey' abductions, Keith Basterfield published a book entitled *UFOs: The Image Hypothesis*, suggesting a psychological theory that did not dent American ufology. He proposed that the experiences were a form of vivid and unusual hallucination. Later he worked with psychologist

Fate magazine 1992. This special issue on UFO abduction shows the modern abduction mania.

Dr Robert Bartholomew to pioneer the concept that witnesses to abductions were what are called 'fantasy-prone personalities' – a small section of humanity known to possess such vivid fantasy lives that they find it hard to distinguish some of their imaginative memories from real ones. This theory is in retreat, but it was important that such a concept should be tested by ufologists.

In 1988 Jenny Randles published a book entitled *Abduction* which had minimal impact in the USA. It pointed out the human dimension to the abduction, the psychic overlap, the way in which witnesses were being found to have a high level of visual creativity and the need to seek a solution that explained all such aspects of the mystery as well – not just the domineering but rather one-dimensional approach of American research.

Almost no alien abductions are known from India, Japan and other eastern countries. Nobody knows why.

Some feel that positive and negative outcomes can occur, and the rather hackneyed format of the 'little grey scientists performing medical experiments' is a direct result of this evaluation being imposed upon the data by ufologists, notably in the USA. In other cultures where that is less prevalent witnesses evaluate their experiences differently and tend to have other (often more user-friendly) types of spacenapping encounters.

A beacon of hope also emerged from folklore researcher Dr Eddie Bullard at Indiana State University. He attempted to establish that the abduction was a modern mythology by comparing it with the genesis of folk tales throughout history. He failed to prove this and believes there is an underlying reality to these cases. But he did stress the importance of the anomalous findings and conducted a major study of eight hundred abduction cases that were available by 1992. This finally persuaded some elements of the American UFO movement that the situation was a lot more complex than it might seem.

Also in 1992 psychologist Dr Kenneth Ring from the University of Connecticut discovered the human side to the abduction mystery. He had been a leading expert in the NDE (near death experience), where people on the verge of death but who survive to tell the tale were frequently reporting vividly real visions. These included bright lights, abduction into a strange world and contact with entities. The comparisons with alien abduction had already been spotted by some ufologists, but Ring used his influence in a major comparative study of the psychological profile of each group. His conclusions appeared in *The Omega Project* and proposed that both NDE and abduction were part of a spiritual puberty through which some 'advanced' members of the human race were passing. Whether his theory eventually proves any more valuable than the simplistic view of alien spacenappings, Ring has again emphasised the work of non-American ufologists for the American audience and may have ensured that more sophisticated work will continue in the future.

The alien abduction phenomenon is a deeply mystifying experience. It may not even relate to the UFO phenomenon in its basic form at all – except by the modern cultural inference that it must do. It shows many differences from simple lights in the sky. These may well be physically real, even if spacenappings are 'only' phenomena of an inner space reality.

CIRCULAR REASONING

*In July 1983 a dramatic
five-pattern crop circle
appeared.*

Although alien abductions dominated ufology in the USA during the 1980s, another issue was to the fore in Europe, especially in Britain.

Flattened crops

In August 1980 a farmer at Westbury in Wiltshire discovered three swathes of gently flattened oat crop on his land. They formed circles about sixty feet across, with neat swirled centres and edges still standing erect. It looked as if something had descended from the skies and squashed the field: the resemblance to a UFO was obvious. The area was inspected by ufologists, including Ian Mrzyglod from the group Probe. Then the farmer harvested the fields and the mystery was over.

Mrzyglod and his team checked the matter sensibly. After consulting physicist Dr Terence Meaden, a specialist in wind damage from tornadoes, they concluded that the circles were probably the result of an unusual type of rotating air vortex called a 'fairweather stationary whirlwind'.

Sporadic circles appeared in 1981 and 1982 at other locations in Hampshire and Wiltshire. Reports in the *Journal of Meteorology* dismissed the idea of a spaceship which was being voiced by some ufologists.

Then, in July 1983, everything changed. Suddenly a dramatic five-pattern formation appeared – with a central circle and four satellites. It looked blatantly artificial, but Dr Meaden sought the cause in more complicated air vortices. Further examples appeared during the next few days as public interest grew.

The weather theory falls down

Ufologist Pat Delgado took the story to the media, stressing the idea that an intelligence (presumably alien of some sort) might be producing the marks for unknown reasons. Immediately a new subject was born. The weather theory, which worked well for simple circles, looked feeble in the face of these 'quintuplets' and the media revelled in the silly season story that they were handed, linking the marks with the popular movie *ET* which was then on release.

Delgado later joined forces with another newcomer, Colin Andrews, and wrote pieces for *Flying Saucer Review* magazine which sought evidence to support such ideas. Each summer brought new formations and increasing numbers via aerial surveillance, usually focused on southern England. Rings appeared around circles, then double and triple rings. The image of someone having a joke at the expense of the eager media and growing band of circle watchers (many of them former ufologists) is obvious in hindsight.

Some ufologists gave strong support to Meaden's weather theory for the simpler patterns but began to uncover a trend of hoaxing. Mrzyglod exposed the first, in August 1983, when a national newspaper paid for the creation of a quintuplet to try to fool a rival paper. This was never reported, as the media had soon lost interest. A real mystery was left in people's minds.

By the end of the decade the crop circle mystery was an internationally recognised phenomena with tourists flocking from all over the world to see the latest formations in southern England. Complex formations such as this co-called 'pictogram' began in 1989 and enterprising farmers charged entrance fees for people to walk inside them. This is a famous pattern found at Alton Barnes, Wiltshire in July 1990.

Cerealogical celebrities

In 1989 Andrews and Delgado, with the help of pilot 'Busty' Taylor, produced a book full of spectacular aerial photographs. *Circular Evidence* played on the mystery, adding many side-issue stories (from dogs getting sick inside circles to aircraft crashing in nearby fields long after the circles were harvested). This, plus the undoubtedly challenging visual enigma which was there for all to go and see each summer, ensured that their clarion call for circle research became a bestseller.

The two men were now celebrities in their own new field, soon christened cerealogy: it spawned three magazines and countless societies. Meaden produced *The Circles Effect and Its Mysteries*, a scientific text which he published himself. Only a few took seriously his theory that the weather could explain virtually everything, including the increasingly complex circular formations.

Hoaxes

Ufologists Jenny Randles and Paul Fuller self-published their own thesis, the only book to explain the social background and take hoaxing seriously. It suggested that Meaden's vortex was creating some circles and hoaxes others, notably the more recent weird shapes. But it still undersold the importance of hoaxing, which nobody had recognised.

The circles changed in direct response. From 1990 they became pictograms – with arcs, straight lines and geometric shapes emphasising that they were the product of an intelligence. In 1990 numbers rose to over five hundred and formed all over Europe, with resultant increased media attention.

Meaden still tried to fit his weather theory into the by now absurd array of patterns. Andrews, Delgado and other rising stars of the circle world were delighted by the pictograms, which to them proved their case.

For most cerealogists the new marks were proof that someone was conveying a message. Fascinated Americans would arrive in Europe each summer and buy fields where they would carve out symbols and await replies in the crop. In 1993 they claim to have got an answer – the sign for a disabled toilet! Another team armed with lasers tried to initiate contact with the circle makers. One UFO group even claimed a success, with aliens who gave – via automatic writing (words transmitted through the mind of a medium directly on to paper using the medium's hand and a pen) – a self-portrait as a kind of invisible dentist's drill!

The ridiculous level to which the phenomenon had descended was shown through smiling faces, whales, dolphins, flowers and so on – clear frauds turning up in many fields. There was even a message in English saying: 'We are not alone.' Randles and Fuller realised that if this was from an alien visitor it should have said '*You* are not alone'!

Paul Fuller issued a warning in a new magazine of hard-hitting investigation, *The Crop Watcher* and in a further book written with Jenny Randles, *Crop Circles: A Mystery Solved*, both of which appeared in 1990. They were slammed by the cerealogists, but their timely words predicted the coming pictograms, emphasised the need to take hoaxing seriously and pointed out 'name games' being played by what were now clearly human tricksters jousting annually with the cerealogists. But the warnings went unheeded. Circles turned up near Fakenham in Suffolk and nobody batted an eyelid!

More than 25 groups of crop circle hoaxers have admitted to their escapades in English crop fields between 1976 and 1994. Some hoaxers have odd code names – like 'Bill Barley' and 'Spiderman'.

The fraudsters come forward

The come-uppance was inevitable. In September 1991 two elderly artists, Doug Bower and Dave Chorley, came forward to claim that they had faked hundreds of circles. After the ones at Westbury had been reported, in 1980, they had constantly elaborated their designs to try to egg the researchers on. The pictograms were expressly designed to kill off Meaden's weather theory, which was getting too much serious exposure for their liking. By 1991 thousands of circles had appeared; Doug and Dave professed to have made about 10 per cent of them and to have largely manipulated people's belief in the mystery.

Doug and Dave approached *Today*, a tabloid newspaper, and faked a circle under journalists' supervision. The unwitting Pat Delgado pronounced it genuine; only later was he told the shocking truth. At first he accepted that the game was up, but after talking with Colin Andrews changed his mind. Thousands of cerealogists breathed more easily. Soon afterwards the partnership split and Andrews moved to the USA, where he was in constant demand to lecture.

Doug and Dave were largely ignored by the cerealogists, despite their evidence. They possessed photographs of earlier circles which they had faked and nobody else had filmed. They said they had signed the last few before 'retirement' in 1991 with big letter 'D's. There were indeed many examples that seemed to support this.

A few small circle groups gave up altogether after *Today*'s exposure, but most fought on as if nothing had happened. A bizarre series of stories were published in the specialist literature, intimating that Doug and Dave were pawns in some secret operation by the British government, out to discredit cerealogy and leave Whitehall free to do their

One of the photographs from *Today*, showing how Doug Bower and Dave Chorley made their circles.

own research. We find this suggestion absurd – although it has helped cerealogy to ride the storm into the 1990s. But the media attention has gone and, indeed, only a fraction of the circles that used to appear every summer are now found.

Some truth in the matter

Crop Watcher magazine quickly accepted Doug and Dave's story after they examined it; this was in fact easy, as they had stressed hoaxing for some time. However, they do believe that a few simple circles are (and always have been) the result of an atmospheric effect which can also trigger UFOs.

There is good evidence for this. Crop circles have been traced back in scientific journals and through other data to long before Doug and Dave were born. There are even folk tales from the Middle Ages which may relate to them. Single circles swirled into crops have appeared all over the world on a sporadic but regular basis.

Ironically, on the day Doug and Dave were telling the world of their

Crop circles came to world attention during the 1980s but they may not be an entirely new phenomenon. Reports of them have been traced back into previous centuries and this woodcut dating from August 1678 seems to suggest that they may have existed in the Middle Ages, where they were interpreted as the work of 'mowing devils'.

spoof Jenny Randles was in the Queensland bush in Australia investigating a reed swamp near Tully. It was a circle which formed here in January 1966 that was, the two admit, the trigger for their trickery. But they did not hoax the original. It formed in a remote area infested with deadly snakes and aboriginal legends tell of strange lights seen here. Many circles have repeatedly formed locally. Other photographs that pre-date the first hoax by Doug and Dave have also been traced.

Randles and Fuller updated their book in 1993, reviewing all of this evidence and including laboratory experiments by physicists in the USA and Japan who were re-creating the circle-making force. It seems, after all, that a real phenomenon may have been behind a few circles amidst the many hoaxes.

WHITLEY STRIEBER – A BREACH IN REALITY?

One of the most controversial and acrimonious abduction cases involved best-selling horror novelist Whitley Strieber, who wrote two books on the affair. The first, *Communion*, was published in 1987, followed by *Transformation* a year later. According to the author, the watershed event occurred over Christmas 1985. The Striebers had an apartment in New York and a 'cabin' in the woods in an isolated part of the state, which was where the main events occurred.

Christmas visitors

On 26 December Whitley and his wife, Anne, went to bed at ten o'clock; their six-year-old son had gone much earlier. In the middle of the night Strieber was woken by a whooshing, whirling noise coming from downstairs. There seemed to be several people moving about. He checked the burglar alarm panel beside the bed, but no door or window had been breached. A short time later the bedroom door opened and a figure entered the room.

The creature was wearing a sort of breastplate and a skirt which came down to its knees. As the being rushed towards him, Strieber blacked out. He then remembers being carried, or floating, naked through the woods. After a further loss of consciousness he found himself sitting in a depression, paralysed, with his eyesight not functioning properly. Opposite him was one of the creatures, wearing some sort of face mask, and beside him, doing something to his head, was another. This one seemed feminine in some indefinable way, and wore dark blue overalls. Then the treetops rushed away beneath him and he was on the grey floor of a 'messy' domed room with a 'lens' at its apex.

Medical experiments

Strieber became terrified as several of the small beings moved about him. The terror was well founded. One of them produced a long, thin needle from a box and 'told' him they were about to insert it into his brain, via his nasal cavity. He argued, but they went ahead and did it anyway. Altogether there were four types. The one in his bedroom had seemed robot-like, while the main group were short and stocky, with deep-set glittering eyes and pug noses. Inside the 'room' he had seen some five-foot-tall creatures with large, almond-shaped black eyes, and a smaller one with round button eyes. The last thing he could recollect about the experience was a feeling of anger as they inserted a long triangular object up his rectum.

When he awoke as normal on the 27th, he had a feeling of unease and a bizarre memory of seeing a barn owl staring at him through the window during the night. Of the abduction he remembered nothing. Yet when he looked for claw marks in the snow on the window ledge there was nothing. Strieber was later to come to the conclusion that the owl was a 'screen memory' to hide what really happened.

Author and abductee, Whitley Strieber.

The terrible aftermath

He then went through a downward personality change. As vague, disturbing images pierced the screen memory, and inexplicable physical symptoms emerged, he believed something awful had happened. He turned to a Christmas present from his brother – *Science and the UFOs* by Jenny Randles and Peter Warrington – and found similarities between their description of an archetypal abduction and his own experiences. In fact the similarities were so close that Strieber says he was 'shocked'.

After discovering that a number of UFO sightings had taken place in the area of the cabin Strieber contacted Budd Hopkins, an American ufologist who uses hypnosis extensively to aid recall. Hopkins prompted him to remember vague details of a previous incident in the cabin. That had occurred on 4 October 1985, when the family had entertained Jacques Sandulescu and Annie Gottlieb as weekend guests.

Strieber remembered an intense light surrounding the cabin during the night, which made him think the roof was on fire. A loud 'bang' had woken them all up. A week later Strieber had a 'memory' of a huge crystal hovering over the cabin, glowing with blue light.

After seeing Hopkins, he phoned up his friends and asked them if they remembered the night in the cabin. Jacques vividly remembered the light. His watch had said it was four-thirty, but the trees and bushes had been lit up as if it was ten in the morning. More disturbing were the recollections of his son. He had suffered a 'dream' where a group of 'little doctors' had taken him outside and put him on a bed. When he grew afraid, they repeated over and over in his head: 'We won't hurt you . . .'

What followed for Strieber were terrible dreams and stress that almost destroyed his marriage. Finally he went to see Dr Donald Klein of the New York State Psychiatric Institute, wondering if he was insane.

Further abduction memories

Next came hypnotic regression which added details to the October and December incidents, but also uncovered another dimension in the process. Apparently the twelve-year-old Whitley, together with his father and sister, had been abducted from a train in 1957! This led him on a trail of investigation into his own past, which uncovered several other anomalous experiences, remembered in part by childhood friends. There were strange memories of seeing wild animals, which he became convinced were camouflage for terrible experiences. The experiences continued beyond the 1985 Christmas watershed.

Whitley Strieber published his account of events up to 1987 in *Communion*, a title allegedly communicated to him by his wife, speaking in a strange voice whilst in a deep sleep. The book had several immediate effects – it became an international bestseller, precipitated a flood of correspondents who thought they too had been assaulted by 'visitors', and attracted a furious backlash by critics from within the UFO community and outside it. Some of the more extreme sceptics were Strieber's former colleagues in the science fiction and horror genres. Strieber is a major horror *fiction* writer. Although he reported this story as horror *non*-fiction, many of his peers were confused and presumed it was another *Amityville* hoax, a nub of truth embellished to make a better story. Strieber flatly denied this charge.

Dr Klein suggested to Strieber that his experiences might be due to an abnormality in the temporal lobe of his brain. Sufferers often exhibit a lack of humour, report strong smells, and experience vivid hallucinatory journeys and unexplained panic. Strieber underwent tests by two different neurologists. According to him, neither could find evidence of brain abnormality. If indeed there are witnesses to parts, or some, of the experiences, then 'hallucinations' was an untenable explanation anyway.

Strieber subjected himself to some painful laboratory tests and reportedly came out with a clean bill of health. Indeed, Donald Klein provided him with a statement for use in *Communion* which said that 'he is not suffering from a psychosis'. But UFO debunker Philip Klass takes issue with this in his book *UFO Abductions – a Dangerous Game*. Klass states that there is some confusion in the dates provided by Strieber of when the tests took place. In Appendix One of *Transformation*, Strieber states that all the medical findings have been turned over to a Dr John Gliedman. He has been given permission to discuss these findings with enquirers who have proper medical and scientific credentials. Klass has tried, however, to obtain Strieber's permission for access to the complete records, but has so far failed. This is perhaps not surprising, as Strieber might fear that Klass would use the material selectively, to bolster his anti-abduction stance.

An illustration from *Communion* as seen by Whitley Strieber.

Beyond *Communion*

Transformation takes us beyond *Communion*, chronologically and in terms of credulity. While researchers in the field are used to dealing with extreme material, to outsiders and critics this must have seemed 'beyond the boggle threshold'. Here the 'visitors' were woven in with dream material and the very worst nightmares of horror writer H.P. Lovecraft. The visitors began to look less like extraterrestrials and more

Communion was later made into a film. Strieber had a hand in its production, and Christopher Walken played the part of the abductee.

like the ghouls and succubi of demonology. This was no longer the straightforward abduction of a human being for experimentation aboard a spacecraft, but a twisted journey through the subterranean dimensions of inner space. More than ever, the edges of the fact/fiction interface were blurring.

Lecturing on the British Empire

One of the strangest events happened on 1 April. Strieber 'woke up' walking along a corridor with a tingling sensation going through his body. He was being led by two small dark blue beings, and he was dressed in a long flowing garment made of paper. The corridor was the colour of flesh. When Strieber commented to the creatures about their colour, one of them replied: 'We used to be like your blacks but we decided this was better.'

The corridor was lined along one wall with drawers. Strieber felt it was a beautiful place, and wondered if in some way it was alive: 'The *place* seemed conscious. Was I actually inside some kind of creature?' He was then led into a room with louvred windows, 'something like a round version of a regimental dining room from the days of the British Raj in India'. The place was filled with translucent white beings who seemed to be in pain. Their leader led Strieber to the centre of the room where he was asked to give a lecture on why the British Empire had collapsed! He complied, but his efforts met with sarcasm and 'cold indifference'.

Out in the corridor again, one of the blue beings pulled open one of the many drawers. It was full of alien bodies wrapped in cellophane. Strieber admits: 'I would be the first to agree that my perceptions may not reflect the objective reality of the experience.'

Dancing inside others

Similar weird experiences are claimed by Strieber later in the book. He remembers a strange journey on an 'aircraft' in 1968. During the turbulent flight, 'a nurse or stewardess' administered some medicine for nausea on his tongue from an eye dropper, and a blonde-haired passenger next to him 'read aloud from a book made of limp cloth'. At his destination he was met off the craft by several of the small entities.

He was in a desert and transported to an oasis. One of the entities showed him a tumbledown building, which was apparently some sort of university. At first a more fearsome alien refused him entry, saying that Strieber 'was not ready yet'. But the being went, and they entered anyway. Once again he was in a corridor, then he was taken into a room where he began to dance. 'When I danced I found myself for moments inside other people and their lives.' Later he met two khaki-uniformed 'Americans', one of whom was using a ciné camera apparently to film Strieber.

In another episode he was transported to a stone room, where a man was shackled on to a stone table and then whipped. This, he was informed, was punishment for failing to get Strieber 'to obey'. As the man was beaten to death, the entity told Strieber: 'It isn't real, Whitty, it isn't real.'

Problems of analysis

Transformation goes much further than *Communion*. If abduction by alien beings aboard a UFO was hard enough for some critics to swallow, then this was sure to stick in the throat. There are other things, too: apocalyptic visions, levitation, out-of-the-body experiences, disembodied voices and other poltergeist activities.

Strieber is a successful and commercially viable writer. However, his experiences seem essentially visionary and do not seem to be literally true, or, for much of the time, objectively true. This is a point that Strieber himself appreciates. If there really is no evidence of mental illness – a problem he confronts again and again – then either the experiences are a product of some higher self, or they really do originate from an outside source.

But there is a problem in this explanation, too. Strieber lists the names of witnesses who have, to a lesser degree, taken part in his experiences. One of the latest incidents took place in his forest cabin, where, allegedly, some journalists were present. Apparently the front door flew open and two of the journalists became paralysed. They watched in horror as several of the small entities came into the room and lifted up a bed containing a third person.

Strieber himself changes his mind a lot regarding the source of his experiences, and concludes that they are both subjective and objective – an objective source that can manifest to the percipient subjectively. Strieber has made some challenging and wonderful remarks. In *Transformation*, he came up with this speculation: 'I think that they must normally exist in some other state of being and that they use bodies to enter our reality as we use scuba gear to penetrate the depths of the sea.'

In a late night discussion programme called *After Dark*, broadcast on Channel 4 early in 1990, he said: 'It's the same experience described by

St Paul, except I was visited by aliens. It is the same net effect – a mechanism that seeks to control and bring about change ... I have experienced a breach in reality.'

— 28 —

INCIDENT ON ILKLEY MOOR

In December 1987 a former policeman was apparently abducted by alien entities on the Moor.

The apparent abduction by entities of a former policeman on Ilkley Moor in Yorkshire allegedly occurred on 1 December 1987. It is one of the most contentious abduction cases in Britain – due, oddly, to a photograph which the man took of one of the beings. Documentary evidence should have made the case more acceptable to the UFO community, but the reverse happened. It is ironic that the incident would have been readily embraced into the body of abduction literature if there had been no picture. The case, investigated and examined in depth by the authors, is vastly complex, and there is only room for an outline here.

Two lost hours

The victim, referred to as 'Philip Spencer', left Ilkley just after 7.10am to walk across the moor and visit his father-in-law who lived in a village on the far side. He took with him a compass, for safety reasons, and a camera, which he intended using for taking pictures of Ilkley town from the moor tops.

He passed the White Wells baths, which is now a museum, and made his way along a stand of trees up over a ridge into a small overgrown quarry. A movement caught his attention, and he turned to see a small 'green creature'. It scuttled away, then stopped, and made a dismissive movement with its right hand. It is at this moment that Spencer took the photograph.

The creature disappeared around an outcrop, and Spencer gave chase. When he arrived there, however, the entity had gone, and he was confronted with a hovering silver disc with a box-like object sliding into the domed top. In a split second it rose at a terrific speed and dis-

Enlargement of the 4′ 6″ entity a former police officer claims to have photographed on Ilkley Moor in December 1987.

appeared into cloud. Bewildered, Spencer returned to Ilkley instead of continuing his walk, and there discovered a discrepancy of almost two hours.

The negative was examined by several photographic experts, and computer image enhancement was attempted by Geoffrey Crawley of the *British Journal of Photography*. The shot was slightly under-exposed and blurred due to camera shake. All that Kodak could say with certainty was that the negative had not been interfered with.

Reversed magnetic fields

Spencer discovered a couple of days after the encounter that his compass was reversed. Instead of pointing north, the needle now pointed south. An electromagnetic field had reversed its polarity.

Peter Hough contacted the University of Manchester Institute of Science and Technology (UMIST), where Dr Edward Spooner, head of the Department of Electrical Engineering and Electronics, agreed to carry out some experiments with a similar compass. Hough and investigator Arthur Tomlinson spent the morning in Dr Spooner's laboratory; eventually he did succeed in reversing the compass. In his report, Spooner wrote: 'The intensity required is not great by some standards; in fact we could not produce a field sufficiently low as not to reverse the polarity of the needle. The minimum field we applied had a flux density of about 0.1 Tesla; this is still about 2000 times greater than the Earth's field.'

The tests had two ramifications. Reversal could be brought about using equipment found in the home or garage, but specialist knowledge was required and there was potential danger from electrocution and fire. Strong industrial magnets had no permanent effect on the compass, causing Dr Spooner to speculate that only a pulsed magnetic field would work. At a later date some new, more powerful magnets were obtained from Japan which did bring about a reversal. However, these were not obtainable outside the industry, and not available at all in 1987.

If an electromagnetic phenomenon connected with the flying object was responsible, it would also have left detectable magnetism in the surrounding rocks – assuming the change had been effected on the moors. Later 'evidence' indicated that it had happened 'elsewhere', thus making a magnetic survey of the location unnecessary.

Hough took a scientist from the Radiological Protection Service to the location. The area was tested for radiation and rocks were taken away for examination, but the results were negative.

Revelations under regression

Some months after the abduction, Spencer starting complaining that he was having dreams of a starry sky, and was concerned about the missing one hour and three-quarters. He wondered if hypnosis might help him remember. Journalist Matthew Hill contacted clinical psychologist Jim Singleton, who agreed to help. Singleton was amazed by the story which emerged during the subsequent hypnosis, although the UFO investigators present were not. It was a classic abduction scenario – although it did have one surprise. The much maligned photograph was taken at the *end* of the experience.

Under hypnosis, Spencer described being approached by the creature earlier in his walk, as he drew level with the trees. He became paralysed, then found himself levitated a few inches off the ground, following the being up the rise and over into the small quarry. There he

Ilkley Moor seems to be a hot bed of activity. Amongst other happenings, there is a strong rumour that another police officer suffered a UFO experience on the moor.

saw the hovering disc and an opening appeared in it. At this point everything went black, and he found himself in a white room. A voice told him over and over again not to be afraid.

Next he was 'put' on a table by several of the beings. A brightly lit horizontal tube then moved over the contours of his body and he closed his eyes. In this state he remarked that his 'nose feels uncomfortable'. Then he was allowed off the table and given a conducted tour of the 'craft'.

Through a 'window' he saw the Earth and realised he was in space. Next Spencer was taken into 'a big round room', where he described some sort of gyroscopic apparatus which provided the motive power for the craft. It was here that the compass and his camera, on straps around his neck, were pulled towards the centre of the room. Then he was in another room where he was shown two 'films'. The first depicted pollution flowing into rivers, scenes of mass destruction and people starving. It was communicated to him that the beings were very concerned about how we were treating our planet. Spencer would not discuss the second film, neither under hypnosis nor out of it. It was personal to him, and, as he told Jim Singleton: 'I'm not supposed to tell anybody about the film. It's not for them to know.'

Philip Spencer was then returned to the exact spot by the trees from where he was abducted. Under hypnosis he then related walking up the hill, seeing the creature and photographing it. His surprise at seeing the entity is remarkable, as he had described being in their company only seconds previously. The segment of 'missing' time has clearly defined edges.

While Spencer was still hypnotised Jim Singleton asked for a description of the beings. 'They're quite small, about four foot, with big pointed ears and big eyes. They're quite dark. They haven't got a nose and only a little mouth. Their hands are enormous, and their arms are long. They've got funny feet, like a V-shape, like two big toes. They've got three big fingers, like sausages. Big sausages.' Afterwards, Spencer told Hough that the skin of the creatures was rough-looking, and that he had seen no evidence of genitals.

Genuine or a hoax?

Did the incident really happen, or was it a complex hoax? There can be no grey area – no talk of subjectivity here – because the photograph puts paid to that argument.

On the picture, to the right of the figure, is a square-shaped blob.

Hough noticed this and realised it was in approximately the right place to correspond with the 'box' which disappeared into the roof of the disc. Was this further photographic evidence?

A year after the incident two Yorkshire investigators, Philip Mantle and Andy Roberts, visited the location and took site photographs. On one of them appeared the 'blob'. Although it was not as obvious as on the original, nevertheless there was no doubt that it was in exactly the same place. They told the authors: 'It would seem that the lighting conditions and the moisture content in the ground have to be exactly right for the phenomenon to appear.'

It was on the slope of the far bank. When they walked towards it, the illusion disappeared. This satisfied Andy Roberts that the whole thing was a hoax. In his opinion Spencer had noticed the blob in the picture and incorporated the idea of the box into his story, then waited for someone to notice it. This reasoning certainly makes sense, but what are the indicators that the affair might be genuine?

From the start, Philip Spencer was adamant that his true identity should never be revealed; it would ruin him socially and professionally, he said. Spencer has never sought to make any money from his story, even though it was on offer. The mainstay of hoaxers is to see their names in print and improve their finances in the process. The only scenario which would make sense is if Spencer was a front man for a group out to discredit the investigators at a later date. Six years on, no one has come forward.

Despite the reference by debunkers of 'little green men', there are hardly any cases where entities have been described as such. Does this validate, or invalidate the Ilkley case? It is interesting that the colour of the figure almost camouflages it into the background. Is this accident or design?

Further incidents

But there were two other major incidents that same year up on Ilkley Moor, neither of which had any publicity. One, incredibly, involved another police officer, who may also have experienced an abduction. The other, in the summer of 1987, involved a local couple driving home.

The Cow and Calf rocks are just a quarter of a mile from where Philip Spencer was abducted. This outcrop overhanging the moor has been the location for several sightings of strange lights. Researcher Paul Devereux believes that such phenomena are a natural earth energy connected with seismic stress. On this occasion, the middle-aged couple were on the Addingham road when they became aware of a mass of white lights hovering over the rocks. Mrs Robinson tried to rationalise the sighting and said to her husband: 'I don't remember there being a farmhouse up there?' Mr Robinson, a fireman, confirmed there was nothing near the rocks to account for the lights.

They continued home, and the lights were still apparent. Although they lived just two minutes drive from the location, the couple decided not to investigate, although Mr Robinson afterwards regretted this decision.

Do these additional experiences validate Philip Spencer? Sometimes motivations for hoaxing are far from clear. Critics have said that such a hoax could have been the result of an abnormal state of mind, although that does not accord with Jim Singleton's observations. Singleton stated that he found Philip to be of a sensitive disposition, and went on to say: 'He was certainly recounting the incident as something which had actually happened. He described things typically as someone would recall a past event. He compares very well with other non-UFO subjects.' While accepting that people under hypnosis can modify and vary their recall, he went on to state: 'However, here I think I've helped Philip to recover memories that were hidden more deeply in the mind.'

Jim Singleton was as certain as he could be that Philip Spencer was not faking the hypnosis. There is another detail, too, which in its own small way strengthens the case. Under hypnosis, Spencer described seeing a door in the object, but did not recollect actually going through it. This 'doorway amnesia' is a component of most abductions. Anyone making up a story would automatically describe going into the 'space-ship'. In 1987 the term 'doorway amnesia' was not around, since ufologists had not yet widely recognised this component, so it is highly unlikely that Philip Spencer would have been aware of it either.

The Ilkley incident is potentially one of the most important abduction accounts. Here, for the first time, a victim may have taken a photograph of one of his abductors, proving the physical reality of the UFO phenomenon.

—29—

HOT AND COLD IN GULF BREEZE

In November and December 1987 UFOs of classic design were captured on film by Ed Walters.

It was the year of the UFO. Whitley Strieber's book was 1987's number one bestseller in the USA and the subject was on every chat show almost every week. In Britain Tim Good was heading the lists with *Above Top Secret*, which claimed a government cover-up of alien contact.

A new big case had to come. It struck the quiet and rather prim coastal town of Gulf Breeze, Florida, across the bridge from Pensacola with its massive naval air station.

Excellent photographic evidence

The story had unique features which assured notoriety. A large number of photographs were taken on Polaroid film during November and December and given to the *Gulf Breeze Sentinel* by local builder Ed Walters. He claimed to do so on behalf of an anonymous witness, which later proved to be himself.

The pictures were colourful and spectacular, certainly more so than the disappointing fare that had reached UFO groups for many years. Indeed some cautious ufologists were concerned about why, with better cameras and film now available to most of the population, the number and quality of UFO photographs submitted to them was falling – and not rising as expectation should decree.

The Gulf Breeze case changed all of that. Silhouetted against an indigo sky were UFOs of classic design. There were no flickering lights in the sky, such as in the images taken at the Hessdalen window area in Norway and so typical of the UFO photographic cases during the 1980s. These shots were of discs with windows and a complex design.

Gulf Breeze, Florida, is the world's most popular UFO skywatch site. UFO watchers gather every day to scan the skies for visitors.

Sometimes there was a single object, sometimes a flotilla. On one a UFO even appeared partially behind tree branches.

The media loved it. Big-name ufologists largely expressed their delight with the case, putting their reputations on the line by endorsing the images. Some wrote sections in a big-budget book about the case (*The Gulf Breeze Sightings*, published by Bantam in 1990). There were dissenters, mostly outside the USA, but they became a repressed minority barely tolerated by most ufologists.

Those who expressed concern were worried by the semi-transparent feel to the photographs, which had an unusually elaborate look about them. Furthermore, the whole history of ufology taught that UFOs never turned up in identical fashion week after week in one place to be filmed by the same man in a variety of poses. If they had done so here, as he claimed, then this case represented a dramatic new direction for the phenomenon.

Eventually, the identity of the photographer was revealed. Walters and his wife professed multiple experiences between autumn 1987 and spring 1988, many of which Walters had captured on his Polaroid camera. In one shot Ed, wrapped in a bath towel, shakes his fist at one of the UFOs, while in another a blue beam is projected down towards the house. The most remarkable of all is the so-called 'Road shot', on which a UFO is seen hovering only feet above a highway, casting a pool of light on to the ground. Walters took it from only a few feet away, crouching by his truck, apparently terrified. It is undoubtedly most impressive, but the angle of the illuminated patch on the road surface seems to some researchers not to match the orientation of the hovering UFO, although other experts have challenged that interpretation. Walters also professed to see aliens (whom he did not photograph) and even to have what appears to have been a near abduction experience.

Testing the evidence

Sceptics were accusing Walters of a double exposure trick – of taking a photograph of a model UFO in an otherwise darkened room and then refilming the background. When such a picture is processed, the two blend together. There were claims (which Walters denied) that he had created hoax photographs of a ghost in the past. Unfortunately a Polaroid camera has no negative, so meaningful analysis was very difficult in this case.

Dr Bruce Maccabee, an optical physicist who worked with the US Navy and has been a renowned investigator of UFO photographs,

GULF BREEZE

Display boards showing UFO photographs taken at Gulf Breeze, Florida, at MUFON UFO Symposium in 1988.

provided Walters with a specially constructed three-dimensional Polaroid camera which enabled him to try to film more UFOs. Simultaneous images would be secured and this would allow hard data about size and distances of the UFOs to be obtained.

Walters did succeed in taking a few pictures this way in March 1988, but not of the same kinds of object as seen before. Measurements indicated smaller dimensions. None the less, Maccabee was satisfied by the evidence that he saw and insisted that Walters really was filming strange objects. Walters also passed a lie detector test sprung upon him by surprise.

After spring 1988 the Walters's experiences ceased and they concentrated on writing their book, for which they were well paid. However, they were supported in their claims by other witnesses in the town, who described seeing UFOs like those that the Walters couple had filmed. Another anonymous photographer (whose identity has never been revealed and who simply called himself 'Believer Bill') supplied the local paper with pictures that were very similar to Ed Walters's Polaroids.

This case has been a source of great controversy within the UFO world. Some researchers, particularly the UFO group MUFON, staunchly defend it, while others, notably the J. Allen Hynek Center for UFO Studies, express doubts – although these were moderated after a time.

After the Walters moved home, evidence of the creation of a model UFO was discovered sketched on a piece of paper. A local youth also came forward to claim that he had helped create a hoax. Ed Walters denied all of this and offered some counter-evidence. His supporters contend that the incriminating material was planted there to discredit him – as indeed it could have been.

By 1993 regular skywatches were taking place by the Pensacola Bay bridge. Quite a few sightings have been alleged and Bruce Maccabee filmed something with his camcorder in May 1992, as have several others. However, some ufologists believe that many of these new sightings result from prank balloons, perhaps manufactured by unknown locals, then set alight and then allowed to drift over the bay in the knowledge that they might stimulate UFO sightings. If true, the motive may be to keep Gulf Breeze on the tourist map. At least one film depicts in close focus what appears to be burning debris from such a man-made 'UFO' dribbling down towards the ground as the glowing reddish light drifts gradually across the sky with the wind.

Whatever the full truth about the Gulf Breeze photographs and the Ed Walters saga, this case has already won a guaranteed place in UFO history.

—30—

THE MAJESTIC TWELVE

In 1987 copies of an official-looking document, classified top-secret, were sent anonymously to several prominent ufologists.

Disinformation seeded into the UFO community by persons unknown included some official-looking documents from just after World War II which referred to a secret panel of politicians and scientists known as the Majestic 12 or MJ12. According to the papers their job was to act as a think tank on the UFO phenomenon, and to report directly to President Truman. Copies of the nine-page report, which was dated 18 September 1947 and classified top secret, were sent anonymously during 1987 to several prominent ufologists, including Timothy Good. It named the twelve members who supposedly dealt with general UFO reports and the Roswell case in particular (see Part Four).

The twelve were all highly credible, and just the sort of specialists who would be brought together to study the phenomenon. They included top nuclear scientist Dr Vannevar Bush; Rear-Admiral Roscoe Hillenkoetter, a Director of the CIA and a firm believer in the reality of UFOs; and General Nathan Twining, who, according to other released documents, cancelled a previous appointment and rushed to New Mexico on the day of the Roswell saucer crash.

Towards the end of 1986 Peter Hough and Jenny Randles became embroiled in a strange affair. A man telephoned Jenny and claimed that his commanding officer in the British Army had given him certain documents to hand over. There were six reports totalling 600 pages. During the conversation certain names and codes were mentioned which later tallied with the MJ12 documents. The papers offered here supposedly contained data from a scientist who had conducted biological analysis of alien bodies retrieved from UFO crashes. This report was dated 1948, and another file, from October 1977, was reputedly entitled 'Elimination of Non-Military Sources'.

John's story

Eventually a meeting was arranged between Randles, Hough and the man, referred to here as John, at a pub near Manchester. Over several hours he gave them a detailed account of the files and how he had come to be in possession of them. His answers to some very hard questioning were detailed and confident.

John had been in the Army until February 1985. His commanding officer had spent time on attachments in America where he had befriended a US Air Force officer at Wright-Patterson Air Force Base. This officer was a computer technician, and claimed he had accidentally accessed some secret UFO files; he copied them, but was arrested. His British friend found where they were hidden and brought them to England. Both officers believed the information should be released into the public domain. The American allegedly died in a car accident, although his friend thought he had been murdered.

Wondering how the files could be released, the officer tested each of his men to ascertain whom he could trust to assist him. It was not until John had left the Army, and returned for reservist weekend training, that his former commanding officer told him the full story. John agreed to help, and was told where the files were hidden and whom to contact.

John did not have the documents on him the day he met the authors. He claimed that fear had driven him to split them up and hide them in several different locations. Now he was wondering whether he should go ahead and just hand them over as originally planned. However, Randles and Hough demanded proof of their existence and a second meeting was arranged at which they would see 'samples'. This was arranged at a country park – but John never turned up. The investigators just wrote the whole thing off as an elaborate hoax.

Eleven days later, however, Jenny Randles received a letter from John in which he apologised for not attending the meeting; at the time he was taking part in an internal investigation. Two days after the meeting, John claimed he was taken to his base where he was interrogated about 'sensitive' documents which were 'the creation of an educated prankster' to which 'no credence could be attributed'.

This turned out to be perhaps more truthful than was apparent at the time. Central to the authenticity of the MJ12 documents was the signature of President Harry Truman. Supporters of the authenticity of the files pointed out that the signature could be genuine because it was identical to Truman's signature on another, non-UFO paper. But sceptics Joe Nickel and John Fischer claimed that the opposite was true

The UFO subject is littered with examples of interference by 'government officials'. Bogus documents, anonymous phone calls and letters seek to reinforce a belief held by many ufologists that we are being visited from outer space. That this should be attempted at all demonstrates the seriousness with which the authorities view the phenomenon. But are they encouraging a belief in extraterrestrials because the truth is even worse?

– the identicalness was proof that the signature was not genuine. They pointed out that no one signs their name exactly the same twice running. Further, they reasoned, if the signature was a forgery then so were all the MJ12 documents.

The real question that should be asked is this. Who forged the documents, and why did they think it necessary to do so?

UFO GLASNOST

Between 21 September and 28 October 1989, in the Western Park in Voronezh, there were six landings and one sighting, with the appearance of 'walking beings'.

Two of the largest nations on earth – China and the former USSR – were virtually unknown territory where UFOs were concerned for a very long time.

In communist-ruled China that remains true – although there are plenty of rumours of UFO reports of all complexions within the boundaries of this vast landmass.

As for the Soviet Union, we were a little more knowledgeable here thanks to visits paid by computer scientist Jacques Vallée and the testimony of ufologists who had fled to the west. Indeed one, Juri Lina, even set up a fake marriage to a Finnish girl in order to emigrate and escape the attentions of the KGB after private UFO group meetings in Moscow had been raided.

Despite restrictions on civilian ufology there was an intense military interest in the subject. Vallée discovered that there had been over ten thousand cases even by the mid-1960s. Several commissions were set up by the Academy of Sciences in Moscow, and a behavioural science researcher with government clearance spent time seeking Western UFO data from his base at a secret establishment in Novosibirsk during the late 1970s.

In the early 1980s a military investigation team was mounted and cosmonaut Marina Popovich was put in charge. Since democratisation she has attended UFO conferences and filled in many of the gaps.

UFO chases in Soviet air space

In November 1993 Tim Good claimed to have talked with a top official from the Russian defence establishment, who confirmed persistent rumours about Soviet jets sent in pursuit of UFOs they were tracking on radar. According to Good's source, so many have occurred that the authorities issued clear instructions to air bases: at first they were just to observe, and only later to intercept. Good was told that several aircraft had been shot down and that two pilots had died in pursuit of UFOs; although whether this means they were chasing something identifiable or extraterrestrial is another matter.

This information may relate to a startling episode over Gorky in spring 1983. A UFO was tracked on radar as it crossed secret air space and was merely observed; it continued its flight. A few months later, a similar unidentified target was observed on radar over another patch of secret Soviet air space – Sakhalin Island – but now an interceptor was sent. The object failed to respond to radio warnings and was shot from the skies. As the world knows, this 'UFO' was, in fact, tragically a Korean Airlines jumbo jet packed with passengers, who as a result of this mistake all died.

Of course, when flight KAL 007 went down in 1983 there was a global outcry. But it was noticeable that the fury expected from the White House and the Pentagon did not burst forth, and there were few repercussions. Perhaps the Americans secretly knew that UFOs were a complicating factor. If the Soviets had been 'tested' by several UFO overflights shortly before (as at Gorky), and had even lost pilots in jet chases when their electrical power was snuffed out by the phenomenon, it would be more understandable that they would regard as a threat an unknown object flying where it should not be.

Openness at last

Although much about Soviet ufology post-dates glasnost, 9 October 1989 was a turning point because it marked the transition. The Soviet Union, on the verge of dissolution, joined the ranks of UFO-reporting nations in an open fashion.

Indeed, the case that took place at the industrial city of Voronezh was officially reported and confirmed by TASS, the Soviet press agency. Whilst TASS was notorious for its propaganda, the last thing it could be described as being was a source of wild tales about flying saucers. As a consequence, its pronouncements about the Voronezh affair shook the world's media. Responsible newspapers, from the London *Times* to the *Washington Post*, carried the story in sober fashion. TASS were asked if they meant what they said and a spokesperson, looking suitably offended, intoned: 'TASS *never* jokes.' It was said in such a way that nobody would disbelieve him.

Dr Jacques Vallée was the first scientist to appear on Soviet TV to discuss UFOs. Even then, in 1965, tens of thousands of cases were known by the authorities but kept secret.

As a measure of the impact of the case it was the subject of items on serious news magazine programmes. Jenny Randles was interviewed live in an ITN studio as a politician might be on the national news.

What had caused this remarkable change of attitude by the Western media? They reported only a few scattered facts about an incident that was really part of a major wave that had struck this part of Russia that autumn. TASS had simply legitimised one case. That was what made it unique.

The full picture was gathered later, and we thank Dr Henry Silanov from the geophysical laboratory at the University of Voronezh for providing first-hand assistance. He says that

> between 21 September and 28 October 1989, in the Western Park [area] in Voronezh [there were] six landings and one sighting [hovering] ... with the appearance of walking beings ... We have no doubts [that the witnesses] are telling the truth in their accounts, because details of the landings are recounted by [them] ... [that] could otherwise have only come from specialist UFO literature, which is not published in our country.

The main events occurred between 23 and 27 September and involved various similar reports, notably a red sphere surrounded by a misty vapour ('like a bonfire in fog', one witness termed it). Many people saw it come down towards a tree which it forced to bend as it tried to land.

From the object several nine- or ten-feet-tall figures in silvery suits emerged and clambered down the tree. The entities were nothing like the Greys of American UFO lore nor even the Nordics so common in the rest of Europe. In fact they were more akin to beings from Russian folk tales about ogres in the woods. They even had three eyes. This may be very significant. We might predict that, with later exposure to Western UFO literature, the Russians will eventually start to report similar abductions with Greys.

The giants did some very weird things before returning to the sphere, including freezing a boy in mid-step. Another person, walking to a bus stop, was supposedly made to vanish until the UFO had left, when he reappeared and carried on walking as if no time had passed at all.

The other stories also featured similar UFOs and entities. In one case a robot appeared; in another, human-sized figures with wrinkled faces. One object swayed from side to side on descent in the falling-leaf motion so often reported in Western UFO cases but probably unknown to Russian citizens.

The 1989 sightings at Voronozh achieved a unique distinction in Britain. All four terrestrial TV channels treated it as a serious news item. Ufologists such as Jenny Randles (ITN News) and Mike Wootten (BBC Newsnight) were called in to the studio to debate it.

Giants from outer space take robot for walkies in a Russian park

by DAVID LAWSON

THE aliens have landed. A leading Russian scientist says there is no doubt that they stepped out of their spaceship and went for a walk in a park.

Three giant creatures 12 feet tall with tiny heads chose spare ground at Voronezh, 300 miles south east of Moscow, for a very close encounter with the human race.

Their arrival was heralded by a shining ball seen by dozens of Voronezh residents.

The UFO landed and out came the giants, similar to humans and accompanied by a small robot.

"They went for a promenade near their spaceship," said official news agency Tass. "Then they disappeared back inside.

"Onlookers were overwhelmed with a fear that lasted several days."

Respected

The landing was authenticated by staff from the Voronezh Geophysical Laboratory, whose head, Genrikh Silanov, is a respected scientist.

Tass said: "Scientists confirmed that a UFO landed. They also identified the landing site and found traces of aliens."

Silanov's men discovered a 20-yard depression in the park with four deep dents, and two pieces of rock.

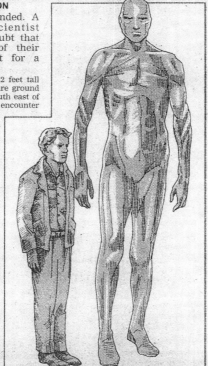

FEARSOME: Alien giant compared with man

Extract from the *Today* newspaper, Tuesday 10 October 1989.

In 1993 Russians launched AURA-Z, a multi-lingual magazine to discuss serious research into cases.

This was the first real Russian wave which became recognised as it was happening. We know that waves feed upon themselves – the publicity of initial events stimulates others to come forward and creates the appearance of a sequence of events. The USSR was living through the series of reports that had struck France and Britain in autumn 1954 and had demonstrated that the phenomenon was global. Now, in the aptly named Western Park, the mystery was showing itself as no respecter of cultural systems either.

— 32 —

THE MANHATTAN TRANSFER

In the early hours of 30 November 1989 a woman was seen floating out of her apartment window in Manhattan and entering a UFO.

Despite there being hundreds of alien abduction stories, there was one significant reason why the presence of spacenappers was not accepted by the world. This was the lack of corroborative evidence.

Although there were many apparently sincere reports from seemingly credible people and even a few multiple witness abductions, there was no real hard evidence – such as something provably extraterrestrial that was removed from the spaceship, or a camcorder sequence taken by the witness aboard a UFO. The history of the subject showed that this was not going to happen, which is why the photograph allegedly taken after an abduction on Ilkley Moor (see page 243) was regarded as so sensational by ufologists.

However, what ought not to have been impossible was the existence of uninvolved witnesses who chanced to see the abduction taking place. In the terrible abduction and murder of Liverpool youngster James Bolger police enquiries proceeded quickly because over thirty people had seen the child as he was led away. They did not realise what was happening at the time, but they saw what they saw. The same is true of a bank robbery in the high street, for example. Passers by are simply bound to witness something.

Personal visions?

Yet in the countless examples of alien abduction this was never the case. There were near-misses. In the case of Alan Godfrey's experience at Todmorden in November 1980, several police officers on moors a few miles away spotted a light in the sky. But nobody on Burnley Road in Todmorden itself saw the UFO hovering over the police car or the abduction that followed. Nor, despite subsequent widespread publicity, has anyone come forward who even saw the empty patrol car in the middle of the road.

Indeed, the problem was worse for the reality of spacenapping. In six cases independent observers saw the witness during the period when they felt they were on board the UFO. None of these witnesses had been inside a UFO when testimony suggested they ought to be!

In fact, these people were just where they were before the experience began. In one case, from Brazil, the witness was prone on the ground, seemingly in an altered state of consciousness (in fact presumed drunk by the person walking past). In another example, from Wales, the witness was seen in a near-catatonic state prone on her bed. In an even more extraordinary episode, from Australia, a woman had an encounter with a UFO and entities. Two witnesses who were with her at the time saw her interacting with these beings and then 'enter' the UFO as if abducted by it. However, she never physically went anywhere. She remained in their view seemingly talking to thin air encountering an object that neither of them could see and which, by standard definitions of reality, was not actually there.

This litany of evidence seems to prove that the alien abduction experience, however real it appears to the witness at the time, occurs at an inner level and not in the real world. In other words, it is some form of very strange visionary phenomenon but definitely not physical reality, such as that which underpins some less exotic types of UFO phenomena.

But then, on 30 November 1989, a case occurred that reversed this visionary trend and had a major impact on the UFO world. Like the Ilkley photograph and the Gulf Breeze affair, it instantly overturned a golden rule of ufology and posed a stark choice. Either such anomalous cases are hoaxes, or the phenomenon has undeniably altered its character in a very significant way over the past few years.

Perhaps this new phase of overt activity, concentrating on much fewer but far more individually dramatic cases, was a genuine step forward towards an acclimatisation of the mystery within the human mind.

Floating above Manhattan

The witness to this epic new case was Linda, a young mother who lived in a high-rise apartment in Manhattan. She had already undergone alleged abductions by Greys and been investigated for some time by

Budd Hopkins. So when she called him to talk about another episode, the morning after it had occurred, it appeared to be nothing special and was subjected to the usual follow-through, including hypnosis, but no more.

In brief, Linda claimed that the entities floated her through her shut bedroom window and surrounded her high above the streets of the city. They then transferred her into a UFO hovering over the tower block and did their usual testing before replacing her in bed. She could not recall how, but did describe the terror on noticing that her two young children had been immobilised. She thought the aliens had killed them,

Abductee Linda Napolitano, who has made appearances at UFO conferences to support her story.

Famed psychologist, Dr John Mack, of the Harvard Medical School, received a big pay out to put his Pullitzer Prize winning talents to bear on the abduction mystery. His resultant book, Abduction, *was published in the UK in May 1994.*

and had to satisfy herself that they were still breathing by holding a mirror to their noses. They were merely deeply unconscious and remembered nothing.

Evidence from the NYPD

This would have been just another 'believe it or not' tale to add to hundreds of others that Hopkins has collected. But in March 1991 Hopkins had a letter from two men claiming to be police officers. Although he had other subsequent correspondence with them (including a tape) they would not meet the ufologist face to face.

These two men claimed to have been parked in a car in the early hours of 30 November 1989 when they had seen a woman floating out of her apartment window in Manhattan and entering a UFO. They saw it fly into the nearby river, submerge and never come out again. The men thought that they had just witnessed a woman being spacenapped by aliens and, for all they knew, murdered. They claimed to feel guilty that they had been unable to do anything about it despite their training, but told Hopkins they could point out the exact apartment involved. Indeed, one of them was in the early throes of a nervous breakdown, having spent weeks parked outside the building trying to summon up the courage to go and knock on the right door and see if the woman existed and knew what they were talking about.

Of course, they apparently had no idea that Hopkins already knew this story and had interviewed the woman herself. As Hopkins tried to check out the story, Linda eventually called him to say that the men had turned up – just as he had warned her they might. They were reputedly stunned by the fact that she was actually expecting them.

Eventually, the two policemen told Hopkins that they were really secret bodyguards for a leading politician. They were ferrying him to the New York heliport when their car stalled, and the incident occurred as if 'stage-managed' for their benefit. This world-renowned statesman had witnessed the entire thing!

A further twist to the tale came when a woman contacted the ufologist to say that she had been driving over the Brooklyn Bridge with some other traffic in the middle of a night two years before when every vehicle's engine stalled, the street lights had gone out, and a group of people witnessed the abduction of Linda from her high-rise apartment. She told essentially the same story to Hopkins as had the two men; although, of course, none of the other affected drivers had gone public with the story in the meantime. Nobody had, as one might expect, even bothered to call the police, and there were no media stories between this dramatic event on the bridge in 1989 and its sudden revelation later.

The most important abduction ever?

Hopkins has considerable faith in this case. He told Jenny Randles when they discussed it at length that he knew the identity of the 'third man', who was of such calibre and integrity that if he chose to tell what had happened to him then the whole world would be convinced about the reality of alien abductions overnight. In August 1993 Hopkins added that he had received a fairly non-committal letter from this man, who has seemingly decided that the time is not right to tell the world. A strong claim published within American ufology is that this man is Javier Perez de Cuellar, the former Secretary General of the United Nations. Hopkins has not endorsed this allegation. Those who have asked de Cuellar to comment have received a flat denial and an insistence that he was not even in New York on the night in question.

An independent team of sceptical ufologists have made their own investigation of the case and presented some disturbing evidence. For example, a newspaper loading bay which is busy all night long is directly opposite the apartment block, but nobody there saw anything. No meetings or helicopter flights were scheduled at the time (although the two bodyguards say this was because it was a top-secret meeting and an unlogged flight). There are a few other nagging questions that are outstanding.

Perhaps more worrying still is that this case fell so conveniently into Budd Hopkins's lap. There is no independent source of contact. All the witnesses came directly to him. He has only their word that they did not know one another beforehand, although there seem no grounds to charge that they did. This is very like the way that 'facts' were so conveniently 'fed out' to Jenny Randles and Brenda Butler after the 1980 Rendlesham Forest case.

Budd Hopkins is very sincere. Linda (Napolitano) has now gone public at UFO conferences and seems genuine. The other witnesses remain anonymous.

With a case of this magnitude it must be proper to express caution. If these witnesses are telling the truth and, especially, if the third man does go public in future, then this may rightly be seen as the most important abduction that has ever occurred. It would confirm our

Author Jim Schnabal claimed in January 1994 that Perez de Cuellor – former Secretary General of the United Nations – has denied being the 'third man' in the Manhatten transfer case.

growing suspicions that the UFO phenomenon has drastically altered its character of late.

Of course, we cannot at present assert any of this. The case remains controversial and will do so until some hard evidence surfaces, perhaps in Hopkins's coming book or the film currently in production. It is intriguing, but sadly not the probative 'case of the century' it has been hailed to be; at least not as it stands.

Part Nine

TOWARDS 2000

THE BELGIAN WAVE

The Belgian sightings were at their most dramatic in March 1990.

The remarkable new 'display mode' which UFOs are adopting took a further stride with the saga of the Belgian sightings between 1989 and 1991. These were at their most dramatic in March 1990. But once again controversy surrounds this affair.

It began on the evening of 29 November 1989 – the very night when, three thousand miles away and about twelve hours later, Linda Napolitano would claim to have been abducted from her Manhattan apartment block in the most incredible spacenapping ever. Whether this is relevant can only be a matter for speculation.

The sightings on 29 November 1989 were investigated by the national UFO group SOBEPS (Belgian Society for the Study of Space Phenomena). Useful independent reports were also published by Wim van Utrecht and Paul Vanbrabant.

A vast, triangular object

Over 120 sightings were reported for that first night alone, mostly around Eupen on the eastern border with Germany. The most important came from two police officers, who saw the object from their patrol car and then pulled into the side of the road to watch it drift overhead before pursuing it.

The UFO was like a dark triangle and had bright lights on each corner, with a reddish glow in the centre. It was huge (sizes estimated by witnesses used terms like 'a football pitch'). It also moved very slowly and almost silently: a faint 'buzzing' or 'humming' was heard by some witnesses. All told, the object was visible for well over an hour and possibly longer. It seemed to be parading up and down the skies as if putting on an exhibition for the citizens of Eupen.

Many more reports followed over the coming weeks, spreading to other parts of Belgium. Most were of a triangular object, although other shapes were seen as well. It is important to point out that triangular objects such as these were not new to this wave. In fact, since the late 1970s they had become an important part of the UFO scene – indeed, more common than 'disc' shapes.

Stealth aircraft?

In Britain a cine film was taken in Leicestershire in October 1978 during a series of reports of what came to be called the 'Silent Vulcan' – because the object, whose outline was picked out by lights, resembled a huge Vulcan bomber but made no sound. This early film is similar to that obtained by certain witnesses with camcorders during the Belgian wave a decade later.

When triangular reports continued to occur, British investigators had suspected the flight of stealth aircraft on secret missions. The profile of these slow-moving, quiet and unusual-looking aircraft was reputed to be triangular with smooth edges and a strange lighting configuration. Aviation sources believed that missions flew from RAF Alconbury, close to the focus of the Leicestershire wave.

During the 1980s more sightings occurred in Britain, where the term 'Manta Ray' was often used as witnesses described the smooth, triangular lines of the object they saw. Important cases were recorded from Ashbourne in Derbyshire and then Alvanley in Cheshire on 23 October 1989, where a senior police officer and his wife observed an object very like the ones to be witnessed in Belgium only five weeks later.

Officially, of course, the theory about stealth aircraft overflying Britain was denied. Indeed, the very existence of stealth aircraft was refuted for many years, although it was an open secret in aviation circles. Eventually, in 1988, the Aurora jet was revealed and it did have the characteristics alleged. But aviation sources interviewed by Jenny Randles in the USA in April 1992 told her that prototypes first flew in the 1970s and that new-generation stealth aircraft were constantly being developed in and around the Tonopah Air Force Base and Groom Lake area of Nevada.

This location was where ufologists were alleging that captured alien UFOs were being test-flown. But she was informed that the technology being spotted here was of human design, albeit with some remarkable capabilities, such as nuclear-powered engines under development, easily mistaken for a UFO.

An internal memo from USAF in Europe to Washington regarding the 1990 sightings over Belgium, officially denying the Stealth bomber claims of some sceptics.

```
RUEAMCC/CMC CC WASHINGTON DC
RUEALGX/SAFE
R 301246Z MAR 90
FM ███████████████
TO RUEKJCS/DIA WASHDC
INFO RUEKJCS/DIA WASHDC//DAT-7//
RUSNNOA/USCINCEUR VAIHINGEN GE//ECJ2-OC/ECJ2-JIC//
RUFGAID/USEUCOM AIDES VAIHINGEN GE
RHFQAAA/HQUSAFE RAMSTEIN AB GE//INOW/INO//
RHFPAAA/UTAIS RAMSTEIN AB GE//INRMH/INA//
RHDLCNE/CINCUSNAVEUR LONDON UK
RUFHNA/USDELMC BRUSSELS BE
RUFHNA/USMISSION USNATO
RUDOGHA/USNMR SHAPE BE
RUEAIIA/CIA WASHDC
RUFGAID/JICEUR VAIHINGEN GE
RUCBSAA/FICEURLANT NORFOLK VA
RUEKJCS/SECDEF WASHDC
RUEHC/SECSTATE WASHDC
RUEADWW/WHITEHOUSE WASHDC
RUFHBG/AMEMBASSY LUXEMBOURG
RUEATAC/CDRUSAITAC WASHDC
BT
CONTROLS
████████████████        SECTION 02 OF 02 ████████  05049


SERIAL:  (U) IIR 6 807 0136 90.

BODY
COUNTRY:  (U) BELGIUM (BE).

SUBJ:  IIR 6 807 0136 90/BELGIUM AND THE UFO ISSUE (U)

MAR TV SHOW.
```

PAGE:0015

```
6.  (U) DEBROUWER NOTED THE LARGE NUMBER OF REPORTED
SIGHTINGS, PARTICULARLY IN NOV 89 IN THE LIEGE AREA AND
THAT THE BAF AND MOD ARE TAKING THE ISSUE SERIOUSLY.  BAF
EXPERTS HAVE NOT BEEN ABLE TO EXPLAIN THE PHENOMENA EITHER.

7.  (U) DEBROUWER SPECIFICALLY ADDRESSED THE POSSIBILITY
OF THE OBJECTS BEING USAF B-2 OR F-117 STEALTH AIRCRAFT
WHICH WOULD NOT APPEAR ON BELGIAN RADAR, BUT MIGHT BE
SIGHTED VISUALLY IF THEY WERE OPERATING AT LOW ALTITUDE IN
THE ARDENNES AREA.  HE MADE IT QUITE CLEAR THAT NO USAF
OVERFLIGHT REQUESTS HAD EVER BEEN RECEIVED FOR THIS TYPE
MISSION AND THAT THE ALLEDGED OBSERVATIONS DID NOT
CORRESPOND IN ANY WAY TO THE OBSERVABLE CHARACTERISTICS OF
EITHER U.S. AIRCRAFT.
```

Of course, test flying such a device in the Nevada desert is one thing, but doing so over Cheshire or Belgium seems rather more difficult to justify. One interesting possibility is that the UFO phenomenon was being deliberately used as a smokescreen for test flights in areas where it was desirable to fly new models but where population density would otherwise preclude it. If the aircraft were seen, it would appear so unusual that it would be reported as a UFO. So new military aircraft could fly with impunity, the authorities knowing that rival military powers would probably not pay too much attention to one more UFO sighting.

Belgian investigators were quick to consider this option for their sudden wave of triangular UFOs. The US Air Force were equally speedy in refuting the claim.

Yet despite these flat denials, such as one in December 1989 that 'the F-117 stealth fighter has never flown in the European theatre', some experts have expressed a different view. Consider, for instance, the comments by former French Minister of Defence Robert Galley (see page 201), and an interesting and seemingly unambiguous comment made on 21 April 1990 by Colonel Tom Tolin, a USAF officer who was speaking in France about the then current Belgian wave. He said that 'F-117s are flying in Europe during night missions, sometimes piloted by United Kingdom RAF pilots, but we are not authorised to tell you where.'

Concerted efforts at investigation

Nevertheless, taking the official denials seriously, the Belgian government set up a remarkable experiment. Not only did they create a system whereby all incoming UFO reports were sent immediately to UFO investigators, but they opened up contacts at radar stations and other facilities to allow the ufologists to do their job. This was a unique joint effort to try to resolve the problem that was clearly vexing the nation.

The outcome was an amazing decision to mount a fully coordinated skywatch over the Easter weekend in March 1990. The public were encouraged to report sightings. The ufologists were allowed to set up a temporary HQ at Bierset airport near Liège. Two military aircraft were put on standby alert – one equipped with sophisticated cameras. On the ground across eastern Belgium the ufologists had teams in contact with one another via mobile phones and ground-based video-recording systems. Belgium was ready for the UFOs!

During 1991 Eastern Belgium topped a poll of the top 10 most active UFO hot spots in the world, narrowly beating Gulf Breeze (Florida) and Todmorden (West Yorkshire).

During the four-day experiment there were a few sightings but little corroboration. However, a detailed study of one incident led SOBEPS to the conclusion that an important event had taken place.

Between 11pm on 30 March and 2am on the 31st a series of police officers around Wavre, 15 miles south of Brussels and 40 miles west of the base at Bierset airport, spotted lights in the sky. These do not seem to have been as exciting as many of the other reports and resemble stars observed through expectation and unusual atmospheric conditions. However, two F-16 fighters were scrambled in response and just after midnight reported radar lock-ons. The pilots saw nothing visually.

Analysis of the film of the onboard computer radar graphics and that of three ground-based radar systems which also tracked the objects did seem to match up. However, the contacts were sporadic and intermittent rather than continuous, and never lasted longer than about twenty seconds. Various echoes were seen moving about the screen at what might be interpreted as incredible speeds – although that does depend upon whether these are material objects, rather than spurious targets on the radar, differing emissions at different points.

Opposing conclusions about this case have been drawn. Some researchers were convinced that this was vital proof of a strange encounter. Others decided that the lights seen by the police were too close a match to the stars and planets in the sky plotted by computer to show what was visible on that night. A SOBEPS scientific expert given full access to all the radar data also concluded that the night's events did not prove anything extraterrestrial, although he suspected that a rare meteorological and atmospheric effect might have stimulated the sightings. Whatever the case, the bold experiment seemingly failed to snare the mystery triangle.

Sightings continued into the summer of 1991, but faded to a trickle. Some thirty films and camcorder images were analysed during that time, but all bar three were misperceptions – of ordinary aircraft, for instance. Sadly, nothing spectacular was obtained despite all the attention. One man did film a triangle of lights crossing the Brussels skyline about ninety minutes after the F-16 radar lock-ons, but some ufologists argue that this was a jumbo jet.

The triangular form of UFO, as seen during the Belgian wave, has by 1994 become more frequently reported than the traditional UFO categories of 'saucers' and 'cigars'.

A further theory: refuelling aircraft

Theories about the Belgian wave are still split among stealth aircraft, alien objects and a piloted microlite being used to simulate UFOs. A similar theory to this – involving a formation team of night fliers – was used by some ufologists to explain another major wave of triangular lights that were seen in the Hudson Valley, New York area in 1985. So the idea may not be as wild as it appears.

One option not widely considered has been borne out by British investigators and might be very appropriate. On several occasions during the period of the Belgian wave very similar large formations of lights were witnessed over central and eastern England. Staffordshire MP William Cash, even asked questions in the House of Commons about them. Witnesses described a huge dark object speckled by lights moving silently and with unusual slowness on its course; they also used phrases like 'the size of a football pitch'.

Investigation proved what these witnesses had seen, although many have refused to accept that answer. It was a formation of aircraft involved in a series of mid-air refuelling exercises, necessary to mount long-distance bombing raids to the Middle East during the Gulf War without having to land en route and waste time. These were secret operations, relatively tricky and dangerous. They are supposed to occur over the North Sea, between England and Belgium, but witnesses saw the aircraft lining up before refuelling actually began.

In these exercises large tanker aircraft full of fuel are linked by umbilical cords to several smaller fighters that surround the tanker as close as possible and use it as a flying fuel station. Because it is such a difficult exercise, especially at night, the aircraft are covered in an unusual and very bright array of lights. Such refuelling also takes place at a considerable height.

On clear nights witnesses will see this very strange formation drifting over. The aircraft are flying as slowly as possible to retain proximity to each other, and relatively slowly because of their great height. As nobody on the ground is expecting to see many aircraft spread over a huge area of sky in a very odd formation, they always misinterpret the lights as being on one huge, and (because of the flying formation) often triangular, object – that is dark and silent, or perhaps making a faint noise as would a dozen high-flying aircraft engines even if miles up in the sky.

Some of the Belgian sightings may also be explicable in this way.

In December 1993 and January 1994 a repeat run of triangular UFOs provoked a major wave over Lincolnshire. Witnesses included a senior officer at RAF Donna Nook. The MoD investigated but found no explanation for the sightings.

—34—

MID-AIR CONFLICT

Six British incidents of mid-air encounters are on record between 1991 and 1993, others have almost certainly occurred.

On 21 April 1991, just after 9pm, an Alitalia MD-80 jet carrying fifty-seven passengers from Milan to London Heathrow was crossing the Kent coast near Lydd. Suddenly Captain Achille Zaghetti spotted a cigar-shaped object above and ahead of him. It flashed past them on a dangerously close path. The object was unlike anything he had seen before, but from its lozenge shape and great speed he feared it might be a missile.

At Heathrow, radar was tracking the aircraft through 22,000 feet on its steady descent. Now they picked up an unidentified object on screen just as the captain reported the frightening incident. The UFO was about ten miles behind the jet and disappearing fast. They had no idea what it was.

This case was effectively hushed up by both the Ministry of Defence and the CAA (Civil Aviation Authority) as they started enquiries, although Zaghetti submitted an official report. He then chose to talk about it back in Italy and the British authorities were forced, perhaps reluctantly, to go public about their investigations.

The CAA confirmed that 'extensive enquiries have failed to indicate what the sighting may have been'. They had ruled out all possibility that it was a rogue missile from a range on the Kent coast. These could not reach the height of this object. The MoD were equally explicit. They said: 'What happened was a mystery. It was yet another UFO.'

A series of near-misses

Indeed so, but it was not *just* another UFO. What these reports fail to reveal is that this near-disaster was merely one of a whole spate of mid-air encounters that have been occurring since the middle of 1991, and which have rapidly turned into something of a dangerous trend. The public are generally unaware of them. Nobody is going out of their way to tell you of the incidents if you choose to fly. But they clearly represent yet another strange step into the limelight by the UFO phenomenon, now demonstrating their amazing manoeuvrability in close proximity to our passenger aircraft.

Reports of these objects have come from all over the world since 1991. The French military helicopter encounter over Brignoles in 1992 is described on page 208. There have been similar encounters over Tasmania, New York, Russia and the California desert. Indeed, in the last case one crew member even took a photograph of the dark cylindrical mass as it shot through the air at a quite remarkable speed.

However, we have paid particular attention to gathering cases from Britain. Six incidents are on record between 1991 and 1993 – although these seem merely to be the ones that have been traceable, and others almost certainly have occurred and remain unknown. Pilots are notoriously reluctant to report UFOs because of the problems that can result. Airlines are also not particularly keen in case it should have an adverse effect on passenger bookings in the cut-throat economic climate.

Yet no airline seems to have been singled out for a close encounter. Over a two-year period we have reports involving Aeroflot, US Air, Qantas and, in Britain, Dan Air, Britannia and British Airways. It seems likely that most airlines have had a close encounter at some stage. Two of the British incidents are particularly important because they again involve radar trackings.

In July 1993 it emerged that a British Airways Boeing 767 on an internal flight from Edinburgh to London had observed a similar object when passing over north-west England at about 30,000 feet. The air traffic control centre based at Manchester Airport had apparently tracked the object briefly, but no further information on this matter has been made available as it was still 'under investigation'.

On 15 July 1991 a Britannia Airways Boeing 737 was descending through 15,000 feet on its way into London Gatwick with a group of holidaymakers returning from Crete. It was passing the Sussex coast at the time on a sunny afternoon. The co-pilot observed, yet again, a dark, lozenge-shaped object on what seemed to be a collision course with the jet. He yelled out. The pilot looked up to see the object sweep past the wing at an estimated distance of only a few hundred feet. In aviation terms that is about as close to a disaster as you can get. The object was thought to be quite small.

In December 1978 the Kaikoura area of New Zealand generated UFOs that were seen by regular cargo air flights. Later they took an Australian TV film crew up who captured some of the most famous video images of UFOs ever recorded.

The most frightening aerial encounter was in 1986 when a Japanese Airlines jumbo had a lengthy term contact with a giant object over the North Pole during a long-haul flight.

The crew reported the matter immediately and London radar had the UFO on screen. It resembled a small aircraft but was not giving out a transponder signal, the electronic code used by all traffic to indicate a known aircraft type. The UFOs speed was just over 100 mph, refuting later speculation that it might have been a balloon. London control was sufficiently concerned to order another incoming aircraft to change course, as the UFO was heading out to sea in its general direction.

In a subsequent investigation the matter was taken very seriously by the CAA and the identity of the object was not established. The risk of collision was rated 'high' by their final report. Thankfully, no collision has ever taken place – these incidents appear to be no more than shots across the bow.

It is early days in the investigation of such cases, but they seem to represent a new and rather worrying pattern. Whatever UFOs turn out to be, the provocative way in which they are interacting with passenger aircraft makes their investigation imperative. We cannot afford to joke about something that is paying such close attention to air traffic above densely populated areas of the world. We owe it to ourselves to take the UFO subject seriously.

Perhaps that is the point of this new phase of aerial activity. The world can readily forget about distant lights in the sky or the claim that someone, somewhere was spacenapped by aliens. But if air traffic is in persistent danger from a near-collision with unknown objects then we ignore that fact at our peril.

─── 35 ───

UFOs in Focus

During 1993 there was a noticeable spate of photographic cases.

It is difficult to predict where the UFO mystery will take us next. It now appears to be changing so rapidly that anything can happen. However, during 1993 there was a noticeable spate of photographic cases. The twist was that this new wave of activity was being captured on the new generation of camcorders.

In Britain alone during 1993 no fewer than nine such cases were reported; the same trend is indicated in other parts of the world. Certainly this is partly due to the rapid rise in camcorder ownership, but the similar escalation in the ownership of still cameras was unmatched by any such increase in UFO photographs. So there may be something more behind this dramatic expansion of the evidence.

Venus rising

It is early days to tell whether the pattern will continue, or, indeed, if any of the cases will offer substantial proof of the extraordinary. Most of the objects filmed are lights in the sky, and many have explanations. Venus was a particular source, being unusually bright in the early morning sky for much of 1993. The automatic focus on cameras tried but failed to 'lock on' to this point of light, and as a result produced a fuzzy spaceship-like blob that looks a good deal more mysterious than it ever was.

A case in the Hartcliffe area of Bristol in late June 1993 resulted in a whole street skywatching for UFOs over several days, and a video image of 'the big one' climbing into the dawn sky night after night. This was without doubt the planet Venus – even so, the story got national and some international media coverage and the film was sent for computer enhancement in the USA.

See opposite above
UFO photographs flooded in during the 1950s but little investigation into them was carried out on the misguided premise that a picture was worth a thousand words. This image from Pescara, Italy, taken in September 1957 is typical of those about which we know very little and whose status is now impossible to confirm or deny.

See opposite below
Many UFO-like photographs were taken during the space missions but almost all have explanations – eg as window bolts reflecting the very strong sunlight, junk floating in a nearby space orbit and even waste matter ejected from the capsule and floating in tandem with it. This shot taken by the crew of Apollo 11 in July 1969 does not show an alien entity but some detritus in orbit above the earth.

This image taken at Playa Sangrila, Uruguay on 23 September 1968 shows a common problem with UFO photographs. They often depict nothing but the UFO and surrounding sky. This prevents meaningful analysis by comparison with foreground or background details. However, investigators have learnt to watch for a dark aura that delineates the edges of a UFO image. When present this can demonstrate that it is a small object close to the camera lens rather than a huge disc thousands of feet in the air.

During the 1970s the number of submitted UFO photographs began to fall dramatically. Instead of hundreds of fuzzy black and white shots only a few – often sharp and spectacular and usually colour – images began to reach ufologists. Whether this turnabout increased or decreased the credibility of the evidence was a contentious question. This image was taken by an unknown source over Germany.

Other – perhaps unexplained – things may well have been seen during the Hartcliffe flap, but the camcorder image upon which everybody concentrated their attention was, in fact, easily resolved.

A similar incident occurred in the West Country during August 1993, when a family set off early in the morning for a day trip to London. They saw a light in the sky and filmed it for some minutes. The camcorder recorded the sound as well as the vision, and provided a very useful example of how many other reported UFO sightings must come about.

The witnesses here understandably misinterpreted the light as it grew and then faded through cloud cover. The camera's inability to focus caused it to look bizarre through the viewfinder; as a consequence the witnesses, ranging across three generations, assumed that what they were viewing *was* bizarre. As they talked about the affair, pre-existing social beliefs about UFOs came into play. They presumed the light's origin to be extraterrestrial and feared that aliens might spacenap and operate on them. In the end the object, which was not moving and was certainly Venus, triggered a complex close encounter.

We stress that the family concerned are not to be singled out as wildly gullible or incompetent. What they went through is the process that most human beings experience in these circumstances. Indeed, this has occurred in many close encounter UFO cases in the past. The only difference here is that we have it captured on sound and video and can analyse the genesis of a UFO encounter from the raw material of a distant light in the sky. In many ways that makes this particular camcorder sequence far more important to ufology than an unexplained flickering light might have been.

Caught on security video

However, there have been a few more puzzling encounters captured on camera. In particular two security camera systems set up at major industrial complexes have provided much food for thought.

At a shopping centre site near Warrington in Cheshire in February 1991 a white 'soap bubble'-like object was recorded moving around an alleyway for several minutes (see page 282). As investigators examined the possibility that a camera fault might be responsible a second camera, looking at a different part of the site, produced a longer sequence of the same object the following April. Various experiments proved that it was glowing with infra-red light.

In September 1993 another security camera at a factory unit in south Lancashire recorded a brilliant white glow moving very slowly towards the north-west over the course of several minutes. This was just after 6am and appears to have been travelling much too slowly to be any obvious aircraft.

The figure on the beach

A few days beforehand a very curious film was submitted to Peter Hough by a family who had been for an August day trip to Rhyl in north Wales. In one sequence the camera panned across the sands and picked up a strange figure standing beside a wooden groyne (see page 283). The figure appeared to glow white – or a semi-transparent silvery hue – and could easily be interpreted as an alien entity. There are some

During the 1990s one of the major new trends within UFO study has been the capturing of objects on video camera. This still is taken from a security camera at a shopping mall in Warrington, Cheshire, on 26 April 1991 and depicts a large object tracked around the complex for 20 minutes before disappearing into the sky. Investigation failed to identify the cause.

similarities with the being photographed by Jim Templeton in Cumbria in 1964 (see page 156).

The witness looked up from the viewfinder and failed to spot the entity with his eyes, causing him to interpret (and report) this experience as a possible ghost. However, evaluation suggests that, as the camera was on a telephoto setting and there was a huge expanse of light sky and beach, his eyes, having just focused through the viewfinder, would find it almost impossible to pick out such a small image easily against a non-contrasting background.

These two cases were considered by scientists at the University of Manchester Institute of Science and Technology, who told investigators Peter Hough and Vic Sleigh that they did not consider them mysterious. The scientists thought the UFO was probably just a slow-moving aircraft, and the entity a man wearing a light mackintosh-type coat whose reflectivity produced an anomalous effect on the film due to

a factor inherent within most home camcorders when shooting light materials and colours.

Ufologists are still waiting

Sadly, as yet there have been no amazing camcorder images, filmed in daylight, of what could only be described as a disc-like object or exotically constructed craft. A lengthy sequence taken in a rural area of Ontario in August 1991 was submitted anonymously to ufologists by a man identifying himself only as 'The Guardian'. It allegedly depicts a rotating lighted disc with army trucks down below, although it is difficult to see too much against the dark background.

Superficially this seems very impressive; an American researcher claims that he has checked out the case and that local people do recall military activity cordoning off the area. 'The Guardian' has allegedly submitted reliable material in the past. However, other sources within ufology are more dubious about this story and say that their enquiries reveal no evidence of a UFO encounter, let alone the capture of an alien vehicle by some military unit at the time.

Some brief images of an 'alien face' were also sent, but these are stills, not camcorder images, and are very hard to interpret. The Ontario film is simply the most visually impressive of the influx of camcorder images in the past few years. It is unlikely to remain the most spectacular for very long, and most ufologists hope that someone, somewhere will

There are several key advantages of camcorder film over still photographs. One of the less obvious is that it provides sound. What the witnesses say during a close encounter can be surprisingly revealing.

shortly secure definitive evidence of the kind of unknown object that will offer no possible doubt.

What they want is a UFO that is not a misperception of some mundane stimulus such as Venus, an airship, laser lights, or so on, as 95 per cent of all UFO sightings prove to be; not a flickering light in the sky, which may be some kind of exotic natural phenomena which evidence strongly suggests do exist; and not the technologically clever but ufologically unconvincing hoax shot of a UFO in the dark, as a few photographic cases these days are wont to be.

What ufologists are waiting for is a clear, unambiguous image of a disc-like craft moving across the daytime sky in such a way that it can only be a large constructed object powered by a method that is far beyond us; or, better still, a close focus image of an alien being – be it a Grey, a Nordic or any other type – moving in such a way that its earthly origin is ruled out.

Whether we shall ever receive such a case depends upon one simple truth. It is a truth which, after fifty years of research into this subject, we still cannot prove one way or the other. We *know* that countless people sincerely observe and report UFOs but that many of these things are not really UFOs at all. We *know* that many of the unexplained cases are UAP (unidentified atmospheric phenomena) – natural energies on the fringes of scientific understanding. But we do *not know* whether any UFOs are alien craft or visitors from another place.

If they are, then with our modern technology in the very near future someone must inevitably film one in such a way that there can be no doubt. Then the world will know for sure. But if no such case arrives quite soon we may have to face one simple, if stunning, conclusion – that there are IFOs and there are UFOs, but there are no alien craft waiting to be filmed!

—36—

WHO OR WHAT IS BEHIND THE UFO PHENOMENON?

The arguments will carry on, but one thing is certain – the UFO subject is NOT history.

We are not concerned here with the 90–95 per cent of UFO reports which probably turn out to have mundane expla-nations, such as bright stars or planets, aircraft landing lights, weather balloons, airships and hoaxes. Rather, we are examining the hard core of cases which resist down-to-earth solutions – the 5–10 per cent that cause such heated debate between sceptics and ufologists and even amongst the ranks of ufologists themselves.

There is absolutely no doubt of the objective reality of UFOs *per se*. Convincing eye-witness reports have been received for decades – centuries, some argue. More than this, the public denial of major governments to charges that they have been secretly investigating the phenomenon were shown, by the release of official documents in the early 1980s to be disinformation. We have demonstrated the truth of this beyond reasonable doubt. British military reports declassified under the thirty-year-rule unambiguously describe the scrambling of RAF jet interceptors chasing 'silver discs'.

All this shows that the argument of whether 'they' do or do not exist is long past. Sceptics should now accept this fact, and address the poss-ible exotic explanations. To do otherwise is tiresome and time-wasting.

The extraterrestrial hypothesis

This is the natural explanation for UFO reports, and a favourite with the media who are unable to grasp the subtleties that permeate the phenomenon: UFOs represent visits by extraterrestrials. They are here to study us, to help mankind, or to 'borrow' human specimens for the extraction of genetic material to manufacture hybrid beings.

Many ufologists, particularly those in America, doubt that there

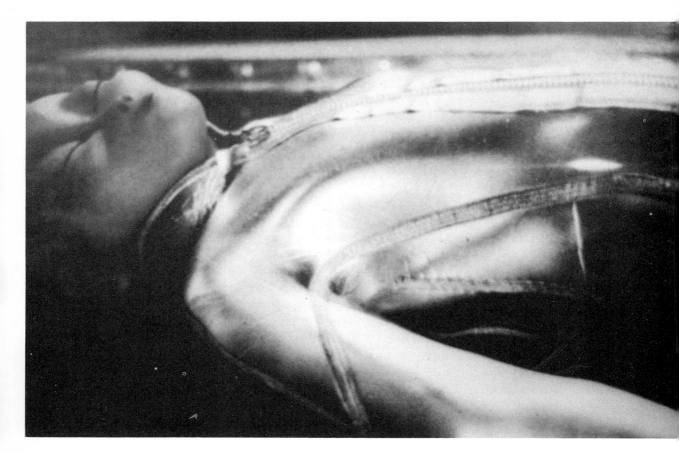

The current debate in ufology rages around the alleged capture of bodies retrieved from crashed UFOs by American security patrols and kept under strict secrecy for up to 50 years. When this photograph hit the media, stories circulated that the final proof had arrived – but this 'alien body' turned out to be a model prepared for an exhibition!

could be any other explanation. The very reason for this belief is also, perhaps, the theory's weakest link. Those in favour of an extraterrestrial explanation cite something obvious in support of their theory: the phenomenon *appears* to be extraterrestrial – it uses all the trappings of 'aliens' and 'spaceships'. Close encounter experiences involve craft which are obviously 'space age', and in contactee and abduction cases the beings inform victims of their extraterrestrial origins. They display star maps, describe their home planets and give terrestrials conducted tours around their flying machines. This must be the answer, if 'they' say so, surely?

The problem with the belief that we are dealing with a culture and technology from another planet is that it is too like us, sometimes to the point of absurdity. 'They' mirror our expectations and our own imaginative excursions into an age where space travel is possible, just as the airship pilots and their craft reflected the expectations of the turn of the last century.

Critics argue that we have anthropomorphised the phenomenon – given it the attributes of our own culture. Genuine extraterrestrials would be so 'alien' they would be beyond comprehension, and not like extras from low-budget SF films. They also point out that the vast distances between star systems would entail journeys lasting centuries – even at just below the speed of light.

Philip J. Klass, an American UFO debunker of many years' standing, makes a point which is perhaps more subtle than he intended. He comments in the Preface of *UFO Abductions: A Dangerous Game*: 'The public has been hoodwinked and brainwashed. I can assure you that there is absolutely no scientifically credible physical evidence to indicate that the Earth is being visited by extraterrestrials – let alone that they are abducting people.'

'The public has been hoodwinked and brainwashed. After having spent more than twenty-two years investigating famous, seemingly mysterious UFO reports, I can assure you there is absolutely no scientifically credible evidence that the Earth is being visited by extraterrestrials – let alone that they are abducting people.' Philip J. Klass – American aviation journalist.

Other dimensions

The phenomenon could *appear* extraterrestrial because the real visitors want us to believe it is. There are many cases in which UFOs and entities have behaved more like apparitions than solid flesh and blood creatures. Flying craft have materialised and dematerialised before startled witnesses, and entities have walked through walls and become visually insubstantial. Far from being located in outer space, the ufonauts seems to arrive and depart from another dimension. They could be sharing this planet with us, but are not on the same plane. This would explain their concern with our potential for destroying the Earth. Major changes to the environment could affect them too. The visitors would lie about their true origins to cover their tracks should we develop interdimensional travel. Who could blame them?

Some speculate that the visitors are time travellers, hiding behind the guise of 'aliens'. The subterfuge could be part of a sociological experiment to observe our behaviour. Under this scenario, UFO abductions could be a reality.

Humans are 'trapped' much in the way that we take animals from the wild. The fuzziness and blackouts experienced at this stage could reflect the administration of drugs or mind control. Once in the 'laboratory' abductees are psychologically tested and medically examined for diseases, the effects of pollution or something introduced into the environment. Finally, after being 'tagged', victims are released back into the wild. This enables them to be picked up again at a later date for re-examination. Of course this could also apply if extraterrestrials were involved.

However, the other-dimension theory would also account for the phenomenon's cultural tracking – its apparent ability to change its cosmetic appearance to suit the times. Victorians had little concept of outer space, but they could grasp the idea of giant airships.

The paranormal option

Some argue that UFOs are not 'nuts and bolts' machines manufactured by flesh and blood beings, but transient paranormal phenomena able to replicate solid objects and entities on a temporary basis. That would explain why UFO encounter scenarios read like third-rate science fiction. The phenomenon would be drawing on information stored in mankind's collective unconscious – a databank containing every human being's thought, first suggested by the Swiss psychologist Carl Jung.

UFO encounters could be a response to wishful thinking, projected fears and hopes – a distorted reflection of man's psyche. If there is an intelligence, it could be attempting to communicate information using metaphors to aid us in our individual and global problems. Intelligence is not even necessary for this theory. The response could be an automatic mechanism, an extension of our own consciousness, capable of physical materialisation for a limited period.

Physical mediums were allegedly capable of bringing spirits into a temporary physical form through the use of a psychic substance called ectoplasm – supposedly an amorphous misty material. Many UFOs have been observed bathed in mist and UFO entities, as we have already noted, often behave like apparitions.

The idea of 'thought-forms' is not new. Tibetan monks apparently had the ability to create entities from their own minds. These beings could eventually take on a life of their own and could be observed by people other than their creators. French traveller and explorer Alexandra David-Neel spent fourteen years in Tibet and called up her own *tulpa*, as they are called. Using meditation and Tibetan rituals she sought to develop the image of a short, fat, jolly monk. This took several months, after which she was rewarded by the materialisation of the monk. But the entity became alarmingly independent and it took several more months to dissolve – during which time others saw it too.

Are all these phenomena interconnected? Researchers, including the authors, have noted some similarities between UFO abductions and near death experiences. Both sets of percipients describe out-of-body states, white lights and encounters with entities. Dr Kenneth Ring, a psychologist from the University of Connecticut, had been doing some comparisons between NDEs and UFO abductions. Ring told Jenny Randles that both sets of experients were 'highly comparable psychologically'. He also noted that, in general, both had an enhanced awareness of psychic phenomena from childhood; this is something that the authors have been aware of in connection with UFO percipients for many years. Dr Ring concludes that they 'may have a common underlying source'.

In his book *The Omega Project*, Ring postulates that both types of experiences are symptoms of the evolution of human consciousness – tools to hone into shape a more advanced form of thinking and awareness. They are driving us towards a state of 'omega'.

The psycho-social theory

This is a reductionist theory that seeks to explain the phenomenon purely in psychological and cultural terms. Carl Jung referred to UFOs as 'a modern myth' and a 'rumour' in his book *Flying Saucers*, published in 1959. He saw the circular shape of some UFOs as having great psychological significance. The *mandala*, Jung noted, is a deep-seated symbol common in dreams and rooted in the unconscious. No doubt, too, if Sigmund Freud had been around to address the issue, he would have interpreted the descriptions of disc- and cigar-shaped objects as a subconscious obsession with the female and male genitalia.

But even Jung was not entirely convinced by his own theory and comments in *Flying Saucers*:

> Unfortunately, however, there are good reasons why UFOs cannot be disposed of in this simple manner. So far as I know it remains an established fact, supported by numerous observations, that UFOs have not only been seen visually but have also been picked up on radar screen and have left traces on the photographic plate. It boils down to nothing less than this: that either psychic projections throw back a radar echo, or else the appearance of real objects affords an opportunity for mythological projections.

Despite Jung's misgivings, there are no lack of supporters for a psychological interpretation of UFO reports and experiences. Advocates believe that individual and group social pressures are exteriorised in a convincing delusion of 'saviours' or 'fiends', which arrive in spacecraft to benefit or abuse human civilisation. The experiences are a

'My own opinions, which developed in the early years of my interest, conform to the psychic hypothesis. Probing the psychiatric and psychic dimensions to UFOs, the UFO-dynamics, promises to give a more comprehensive picture.'
Berthold E. Schwarz, M.D. – UFO investigator.

psychological response to the fears and hopes of individuals in society. They are subjective, internal experiences.

Eddie Bullard is an American folklorist who has studied UFO experiences and compared them with traditional folk tales to determine if they are one and the same. In the February 1988 *MUFON UFO Journal* Bullard writes: 'Abduction reports as a body show far more similarities than accident, random hoaxes or pure fantasies can explain. The consistencies in form and content down to numerous minute details demonstrate that abductions make up a coherent phenomenon, whatever its ultimate nature.'

In his study, Bullard concludes:

> If abductions are stories then the accounts should branch off into a different national version for each geographical area, but they do not. If abductions are stories the investigator should be able to impose an individual style on them ... If abductions are stories they should change according to an expected pattern over time, but their history is steady instead, even to the point of opposing external influences.

In June 1992 Boston's Massachusetts Institute of Technology (MIT) played host to a gathering of UFO researchers, among them Jenny Randles. The delegates also included psychologists and social workers who reported on their studies of the abduction phenomenon. Paper after paper on the results of the psychological testing of abductees was presented: they established that abductees were ordinary citizens, sincere, with no detectable psychopathic disorders.

Australian researcher Keith Basterfield had long been a supporter of the 'fantasy-prone hypothesis'. This suggests that abductees are part of a small group of humanity (not more than 5 percent) who have such rich inner fantasy lives that they cannot separate imaginative experiences from reality. After the results of three different tests had been read out, Basterfield withdrew the theory from further discussion.

Mind-bending earth lights

In 1982 a book was published which was to have repercussions around the UFO community. *Earth Lights*, written by Paul Devereux with the collaboration of geochemist Paul McCartney, postulated a natural energy which could manifest as balls of light and interact with the mind. Devereux drew on an experience of his own when he was a college student in Bromley, Kent. In May 1967, a curious rectangular orange light appeared outside. As he watched, the phenomenon seemed to change and structure itself into a figure with arms outstretched. This was also seen by other students, although the identity of the figure varied depending on the belief system of each observer.

Although there had been a previous work, *Space-Time Transients and Unusual Events* by Canadian researchers Michael Persinger and Gyslaine Lafrenière, Devereux's book was the first to draw together all the pieces of the mystery and present new regional studies. He has since produced several more publications.

Light phenomena appear all over the planet. Earthquake lights were reported – and ignored – for years, and it was not until 1910 that scientists started to take an interest. The phenomenon manifests as balls or aurora-like displays of light in the air prior to or just after an earthquake. Many lights reported as UFOs may be connected with earthquake lights.

Researchers discovered that anomalous lights occurred over heavily faulted lines in the Earth's crust – typical sites of earthquake activity. The Pennines in the north of England, and the Chinati Mountains near Marfa in Texas, are two good examples where hundreds of sightings have been recorded, photographed and even filmed.

The main explanation for earth lights is the 'piezo-electric effect'. Laboratory experiments were carried out where crystal was put under tremendous pressure, and at a certain point electrical discharges were created. It is deduced from this that crystal-bearing rocks put under pressure through subterranean stress would similarly produce electrically charged plasma in the atmosphere. A witness could misperceive the lights as UFOs.

Paul Devereux took the theory a step further, and concluded that witnesses close to the phenomenon would be directly effected. The electrical field of the light form would interact with the observer's brain, and the result would be an empathy between them. The witness, already thinking 'UFO' and bringing forth the appropriate imagery from the subconscious, would have that idea tapped by the plasma which would obligingly structure itself to represent the thought visually.

Michael Persinger, while believing that light phenomena are responsible for close encounter experiences, does not go as far as Devereux. He postulates that electromagnetic fields emanating from the phenomenon would affect the temporal lobe areas of the brain. This could trigger off 'temporal lobe epilepsy'. During a seizure of this kind,

'Of course the flying saucers are real – and they are interplanetary.' Air Chief Marshall Lord Dowding, head of the RAF during World War II, August 1954.

sufferers report hearing disembodied voices, experiencing out-of-body states and observing exotic figures.

Earth light research has generated some fascinating arguments which should be taken into account by ufologists. However, beyond the sensible assumption that exotic luminosities might be mistaken for 'spaceships', the rest is speculation, founded though it is on detailed research.

Certainly there seems more to this phenomenon than Persinger would admit. Earth lights appear to exhibit an intelligence in their movements, and seem to react to witnesses. Some UFO researchers have postulated the idea that UFOs are life-forms that inhabit the upper atmosphere. Kenneth Arnold came to this conclusion towards the end of his life.

Final thoughts

The source of UFO sightings and experiences could be one of the above, a combination, or none of them at all. Voices in some quarters say that UFO sightings and UFO abductions are entirely separate phenomena. It has been suggested that UFO organisations should concentrate on sightings and leave the abduction cases to the psychologists. Some groups concur with this suggestion, while others feel the phenomenon is paranormal and have expanded their interests accordingly. Ufology is coming to a crossroads.

Even psychologists cannot make up their minds. Peter Hough, who has worked with several clinical psychologists, has come up against this dilemma. One concluded that the case he was working on was based on objective reality, while the other thought that his case was internal and a reflection of childhood abuse. Both were abduction experiences.

The dilemma here is that on the one hand we seem to be dealing with hardware that is seen, reflects the sun and can be recorded on radar, and on the other encounters with entities who exhibit nothing new at all. Quite the contrary, they are an amalgam of every fantasy we have read and every science fiction film we have seen. This is fact. We must face it. Nevertheless, the encounters could still be objectively 'real'.

The phenomenon could be so 'alien' it is beyond comprehension. Cultural tracking, first brought to our notice by Jacques Vallée in his 1970 classic *Passport to Magonia*, demonstrates the similarities between the abduction of human beings by fairies, who were taken to 'fairyland', and modern kidnappings by extraterrestrials. Is it a coincidence that toadstools, supposedly the domain of fairies, resemble modern saucer-shape craft? This seems at odds with Thomas Bullard's study, but it is true all the same.

One answer is that witnesses in previous times described extraterrestrials and their flying machines in terms of fairies and toadstools because they had no concept of outer space. Another is this: when the mind is suddenly confronted with an anomaly it struggles to identify it in terms of previous experience and information stored in the subconscious. That is why witnesses initially seek to identify UFOs as terrestrial aircraft or astronomical bodies. But when this fails the mind draws on more exotic possibilities. When an anomaly is utterly alien, beyond anything previously experienced or imagined, the mind will have to impose on it whatever is available – images from science fiction scenarios.

Perhaps this is mankind's saving grace. Such interpretations foisted

Were the fairies and toadstools of bygone ages really extraterrestrials and their flying machines?

on the conscious mind by the subconscious could be protecting us from a horror that would psychologically destroy us if we could perceive it in its true form.

The arguments will carry on, but one thing is certain – the UFO subject is not history. While you, the reader, mull over the contents of this book, and the investigators and researchers argue over who is right, UFOs continue to be chased by Air Force jets, recorded on radar, filmed and photographed. Ordinary men, women and children, from all walks of life, continue to suffer 'missing time' followed by fear and incomprehension as 'memory' returns of being in a white room, undergoing an examination by some abomination better left in the pages of a Stephen King novel.

SOURCES

ALDISS, Brian W., *Billion Year Spree*, Weidenfeld & Nicolson, 1973

ANDREWS, Colin and DELGADO, Pat, *Circular Evidence*, Bloomsbury, 1989

ARNOLD, Kenneth and PALMER, Ray, *The Coming of the Saucers*, Amherst Press, 1952

BARRY, Bill, *Ultimate Encounter*, Corgi, 1981

BASTERFIELD, Keith, *UFOs: The Image Hypothesis*, Reed, 1980

BOWEN, Charles (ed.), *The Humanoids*, Futura, 1977

BROWNELL, Winfield S., *UFOS: Key to Earth's Destiny!*, Legion of Light Publications, 1980

CAMPBELL, Stewart, *The UFO Mystery Solved*, Explicit Books, 1994

CLARKE, David and ROBERTS, Andy, *Phantoms of the Sky*, Hale, 1990

CONDON, Edward (ed.), *Scientific Study of UFOs*, Bantam, 1969

CUFOS, *Plains of San Agustin Controversy*, 1992

DEVEREUX, Paul, *Earth Lights Revelation*, Blandford, 1990

EVANS, Hilary, *The Evidence for UFOs*, Aquarian, 1983

EVANS, Hilary, *Visions, Apparitions, Alien Visitors*, Aquarian, 1986

EVANS, Hilary and SPENCER, John (eds), *UFOS 1947–1987*, Fortean Tomes, 1987

FAWCETT, Larry and GREENWOOD, Barry, *Clear Intent*, Prentice-Hall, 1984

FLAMMONDE, Paris, *UFOs Exist!*, Ballantine, 1977

FREWIN, Anthony, *One Hundred Years of Science Fiction Illustrations*, Jupiter, 1974

FULLER, John G., *The Interrupted Journey*, Souvenir, 1980

GOOD, Timothy, *George Adamski, the Untold Story*, CETI, 1983

GOOD, Timothy, *Above Top Secret*, Sidgwick & Jackson, 1987
HARBINSON, W.A., *Genesis*, Corgi, 1980
HIND, Cynthia, *UFOs African Encounters*, Gemini, 1982
HOBANA, Ion and WEVERBURGH, Julien, *UFOs from behind the Iron Curtain*, Corgi, 1975
HOLDSTOCK, Robert (consultant ed.), *Encyclopedia of Science Fiction*, Octopus, 1978
HOPKINS, Budd, *Missing Time*, Merak, 1982
HOPKINS, Budd, *Intruders*, Random House, 1987
HOUGH, Peter and RANDLES, Jenny, *Looking for the Aliens*, Blandford, 1992
HYNEK, J. Allen, *The UFO Experience*, Regnery, 1972
JACOBS, David, *UFO Controversy in America*, IUP, 1975
KEEL, John A., 'Mystery Aeroplanes of the 1930s', in *Flying Saucer Review*, Vol.16, Nos 3 and 4
KEEL, John A., *UFOs: Operation Trojan Horse*, Putnam, 1970
KEYHOE, Donald, *Flying Saucers Are Real*, Fawcett, 1950
KLASS, Philip J., *UFOs: The Public Deceived*, Prometheus, 1983
KLASS, Philip J., *UFO Abductions: A Dangerous Game*, Prometheus, 1989
MACK, Dr John, *Abduction*, Simon & Schuster, 1994
MONDEY, David and TAYLOR, Michael J.H., *The Guinness Book of Aircraft*, Guinness, 1988
MOORE, William and BAERLITZ, Charles, *The Roswell Incident*, Grafton, 1980
MOULTON HOWE, Linda, 'Animal Mutilation Up-Date', in *Enigmas*, May/June 1993
PAGE, Thornton and SAGAN, Carl (eds), *UFOs: A Scientific Debate*, Cornell, 1972
RANDLE, Kevin and SCHMITT, Don, *UFO Crash at Roswell*, Avon, 1992
RANDLES, Jenny, *Alien Abduction*, Inner Light, 1989
RANDLES, Jenny, *Aliens: The Real Story*, Hale, 1993
RANDLES, Jenny, *From Out of the Blue*, Berkeley, 1993
RANDLES, Jenny and FULLER, Paul, *Crop Circles: A Mystery Solved*, Hale, 1990 (updated 1993)
RANDLES, Jenny and HOUGH, Peter, *Death by Supernatural Causes?*, Grafton, 1988
RANDLES, Jenny and HOUGH, Peter, *Scary Stories*, Futura, 1991
RANDLES, Jenny and HOUGH, Peter, *Encyclopedia of the Unexplained*, Michael O'Mara, 1994

RING, Kenneth, *The Omega Project*, Morrow, 1992

ROBERTS, Anthony and GILBERTSON, Geoff, *The Dark Gods*, Rider, 1980

RUPPELT, Edward, *The Report on UFOs*, Ace, 1956

SACHS, Margaret, *The UFO Encyclopedia*, Corgi, 1981

SAUNDERS, David and HARKINS, Roger, *UFOs? Yes!*, World, 1968

SCHNABEL, Jim, *Round in Circles*, Hutchinson, 1993 and *Dark White*, Hamish Hamilton, 1994

STEIGER, Brad (ed.), *Project Blue Book*, Bantam, 1978

STRIEBER, Whitley, *Communion*, Moraw, 1987

STORY, Ronald D. (ed.), *The Encyclopedia of UFOs*, New English Library, 1980

VALLÉE, Jacques, *Anatomy of a Phenomenon*, Regnery, 1965

VALLÉE, Jacques, *Passport to Magonia*, Neville Spearman, 1970

WALTERS, Ed and Frances, *The Gulf Breeze Sightings*, Bantam, 1990

Recommended publications and research groups

AFU, Box 11027 600, 11 Norrkoping, 11 Sweden

Association for the Scientific Study of Anomalous Phenomena (ASSAP), Hugh Pincott, ASSAP Secretary, 20 Paul Street, Frome, Somerset BA11 1DX

Aura-Z, PO Box 224, Moscow 117463, Russia

Bulletin of Anomalous Experience, 2 St Clair Ave West, Suite 607, Toronto, Canada M4V 1L5

Crop Watcher, 3 Selborne Court, Tavistock Close, Romsey, SO51 7TY

J. Allen Hynek Center for UFO Studies, 2457 West Peterson Ave, Chicago, Illinois 60659, USA

Enigmas (Scotland), 41 The Braes, Tullibody, Clackmannanshire, FK10 2TT

Fate, PO Box 1940, 170 Future Way, Marion, Ohio 43305, USA

Flying Saucer Review, Snodland, Kent ME6 5HJ

Northern UFO News, 37 Heathbank Road, Stockport, Cheshire, SK3 0UP

OVNI Presence, BP 324, Aix-en-Provence, Cedex 1, France

UFO Afrinews, PO Box MP 49, Mount Pleasant, Harare, Zimbabwe

UFO Research Australia, PO Box 2435, Cairns, QLD 4970, Australia

UFO Call is a news and information service provided by British Telecom and BUFORA. Available in Britain only, at information line rates, it is presently written and recorded weekly by Jenny Randles and available on 0891-121886

In June 1994 a group of British ufologists combined to produce a pioneering high quality journal, *The New Ufologist*. Unique in the UFO world this is independent of all groups and non-profit making. It will put any money raised back into a newly created research fund and at regular open gatherings will invite proposals from anyone with an important case needing scientific study or an interesting research scheme waiting to be carried out. A majority vote of those present will distribute funding to any proposals thought to contribute new knowledge to the subject.

The New Ufologist, 71 Knight Avenue, Canterbury, Kent CT2 8PY

Readers who wish to report any UFO encounter (in confidence if preferred) can contact the authors. They will, upon request, put the witness in touch with a reliable local investigator. Write to: 37 Heathbank Road, Stockport, Cheshire SK3 0UP

Please include SAEs or International Reply Coupons when writing to any of the above addresses.

INDEX
